Best Hikes Cincinnati

Best Hikes Cincinnati

The Greatest Views, Wildlife, and Forest Strolls

Second Edition

Johnny Molloy

GUILFORD, CONNECTICUT

For all the hikers who ply the trails of Cincinnati
and the greater Tri-State area

FALCONGUIDES®

An imprint of The Rowman & Littlefield Publishing Group, Inc.
4501 Forbes Blvd., Ste. 200
Lanham, MD 20706
www.rowman.com
Falcon and FalconGuides are registered trademarks and Make Adventure Your Story is a trademark
of The Rowman & Littlefield Publishing Group, Inc.

Distributed by NATIONAL BOOK NETWORK

British Library Cataloguing in Publication Information available

Library of Congress Cataloging-in-Publication Data available

ISBN 978-1-4930-3802-2 (paperback)
ISBN 978-1-4930-3801-5 (e-book)

♾™ The paper used in this publication meets the minimum requirements of American National
Standard for Information Sciences—Permanence of Paper for Printed Library Materials, ANSI/NISO
Z39.48-1992.

Printed in the United States of America

Contents

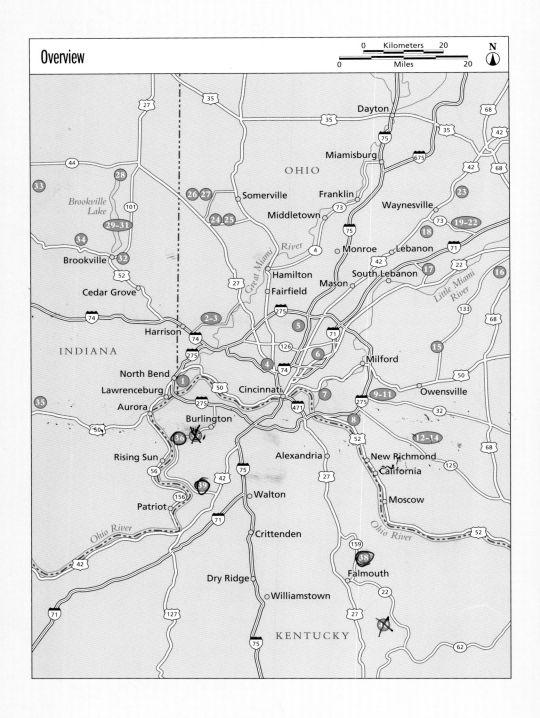

0   Kilometers   20

0   Miles   20

N

Dayton

OHIO

Miamisburg

Somerville   Franklin   Waynesville

Brookville
Lake   Middletown

Monroe   Lebanon

Brookville   Hamilton   Mason   South Lebanon

Cedar Grove   Fairfield

Harrison

INDIANA

North Bend   Cincinnati   Milford

Lawrenceburg

Aurora   Owensville

Burlington

Rising Sun   Alexandria   New Richmond

California

Patriot   Walton   Moscow

Crittenden

Ohio River   Falmouth

Dry Ridge

Williamstown

KENTUCKY

Great Miami River

Little Miami River

39. Big Bone → Nice, but crowded (Buffalo)
38✦ Kincaid → Lake, trails... not crowded!
           Loved this one. Will go Back!!!
36. Middle Creek - Nice 3 mile loop - not to
       crowded. - (close)

#8. Woodland Mound Hike - (Not a favorite; more of a
       park, Then hiking. Nice views of River, water park for
       Toddlers.

Acknowledgments

Thanks to all the people of Cincinnati who shared their favorite places to hike. Thanks to Serra Designs for providing me with a quality tent for camping between hikes. Thanks also to the folks at FalconGuides.

It is easy to see how shagbark hickory got its name.

◄ *Trail scenes like this lure hikers into springtime.*

The wetlands of Spring Valley are a haven for wildlife.

Introduction

Welcome to the second edition of *Best Hikes Cincinnati*. It is an honor to update and improve this hiking guide to a hiker town such as Cincinnati. On first thought, Cincinnati may not seem like a hiker's town. Nevertheless, read on and you may change your mind. Cincinnati is a son of a river, born on the banks of the mighty Ohio, between the points where the Little Miami River and Great Miami River release their waters to the Ohio River. These rivers cut great valleys, giving Cincinnati topographical relief—vertical variation, if you will—that enhances a landscape where the flora and fauna of the East, the Midwest, and the South meld into a mosaic of nature. After starting with an attractive landscape, you add quality parks that preserve not only the plants and animals—the natural history—but also human history. Over time, area residents began to appreciate and acknowledge this scenic beauty in the Seven Hills of Cincinnati and points beyond. They could see that the special places would remain special if they were held by the public for the public to use and enjoy, to create parks and preserves. Luckily for us, the city of Cincinnati and Hamilton County began a tradition of creating parks, from Mount Airy Forest nearly a century back to newer parks such as Fernbank Park. Trails became part of these natural oases.

Additionally, the state of Ohio has established several state parks within easy striking distance of greater Cincy, such as East Fork State Park. The establishment of some preserves extends back to the Great Depression of the 1930s, when the Civilian Conservation Corps came in and built campgrounds, picnic shelters, and other facilities to enhance the already verdant beauty in what became the state parks. Within those parks, they built hiking trails to explore hills and valleys, vistas and waterfalls. The same story was going on in city, state, and county parks in Kentucky to the south and Indiana to the west. Today, we hikers benefit from a cornucopia of parkland throughout the Tri-State. It all adds up to an impressive array of hiking destinations!

It is in Cincinnati and this greater region where the hikes in this book are found. After having the privilege of researching potential hikes for this book, hiking the hikes, taking photographs, finding the ones that made the grade—and the ones that didn't—exploring the parks beyond the trails, mapping the hikes, and then actually writing, completing, and updating this project, I couldn't help but reflect on the wealth of places found within the scope of this book. Shawnee Lookout came to mind first. It is one of the most famous area landmarks. And it is a microcosm of the Tri-State. Shawnee Lookout offers a remarkable hilltop view of not only the Great Miami River but also its mother river—the mighty Ohio, the mother of Cincinnati. Also visible are the green hills of Kentucky and Indiana beyond. Shawnee Lookout harbors not only the natural beauty of the Tri-State but also the human history found here, starting with the Shawnee Indians and the amazing earthworks found at this park.

I reflected on other destinations, recounting all the scenic hikes of greater Cincinnati. I followed the view into Indiana, considering the trails there. Versailles State Park features a rugged network of pathways. The park was originally developed over eight decades back by the Civilian Conservation Corps. The view of the Laughery Creek Valley from an overlook built by the CCC is inspiring not only for the panorama of the vale beneath but also for the story behind the men who made the trails. Brookville Lake has the Adena Trace, a path that encircles the impoundment, including a wilderness section not for the faint of heart. Mounds State Recreation Area also has appealing lake views, but more than that it has Indian mounds built 2,000 years back that add perspective to the hike.

I gazed south to Kentucky. Across the river were nature preserves, such as the Boone County Cliffs, in which grow ancient trees that began as seedlings before anyone had heard of a place called Cincinnati. And there was Middle Creek Park. This place could brag of the most massive trees of them all, sycamores so large it would take several hikers linked arm-in-arm to measure their circumference. The Bluegrass State also has quiet state parks with nature trails and other outdoor activities and facilities that make for easy and alluring outdoor destinations.

And the view came back to Ohio, where hiking destinations ring Cincinnati to the east, the north, and the west. East Fork State Park has an extensive trail network to be envied by other parks. First is the 32-mile Steve Newman Worldwalker Perimeter Trail, named for a local Bethel, Ohio, man who made it by foot entirely around the globe. Other paths were designed for backpackers and nature trails for the casual hiker. East Fork State Park also has equestrian and mountain bike paths. Stonelick State Park has flatwoods trekking and big trees of its own.

The lotus blooms of Cowan Lake State Park shine brightly in my memory. The greater Caesar Creek Lake area has lakeside trails that presented watery vistas, river gorge paths, hikes to waterfalls named Crawdad and Horseshoe. Trailside fossils add an element of ancient history to the hikes. More recent history was revealed at the Caesar Creek Pioneer Village, adding a learning aspect—mental exercise if you will—to the physical rewards of hiking here. And then there is the Big Woods of Hueston Woods State Park. The towering forest, centuries in the making, first bring amazement at the trees' size and number, followed by pride that Ohio forbearers thought to preserve such a place for unborn generations. Human history stands out here, too, as a hike passes by an old sugar shack, where Buckeye State pioneers practiced the art of turning maple sap into maple syrup and other sweet treats.

I then mentally drew closer to the city of Cincinnati, recalling those destinations close to home that make area hiking an easy, quick, and rewarding endeavor. The Creek Trail at French Park features everywhere-you-look beauty as French Creek cascades over layer after layer of limestone. Glenwood Gardens, with its elaborate trailhead, avails wetland splendor among hills in the heart of the metropolis. The trails of Whitewater Memorial Forest exemplify Hamilton County's commitment to great parks. After all, their website is www.greatparks.org.

I came again to the scene at hand, Shawnee Lookout, and considered the physical toil of the nearby earthworks, preserved for generations past, present, and future to admire. The aboriginal Americans knew this as a special spot in a deep valley where the Little Miami, the Great Miami, and Ohio River converge. Today, it is where the city of Cincinnati forms the heart of a special area, where the states of Ohio, Kentucky, and Indiana converge. The physical toil of creating parks and building trails benefited us now. And when combining the history, beauty, and the parks that preserve them, I concluded Cincinnati *is* a hiker's town. The trails offered in this book will help you explore, understand, and appreciate the natural and human history of the greater Cincinnati region. Enjoy.

Weather

Cincinnati experiences all four seasons in their entirety. Summer can be warm, with occasional downright hot spells. Morning hikers can avoid heat and the common afternoon thunderstorms. A smartphone allows hikers to monitor storms as they arise. Hikers increase in numbers when the first northerly fronts of fall sweep cool, clear air across the Ohio Valley. Crisp mornings, great for vigorous treks, give way to warm afternoons, more conducive to family strolls. Fall is drier than summer. Winter will bring frigid subfreezing days, chilling rains, and snows—and fewer hours of daylight. However, a brisk hiking pace and wise time management will keep you warm and walking while the sun is still above the horizon. Each cold month has a few days of mild weather. Make the most of them. Spring will be more variable. A warm day can be followed by a cold one. Extensive spring rains bring regrowth but also keep hikers indoors. But any avid hiker will find more good hiking days than they will have time to hike in spring and every other season. A good way to plan your hiking is to check monthly averages of high and low temperatures and average rainfall for each month in Cincinnati. Below is a table showing each month's averages. This will give you a good idea of what to expect each month.

Month	Average High	Average Low	Precipitation
January	38 degrees	23 degrees	2.7"
February	44 degrees	27 degrees	2.3"
March	55 degrees	35 degrees	3.5"
April	66 degrees	43 degrees	3.8"
May	75 degrees	54 degrees	4.5"
June	83 degrees	62 degrees	3.7"
July	87 degrees	67 degrees	3.2"
August	86 degrees	65 degrees	3.5"
September	79 degrees	58 degrees	3.0"
October	67 degrees	46 degrees	2.8"
November	54 degrees	37 degrees	3.5"
December	43 degrees	27 degrees	3.0"

Flora and Fauna

The landscape of the Tri-State offers everything from deep valleys below river-carved hills to flatland forests stretching toward the horizon to large impounded lakes along which thrive woodland and meadow. A wide variety of wildlife calls these dissimilar landscapes home.

Deer will be the land animal you most likely will see hiking Cincinnati's trails. They can be found throughout the Tri-State. Deer in some of the parks are remarkably tame and may linger on or close to the trail as you approach. A quiet hiker may also witness turkeys, raccoons, or even a coyote. Don't be surprised if you observe beaver, muskrat, or a playful otter along streams and lakes. If you feel uncomfortable when encountering any critter, keep your distance and they will generally keep theirs, especially snakes.

Overhead, many raptors will be plying the skies for food, including hawks, falcons, and owls. Depending upon where you are, other birds you may spot range from kingfishers to woodpeckers. Look for waterfowl in lakes. Since southwest Ohio is the convergence of the North, the Midwest, and the South, songbirds are abundant.

The flora offers just as much variety. Along the trails you will find verdant hardwood forests. In cooler north-facing areas you will see maple, beech, cherry, and other northern hardwoods. Pawpaws will be found under the shade of them. South-facing woods will have more oaks and hickories. In moister areas, sycamores predominate and are found along nearly every stream in the Tri-State. Wildflowers will be found in spring, summer, and fall along watercourses and in drier site-specific situations.

Wilderness Restrictions/Regulations

Hiking in greater Cincinnati is done primarily in city, county, and state parks, and also nature preserves and US Army Corps of Engineers land. The city of Cincinnati has a fine park system, highlighted by Mount Airy Forest. They are operated on a more casual basis and are free and open to the public with few restrictions. Hamilton County, in which lies Cincinnati, has one of the better county park systems in the country. They are well-run, well-maintained facilities with a little bit of everything for everyone, from hiking to camping to golfing. The system is fee-based.

Ohio state parks offer natural getaways with an emphasis on recreation. They also preserve special areas, such as the Big Woods of Hueston Woods State Park. Area state parks are often centered on a reservoir built by the US Army Corps of Engineers. These man-made lakes were built primarily for flood control and water storage. The recreation aspect of the lakes is an important but secondary function. Trails are laid upon the shoreline of the reservoirs. Most state park hiking destinations in Kentucky and Indiana also border reservoirs and utilize land adjacent to the reservoirs for trails. Entrance to the parks, and their trails, are generally free, but you will have to pay to camp, golf, or overnight in a cabin. As a whole, the state park trail systems are in good shape.

Then there are the nature preserves. Ohio, Indiana, and Kentucky all have special programs whereby land is set aside for protection. These lands usually have unique ecological characteristics that deem them worthy of saving and are the most restricted in terms of usage. Luckily for us, hiking is considered passive recreation. Camping is generally not allowed on these lands.

Getting Around

AREA CODES

The Cincinnati area code is 513. Southwest Ohio outside of Cincinnati is 937. Area codes for Indiana areas covered in this book are 765 and 812. The area code for Kentucky areas covered in this book is 859.

ROADS

For the purposes of this guide, the best hikes near Cincinnati are confined to a one-hour drive from the greater metro region. Easterly in Ohio, this stretches to the town of Bethel, northeast to Clarksville, northwest to Oxford, and to the Indiana state line. In Indiana hikes extend out I-74 and to the towns of Versailles and Liberty. Southward, hikes reach into Kentucky, primarily the counties that border Ohio. The entire hiking area is considered the Tri-State, with Cincinnati its epicenter.

A number of major interstates converge in Cincinnati. Directions to trailheads are given from these arteries. They include I-75, I-74, I-71, and I-275—the main loop around Cincinnati.

BY AIR

Cincinnati/Northern Kentucky Airport (CVG) is 13 miles south of downtown Cincinnati, off I-275, near Florence, Kentucky.

To book reservations online, check out your favorite airline's website or search one of the following travel sites for the best price: www.cheaptickets.com, www.expedia.com, www.orbitz.com, www.priceline.com, www.travelocity.com, or www.trip.com—just to name a few.

BY RAIL and BY BUS

Cincinnati is served by AMTRAK. Schedules and pricing are at www.amtrak.com or by calling (800) 872-7245. Southwest Ohio Regional Transit Authority (known as "the Metro") operates rail and bus service throughout Cincinnati and its suburbs. Visit www.go-metro.com or call (513) 621-4455. In addition to the Metro, Greyhound serves many towns in the region; visit www.greyhound.com for more information.

VISITOR INFORMATION

For general information on Cincinnati, visit the official website of the Cincinnati Regional Tourism Network, www.cincinnatiusa.com, or call (800) 581-2260. This covers the Tri-State area, including northern Kentucky and southeastern Indiana as well as Southwest Ohio beyond the city of Cincinnati.

About the Author

Johnny Molloy is a writer and adventurer based in Johnson City, Tennessee. His outdoor passion was ignited on a backpacking trip in Great Smoky Mountains National Park while attending the University of Tennessee. That first foray unleashed a love of the outdoors that led Johnny to spend over 4,000 nights backpacking, canoe camping, and tent camping throughout the country over the past three decades. If you put the days of camping all together that is nearly eleven straight years of camping out.

Friends enjoyed his outdoor adventure stories; one even suggested he write a book. He pursued his friend's idea and soon parlayed his love of the outdoors into an occupation. The results of his efforts are over sixty-five books and guides. His writings include hiking guidebooks, camping guidebooks, paddling guidebooks, comprehensive guidebooks about a specific area, and true outdoor adventure books covering all or parts of twenty-six states.

Though primarily involved with book publications, Molloy writes for magazines and websites. Furthermore, he is an outdoors columnist and feature writer for his local paper, the *Johnson City Press*. He continues writing and traveling extensively throughout the United States, endeavoring in a variety of outdoor pursuits.

A Christian, Johnny is an active member of First Presbyterian Church in Johnson City, Tennessee. He is also a Gideon. His non-outdoor interests include reading, Christian studies, and University of Tennessee sports. For the latest on Johnny, please visit www.johnnymolloy.com.

How to Use This Guide

Take a close enough look, and you'll find that this guide contains just about everything you'll ever need to choose, plan for, enjoy, and survive a hike near Cincinnati. Stuffed with useful local area information, *Best Hikes Cincinnati* features forty mapped and cued hikes. Here's an outline of the book's major components:

Each hike starts with a short **summary** of the hike's highlights. These quick overviews give you a taste of the hiking adventures to follow. You'll learn about the trail terrain and what surprises each route has to offer. Following the overview, you'll find the **hike specs:** quick, nitty-gritty details of the hike. Most are self-explanatory, but here are some details on others:

Distance: The total distance of the recommended route—one-way for loop hikes, the round-trip on an out-and-back or lollipop hike, point-to-point for a shuttle. Options are additional.

Hiking time: The average time it will take to cover the route. It is based on the total distance, elevation gain, and condition and difficulty of the trail. Your fitness level will also affect your time.

Difficulty: Each hike has been assigned a level of difficulty. The rating system was developed from several sources and personal experience. These levels are meant to be a guideline only and may prove easier or harder for different people depending on ability and physical fitness.

- **Easy**—5 miles or less total trip distance in one day, with minimal elevation gain, and paved or smooth-surfaced dirt trail.
- **Moderate**—Up to 10 miles total trip distance in one day, with moderate elevation gain and potentially rough terrain.
- **Difficult**—More than 10 miles total trip distance in one day, strenuous elevation gains, and rough and/or rocky terrain.

Trail surface: General information about what to expect underfoot.

Best Season: General information on the best time of year to hike.

Other trail users: Such as horseback riders, mountain bikers, inline skaters, etc.

Canine compatibility: Know the trail regulations before you take your dog hiking with you. Dogs are not allowed on several trails in this book.

Land status: National forest, county open space, national park wilderness, etc.

Fees and permits: Whether you need to carry any money with you for park entrance fees and permits.

Maps: This is a list of other maps to supplement the maps in this book. USGS maps are the best source for accurate topographical information, but the local park map may show more recent trails. Use both.

Trail contacts: This is the location, phone number, and website URL for the local land manager(s) in charge of all the trails within the selected hike. Before you head out, get trail access information, or contact the land manager after your visit if you see problems with trail erosion, damage, or misuse.

The **Finding the trailhead** section gives you dependable driving directions to where you'll want to park. **The Hike** is the meat of the chapter. Detailed and honest, it's a carefully researched impression of the trail. It also often includes lots of area history, both natural and human. Under **Miles and Directions,** mileage cues identify all turns and trail name changes, as well as points of interest. **Options** are also given for many hikes to make your journey shorter or longer depending on the amount of time you have. Don't feel restricted to the routes and trails that are mapped here. Be adventurous and use this guide as a platform to discover new routes for yourself. **Green Tips** are included to help you help the environment we all share. A sidebar is included with most hikes. This is simply interesting information about the area or trail that doesn't necessarily pertain to the specific hike but gives you some human or natural tidbit that may pique your interest to explore beyond the simple mechanics of the trek. Enjoy your time in the outdoors and remember to pack out what you pack in.

How to Use the Maps

Overview map: This map shows the location of each hike in the area by hike number.

Route map: This is your primary guide to each hike. It shows all of the accessible roads and trails, points of interest, water, landmarks, and geographical features. It also distinguishes trails from roads, and paved roads from unpaved roads. The selected route is highlighted, and directional arrows point the way.

Trail Finder

Hike No.	Hike Name	Best Hikes for Waterfalls	Best Hikes for Great Views	Best Hikes for Children	Best Hikes for Dogs	Best Hikes for Stream Lovers	Best Hikes for Lake Lovers	Best Hikes for Nature Lovers	Best Hikes for Backpackers
1	Hikes of Shawnee Lookout Park		●		●				
2	Shaker Trace		●						
3	Loops of Miami Whitewater Forest			●	●			●	
4	Stone Steps Loop at Mount Airy Forest							●	
5	Glenwood Gardens		●	●		●		●	
6	French Park Hike	●			●		●		
7	Stanbery Park Hike					●		●	
8	Woodland Mound Hike	●	●	●		●			
9	Redwing Loop	●			●			●	
10	Far Ridge Loop		●		●	●		●	
11	Lookout Loop			●		●			
12	East Fork Loop		●			●	●		●
13	Poplar Creek Loop at East Fork State Park						●	●	●

Hike No.	Hike Name	Best Hikes for Waterfalls	Best Hikes for Great Views	Best Hikes for Children	Best Hikes for Dogs	Best Hikes for Stream Lovers	Best Hikes for Lake Lovers	Best Hikes for Nature Lovers	Best Hikes for Backpackers
14	Cloverlick Creek Hike	●				●	●		●
15	Beechtree Loop at Stonelick State Park			●	●		●		
16	Cowan Lake State Park Hike			●	●		●	●	
17	Trails of Fort Ancient		●	●					
18	Caesar Creek Gorge State Nature Preserve				●	●		●	
19	Crawdad Falls/Peninsula Loop	●	●		●	●	●		
20	Horseshoe Falls Hike	●	●		●	●	●		
21	Old Sugar Camp Hike		●		●	●	●	●	
22	Trace Run Double Loop		●		●	●		●	
23	Spring Valley Loop		●	●	●		●		
24	Bachelor Preserve Loop at Miami University				●	●		●	
25	College Woods Loop at Miami University			●	●	●	●	●	
26	Cedar Creek Falls at Hueston Woods State Park	●			●	●			
27	Big Woods Hike at Hueston Woods State Park		●		●	●	●	●	

Hike No.	Hike Name	Best Hikes for Waterfalls	Best Hikes for Great Views	Best Hikes for Children	Best Hikes for Dogs	Best Hikes for Stream Lovers	Best Hikes for Lake Lovers	Best Hikes for Nature Lovers	Best Hikes for Backpackers
28	Whitewater Memorial State Park		•				•	•	
29	Adena Trace Sampler						•	•	
30	Garr Hill Wildlife Wander		•		•		•	•	
31	Glidewell Mound Loop			•	•		•		
32	Wolf Creek Trail from Brookville Dam		•				•		
33	Mary Gray Bird Sanctuary Loop			•	•	•		•	
34	Whitewater Canal Historic Trail		•	•	•	•		•	
35	Versailles State Park Hike	•	•			•			
36	Middle Creek Park Loop				•	•		•	
37	Boone County Cliffs State Nature Preserve			•				•	
38	Kincaid Lake State Park Hike			•	•			•	
39	Big Bone Lick State Park Hike			•	•			•	
40	Quiet Trails State Nature Preserve				•	•		•	

Map Legend

Transportation

══⟨75⟩══	Freeway/Interstate Highway
══⟨50⟩══	U.S. Highway
══⟨56⟩══	State Highway
══[1488]══	Other Road
══ ══ ══	Unpaved Road

Trails

▬ ▬ ▬	Selected Route
- - - -	Trail
▬▬▬▬	Paved Trail
→	Direction of Route

Water Features

⬭	Body of Water
	Marsh
∿	River/Creek
≶	Waterfalls/Cascades

Symbols

⬱	Boat Launch
⏜	Bridge
■	Building/Point of Interest
▲	Campground
♠	Fire Tower
⚲	Gate
🚻	Park Office
P	Parking
⛱	Picnic Area
🚻	Restroom
⚐	Scenic View
⟨20⟩	Trailhead
○	Towns and Cities
❓	Visitor Center

Land Management

▭	State/County Park
— – – —	State Line

Metro Cincinnati

As the name implies, Metro Cincinnati includes the heart of the urban area and populated areas on the periphery. These hikes include Cincinnati city parks as well as the fine Hamilton County park system. The steep terrain created by the Ohio River figures into many of these hikes, and the river highlands present great views of the valley and beyond. These metro hikes vary in distance and difficulty and make for quick getaways that in-town and suburban residents can use. History and panoramas meet at Shawnee Lookout Park. Rock-hop a scenic and wildflower-laden stream at French Creek Park. New places await your discovery.

Metro Cincinnati features trails for exercise, exploration, and simply beauty.

1 Hikes of Shawnee Lookout Park

Shawnee Lookout Park features three rewarding—but relatively short—loop hikes. Though each one is individually worthwhile, their close proximity allows you to make a hiker's triple play. First visit extensive Paleo-Indian earthworks located atop a ridge dividing the Great Miami River and Ohio River and travel to a stellar vista where you can see the confluence of the rivers and three states at once—Ohio, Kentucky, and Indiana. Next, enjoy more river vistas of both the Great Miami and Ohio Rivers on the last two hikes, adding up to nearly 5 miles of walking pleasure.

Start: Shawnee Lookout Trailhead
Distance: 1.4-, 2.0-, and 1.2-mile loops
Hiking time: About 4 to 5 hours
Difficulty: Moderate
Trail surface: Mostly natural surface paths in forested woods, pea gravel in places
Best season: Year-round
Other trail users: None
Canine compatibility: Leashed dogs permitted

Land status: County park
Fees and permits: Parking fee required
Schedule: Open daily year-round sunrise to sunset
Maps: Shawnee Lookout Park; USGS Lawrenceburg, Hooven
Trail contacts: Shawnee Lookout Park, 2008 Lawrenceburg Rd., North Bend, OH 45052; (513) 941-0120; www.greatparks.org

Finding the trailhead: From exit 21 on I-275 west of downtown, take Kilby Road south for 1.0 mile to US 50. Turn right onto US 50 west and follow it 1.7 miles to Lawrenceburg Road. Turn left onto Lawrenceburg Road and follow it 0.7 mile, crossing the Great Miami River. Reach a T intersection. Turn right, still on Lawrenceburg Road, and follow it 0.5 mile to Shawnee Lookout Park, on your left. Turn into the park and climb away from the ranger station, tracing the main park road to dead-end at the trailhead after 1.9 miles. To reach the second and third trailheads, you will have to drive 1.2 miles back toward the park entrance. Trailhead GPS: N39 7.236' / W84 48.516'

The Hike

Shawnee Lookout Park, location of the following hikes, is simply one of the most scenic hiking destinations in greater Cincinnati. Your first trek, to *the* Shawnee Lookout on the Miami Fort Trail, takes you uphill into thousands years of Ohio Indian life. Trailside information signage helps explain the human and natural history of this strategic location. If you are ever going to read trailside interpretive information, do it here and now, even if it is not entirely correct and espouses now controversial theories as to the existence of the fort.

In summer, the ridgetop forest will be quite thick with cherry, locust, and walnut, under which grows copious small pawpaw trees, partially obscuring the earthworks and surrounding views of the Great Miami River and the Ohio River. If you come when the leaves are off the trees, you will be rewarded with not only better river views but also a better lay of the earthworks, which by any measure were done with nearly incomprehensible amounts of human labor, perhaps over many centuries.

The trail leads to the main earthworks, where you make a loop. Undulate along a ridgeline dropping toward the Great Miami River. After leaving the main earthworks, the path continues westerly toward the point of the ridge and views that await you. The first vista overlooks a large wetland of the Great Miami River. Shawnee Lookout Park protects over 250 acres of seasonally flooded riparian habitat along with nearly a thousand additional acres of wetlands below. These wetlands provide habitat for area wildlife as well as migratory waterfowl that use the Ohio River flyway. The best view of all lies at trail's end—Shawnee Lookout. Take a seat on the bench and scan westward. The Ohio River and its wooded ramparts are easily identifiable. Kentucky rises on the south bank. Below, you can see the Great Miami River meandering to add its flow to the Ohio. An imaginary north-south line divides the Buckeye State from Indiana. It runs just below Shawnee Lookout. Anything you see west of the Great Miami River will be the Hoosier State. Given the lay of the land, it is easy to see this area as a highly defensible position—if the earthworks were indeed a fort.

Your return trip takes you by more earthworks. Imagine all the work in moving the soil by hand! At this point you are probably coming down on one side or another of the theories as to why these earthworks were established. No matter your theory, we can all agree that Shawnee Lookout is a great park and hiking destination.

After driving to the second trailhead, you will pick up the Little Turtle Trail, the first hiking trail constructed at Shawnee Lookout Park. The pea gravel path, named after a Miami Indian chief, meanders through level woods of white ash, locust, hackberry, and more. If you think you are walking in a circle, you are three-quarters right. The trail curves three-fourths of the way around a field for reasons known only to the trail builders.

WHO BUILT THE FORT? AND IS IT EVEN A FORT?

Whether you call it Fort Miami or Shawnee Lookout, this area has been visited by local residents, surveyed by archaeologists, and theorized over by nearly everyone. Mounds, earthen walls, and scooped-out areas are visible from the trail. Most of the earthworks are now covered with trees, though some parts have been kept open. The latest theories center on the earthworks being part of a grand water management project. It's easy to see from here that the rivers are hundreds of feet down and area springs simply couldn't meet the water demand of the tribes that lived here for the defensive advantage; therefore, they created ponds and runoff catching areas with canals to enhance the agricultural possibilities of this protected, defensible area on high. Historically, the earthworks were thought purely for defense, while others have declared the mounds constructed for religious reasons. Research continues on this fascinating and beautiful preserved slice of greater Cincinnati.

View of the Ohio River from trailside overlook

Eventually, the Little Turtle Trail breaks northeasterly to reach the loop portion of the hike. An extraordinary number of cherry trees flank the nearly level path. Vines curl and twist among the trees, while trailside brush grows nearly impenetrable during the warm season. Interpretive signage adds an educational aspect to the trek. Soon you will come along a lofty bluff towering over the Ohio River. The trail travels the bluff edge and reaches a cleared vista, where you can peer into the Bluegrass State. Hickories and oaks predominate on this drier ridgeline. Grab one last view before turning away from the river then passing an Indian burial mound. Before you know it you are back at the trailhead.

The third base in your triple play, the Blue Jacket Trail, is also named for a chief. Start on the same side of the road where you parked. Pick up the wooded path as it travels northwesterly away from the road and toward the Great Miami River. Pass under a couple of power lines before curving along a bluff line of the Great Miami. Shortly reach a cleared overlook of the Great Miami River valley, where views stretch well into Indiana. Relax at this vista and mentally compare the scenic river views you've seen here at Shawnee Lookout Park. The Blue Jacket Trail leaves the bluff and makes its way through pawpaw woods before opening to a power line and completing the loop. It is but a short walk to finish your triple play.

Hikes of Shawnee Lookout Park

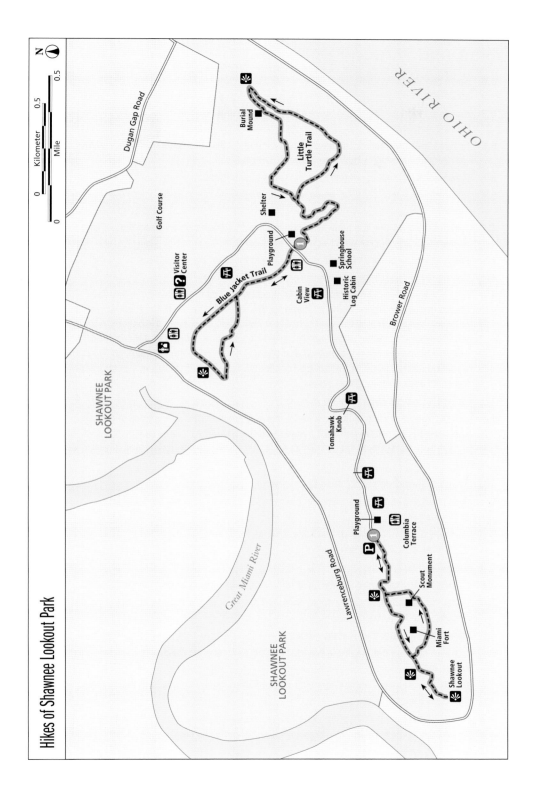

SHAWNEE LOOKOUT PARK

SHAWNEE LOOKOUT PARK

OHIO RIVER

Great Miami River

Dugan Gap Road

Golf Course

Visitor Center

Blue Jacket Trail

Playground

Shelter

Cabin View

Springhouse School

Historic Log Cabin

Little Turtle Trail

Burial Mound

Brower Road

Tomahawk Knob

Lawrenceburg Road

Playground

Columbia Terrace

Scout Monument

Miami Fort

Shawnee Lookout

N

Kilometer

Mile

Miles and Directions

0.0 Begin the Miami Fort Trail, ascending from the auto turnaround and parking area at road's end.

0.2 Reach the loop portion of the hike and the main earthworks after passing a view of the Great Miami River.

0.5 Reach a trail intersection. The loop turns back and circles the main earthworks. However, keep straight, heading westerly to Shawnee Lookout.

0.6 Pass a vista overlooking wetlands of the Great Miami River.

0.7 Reach the Shawnee Lookout, where views of three states open. Backtrack to the main loop.

0.9 Turn right and resume the main loop, curving around the primary concentration of earthworks and bridging a couple of wet-weather streams.

1.1 Pass a monument commemorating one of the founders of the Boy Scouts.

1.2 Complete the loop. Begin backtracking toward the trailhead.

1.4 Reach the Shawnee Lookout trailhead, completing the first hike. Drive 1.2 miles back toward the park entrance to the trailhead for the Little Turtle Trail and the Blue Jacket Trail. From the parking area on the west side of the main park road, cross the park road toward the playground. Near the playground, note the circular stone pit now covered in sand. Its purpose is unclear, but it is surmised that this was once an ice storage pit used by settlers who lived where this park now stands. Look for the Little Turtle Trail sign at a point where the grass ends and woodland begins.

1.7 Pass a fenced deer exclosure on your right.

1.8 Reach the loop portion of the hike and a four-way junction (the grassy track heading left accesses a trail shelter). Turn right here, toward the Ohio River.

2.1 Come along the bluff line above the Ohio River. The trail turns northeasterly, paralleling the bluff.

2.2 Reach a cleared view of the Ohio River valley.

2.4 Pass a second cleared river view. The path then turns away from the bluff line and ascends.

2.5 Pass beside an aboriginal Ohioan burial mound. Paleo-Indian habitation has been documented at least 2,000 years back.

2.8 Bridge a streambed by culvert.

3.0 Complete the loop portion of the Little Turtle Trail, backtracking toward the parking area.

3.4 Reach the trailhead. Cross the main park road and pick up the Blue Jacket Trail. Slightly descend into thick woodland.

3.6 Pass under a power line. Reenter woods.

3.7 Come to the loop portion of the Blue Jacket Trail. Keep straight, passing under a second power line.

4.0 Reach a cleared view of the Great Miami River Valley that points west into Indiana. Soon turn away from the bluff.

4.3 Complete the loop portion of the Blue Jacket Trail, backtracking toward the trailhead.

4.6 Arrive back at the trailhead parking area, completing the hiker triple play.

2 Shaker Trace

This hike utilizes the longest trail at Miami Whitewater Forest, the Shaker Trace. It makes a long and worthy loop within the Dry Fork Whitewater River Valley. The trail travels from the developed recreation hub near the park visitor center and works its way through woods and restored prairie. Later, it enters wetlands, for Miami Whitewater Forest is not merely a recreational park: It also has reestablished and preserved fast-disappearing natural habitat from the greater Cincinnati landscape. You will explore these wetlands then move on through bucolic rolling fields, mixed with stands of trees, where views stretch for surprising distances. Other sections travel alongside Dry Fork Whitewater River.

Start: Miami Whitewater Forest Visitor Center
Distance: 7.8-mile loop
Hiking time: About 3.5 to 4.5 hours
Difficulty: Moderate to difficult due to distance
Trail surface: Asphalt
Best season: Sept through May
Other trail users: Bicyclers, joggers, roller bladers
Canine compatibility: Leashed dogs permitted

Land status: County park
Fees and permits: Parking fee required
Schedule: Open daily year-round sunrise to sunset
Maps: Miami Whitewater Forest; USGS Shandon, Harrison
Trail contacts: Miami Whitewater Forest, 9001 Mount Hope Rd., Crosby Township, OH 45030; (513) 367-4774; www.greatparks.org

Finding the trailhead: From exit 3 on I-74 west of downtown near the Indiana state line, take Dry Fork Road north for 0.9 mile to turn right onto West Road. Follow West Road for 0.2 mile to Timberlakes Drive. Turn left onto Timberlakes Drive and follow it 0.6 mile to Harbor Ridge Drive. Turn left and follow Harbor Ridge Drive for 0.4 mile to the large visitor center, boathouse, and snack bar area on your right. Park in the large visitor center lot. Trailhead GPS: N39 15.500' / W84 44.619'

The Hike

Miami Whitewater Forest, a Hamilton County park, caters to all kinds of outdoor enthusiasts, from hikers to bikers, boaters, anglers, golfers, equestrians, campers, paddlers, picnickers, and on and on. It is truly a recreation complex. The Shaker Trace fits in well with this concept. It offers a nearly 8-mile loop stretching throughout the northern half of the 4,300-plus-acre getaway.

Now to the downside—the trail is asphalt. A natural surface path is preferred, but this could be a great alternative for rainy days or after precipitation has saturated the ground. It is also a safe and sure path, used by women with strollers who might otherwise be reluctant to head into the woods alone or with a young child. Also, a shorter 1.6-mile loop is available for those who want a shorter escape to nature. Since the path is paved, you will be sharing it with bicyclers, runners, and roller bladers—and

Walkers and runners as well as bicyclists enjoy the Shaker Trace.

a surprising number of hikers and exercisers. Exercise stations and contemplation benches are placed at intervals along the path for those who alternatively want additional workouts or a break from their trail treading.

The trailhead can be a busy, confusing place. The visitor center, ranger station, restrooms, and gift shop are at the front of the building. Behind are the bait shop, bike rental, and boat rental area. The snack bar is also here. The bank fishing area lies near the trailhead. The whole area stands on a peninsula overlooking Miami Whitewater Forest Lake.

You will leave this busy area, crossing the first of several roads: two-lane, mostly quiet thoroughfares. Begin your clockwise loop. Trail intersections are clearly marked and mileages have been painted onto the trail to keep you apprised of your distance covered. The asphalt track is divided in the middle with a yellow line, allowing two-way traffic of hikers and bicyclers. In the warmer season, have a shade hat and sunscreen for Sol overhead.

Make sure to stop at the Shaker Trace wetlands. A spur trail leads to a wildlife viewing blind, good for observing waterfowl. The path then meanders in a bucolic pastoral setting. Even the nearby quaint farms add to the tranquility. Begin circling back toward the trailhead beyond your most northerly point. The backdrop continues to be eye appealing and the hills not challenging at all. More road crossings lie ahead. Some of them go under the roads they intersect. In the distance, hills rise along the valley of Dry Fork Whitewater River. The trail feels more intimate there. Finally, you meet the Inner Loop, where other walkers are likely to be. It is but a short distance back to the trailhead.

While you are here, consider indulging in many of the other activities at this inclusive park. The choices are as wide as you will see at one recreation destination. Many of them, such as boating, fishing, biking, or camping, are within walking distance of the Shaker Trace trailhead.

Miles and Directions

0.0 Start on the northeast side of the large parking area, to your left as you face the visitor center building. The Shaker Trace begins near the fishing area and heads left, northwest, away from the visitor center (another paved path heads right, past the fishing area and around the edge of the lake to the boathouse).

0.2 The Shaker Trace splits. Stay left, going clockwise on the loop. Your return route crosses Mount Hope Road, but you travel westerly, parallel to the road. Pass under Harbor Ridge Drive, which spans the trail on a stone bridge. A hodgepodge of field and wood borders the track.

0.7 Reach the Inner Loop of the Shaker Trace. It leaves right, running parallel to Dry Fork Whitewater River before again meeting the main Shaker Trace, creating a 1.6-mile circuit. Stay left here, immediately bridging Dry Fork Whitewater River. Pass through an open prairie with native grasses and ample bird life.

1.2 Tunnel under New Haven Road. Travel along prairie.

1.8 Carefully cross Baughman Road. Enter the heralded Shaker Trace wetlands.

2.0 Don't miss the spur trail leading left to an overlook of the Shaker Trace wetlands. A covered viewing platform peers upon marsh and open water. Interpretive information adorns the platform walls. The trail curves toward Howard Creek, a tributary of Dry Fork Whitewater River, as you roll through prairie and wetland, presenting an attractive landscape.

3.0 Pass a pond on your left that should have water year-round.

3.1 Come to a trailside shelter. It offers a covered picnic area as well as tree-shaded tables. Make sure to look back south across the wetland for a pleasant view.

3.4 Bridge Howard Creek. Keep rolling through a pastoral setting.

4.3 Cross Oxford Road.

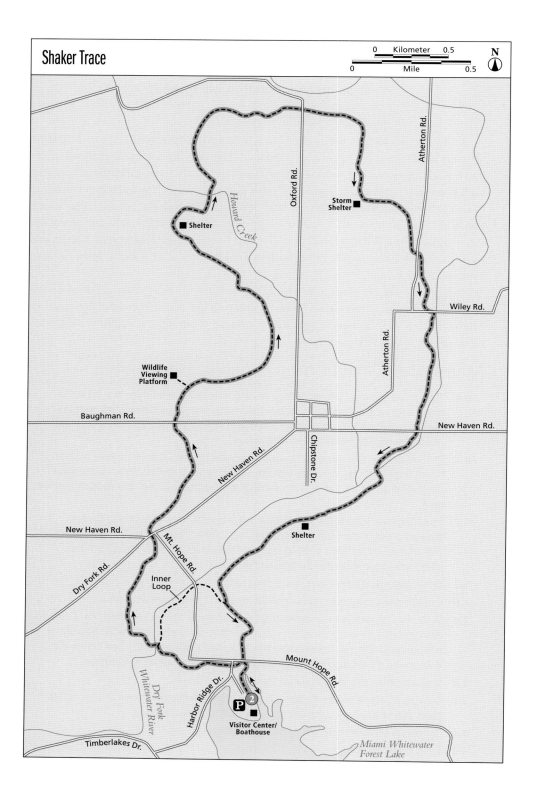

Shaker Trace

0   Kilometer   0.5

0   Mile   0.5

N

Howard Creek

Oxford Rd.

Atherton Rd.

Storm Shelter

Shelter

Wiley Rd.

Atherton Rd.

Wildlife Viewing Platform

Baughman Rd.

New Haven Rd.

New Haven Rd.

Chipstone Dr.

Shelter

New Haven Rd.

Dry Fork Rd.

Mt. Hope Rd.

Inner Loop

Mount Hope Rd.

Dry Fork Whitewater River

Harbor Ridge Dr.

P   2

Visitor Center/ Boathouse

Timberlakes Dr.

Miami Whitewater Forest Lake

4.9 Come to a storm shelter in open terrain.

5.2 Cross Atherton Road. Soon come alongside Dry Fork Whitewater River. Good views open of the watercourse.

5.6 Go under Wiley Road. Watch for bicycles while emerging from under the bridge. Keep southbound, enjoying more looks at Dry Fork Whitewater River.

6.1 Walk under New Haven Road, still along Dry Fork.

6.4 Bridge Dry Fork Whitewater River. You are now on the east bank of the waterway in more wooded terrain.

6.8 Pass by another storm shelter. Stay in a deep, wooded valley.

7.4 Come to the other end of the Inner Loop after climbing a hill. The Shaker Trace will sometimes become more crowded with casual hikers and dog walkers.

7.6 Cross Mount Hope Road and complete the loop portion of the hike. Backtrack toward the trailhead.

7.8 Complete the hike.

GREEN TIP

As you take advantage of the spectacular scenery in greater Cincinnati, remember that our planet is very dear, very special, and very fragile. All of us should do everything we can to keep it clean, beautiful, and healthy.

3 Loops of Miami Whitewater Forest

Make three loops on three different trails starting from the same trailhead at this 4,300-acre county forest that includes not only hiking trails but also camping, fishing, boating, and more. Your hikes travel through hilly terrain with frequent elevation changes, adding to the hiking challenge. What value—three hikes in one destination! Small lakes and wet-weather streams add a watery aspect to the wooded setting.

Start: Timberlakes Trail Shelter
Distance: 3.8-mile triple loop
Hiking time: About 2 to 2.5 hours
Difficulty: Moderate
Trail surface: Natural surface paths in forested woods
Best season: Year-round
Other trail users: None
Canine compatibility: Leashed dogs permitted

Land status: County park
Fees and permits: Parking fee required
Schedule: Open daily year-round sunrise to sunset
Maps: Miami Whitewater Forest; USGS Shandon, Addyston, Harrison, Hooven
Trail contacts: Miami Whitewater Forest, 9001 Mount Hope Rd., Crosby Township, OH 45030; (513) 367-4774; www.greatparks.org

Finding the trailhead: From exit 3 on I-74 west of downtown near the Indiana state line, take Dry Fork Road north for 0.9 mile to turn right onto West Road. Follow West Road for 0.2 mile to Timberlakes Drive. Turn left onto Timberlakes Drive and follow it 1.0 mile to the Timberlakes shelter and trailhead with a large parking area on your left. Trailhead GPS: N39 15.026' / W84 44.903'

The Hike

Each of the three trails on this hike is classified as a nature trail by the Hamilton County parks department. And I agree, they offer quiet walks in woodlands. For better or worse, you will be returning to the trailhead between each of the three hikes. The trailhead features a picnic area, a covered shelter, restrooms, and water. Your first trail, Timberlakes Trail, is the most water oriented. It passes by a small dammed pond and comes near the big body of water at this park—Miami Whitewater Forest Lake.

It is but a short downhill jaunt on the Timberlakes Trail through hickory-oak woods to reach the dammed pond. The trail actually crosses the dam, and you can gain views of the impoundment from there. The hike then takes you up to a ridgeline where the trail offers easy walking. It comes near the access road for Miami Whitewater Forest Lake before running parallel to that impoundment. Return to the ridgeline, traveling south through rich deciduous woods before looping down to the small pond you were at earlier.

Next up is the Oakleaf Trail. It loops by the aforementioned pond, as well as a different smaller pond, with cattails and duck moss during the warm season. A boardwalk leads along the perimeter of the wetland and a steep hill with beech and buckeye. The

Coming to the first of several ponds you will see on this hike

Oakleaf Trail roller-coasters through a hickory-oak-maple complex. A highlight of this trail is the spur to a pond overlook with a contemplation bench perfect for relaxation. A solid climb brings you back to the parking area for your third trail.

Pick up the Badlands Trail across Timberlakes Drive. The Badlands Trail is named for the unusual land formations, which I attribute to erosion from poor land practices in days gone by. Sometimes it's hard to look at a forest and think of it as once being cleared, but this was likely pasture or farmland that lost topsoil following storms. You will be traveling into drainages that flow during winter, early spring, and following heavy rains. Bridges span some of the rocky streambeds. These drainages divide wooded hills over which you ramble. If you are tiring, take the Badlands Trail shortcut. Otherwise stick with the whole loop and earn the complete 3.8 miles of the hike.

GREEN TIP
Pass it down—the best way to instill practical physical health habits in your children is to set a good example. Take them on a hike!

MIAMI WHITEWATER FOREST

Run by Hamilton County, Miami Whitewater Forest contains a whopping 4,345 acres. A multiplicity of recreational opportunities lies within its boundaries. In addition to the three nature trails described here, the park also has a Parcours fitness trail, with exercise stations that add to the walking. Equestrians have their own path. The Shaker Trace Trail is paved. You can make a 1.2-mile loop or a 7.8-mile loop. It is popular with hikers, bicyclers, and joggers. (Bicycles are for rent at the park.) A highlight of the long circuit is a trip through the Shaker Trace wetlands, 130 special preserved acres. The Shaker Trace also makes its way amid woodland, fields, and old farmland.

Cincinnatians should take advantage of the close and easy camping here, as Miami Whitewater Forest offers a 46-site campground. Each site has electricity, as well as a fire ring and picnic table. Reservations are accepted up to one year in advance. The sites are laid out in a classic loop, with water spigots within reasonable distance of every camp.

Miami Whitewater Lake is the park's centerpiece. The Timberlakes Trail, on this hike, comes very near the 85-acre lake. Electric and gas motors are allowed on the lake, but only up to 4 horsepower. Rent a pontoon or fishing boat. However, self-propelled watercraft abound. Rent a pedal boat, kayak, or even a stand up paddleboard or bring your own canoe or kayak. Cool off at a watery playground. Landlocked anglers can head to the park's fishing pier. As you can read, hiking is just one of the many outdoor opportunities at Miami Whitewater Forest.

Miles and Directions

0.0 From the lower end of parking area, away from the restrooms and Timberlakes Shelter, pick up the Timberlakes Trail heading easterly and downhill.

0.2 Cross the dam of a pond and reach the loop portion of the Timberlakes Trail. Turn left, northwesterly, following the dammed tributary.

0.4 Reach a mini-loop of the Timberlakes Trail on top of a ridge. Saunter north on a level wooded track toward Harbor Ridge Road.

0.6 Come near Harbor Ridge Road before turning back south, hiking a hill above Miami Whitewater Forest Lake.

0.7 Complete the mini-loop and proceed southerly along the ridge.

1.1 Come near the dammed pond.

1.4 Reach the trailhead after crossing back over the pond dam. Stay left and pick up the Oakleaf Trail, which starts near the Timberlakes Shelter.

1.5 Bridge the dam of a smaller pond. Begin the loop of the Oakleaf Trail, passing over a boardwalk.

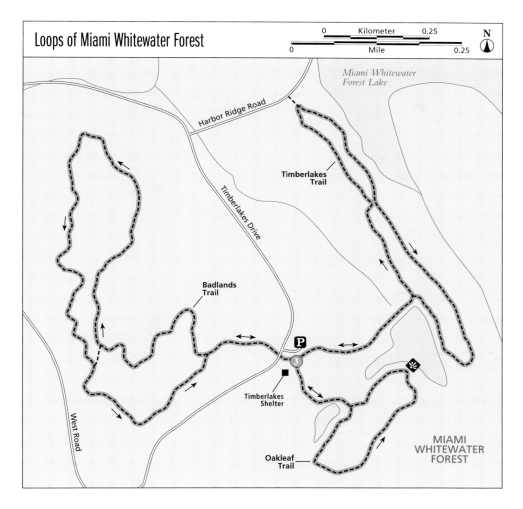

Loops of Miami Whitewater Forest

0	Kilometer	0.25
0	Mile	0.25

N

Miami Whitewater
Forest Lake

Harbor Ridge Road

Timberlakes
Trail

Timberlakes Drive

Badlands
Trail

P

Timberlakes
Shelter

West Road

Oakleaf
Trail

MIAMI
WHITEWATER
FOREST

1.9 Reach the spur trail leading to a contemplation bench at the edge of a pond. The Oakleaf Trail then rises to the trailhead after completing its loop.

2.2 Begin the Badlands Trail on the west side of Timberlakes Drive. Descend on wooden steps to a wooded hollow and the loop portion of this trail. Begin a pattern of dipping into drainages and climbing ridges.

2.3 Stay right at the loop of the Badlands Trail.

2.6 A shortcut leads left to bisect the loop portion of the Badlands Trail. Stay right with the longer circuit.

3.0 Curve back south on a hill well above Dry Fork Whitewater River.

3.4 Pass the other end of the Badlands Trail shortcut.

3.7 Complete the loop of the Badlands Trail.

3.8 Return to the trailhead after finishing all three loops of Miami Whitewater Forest.

4 Stone Steps Loop at Mount Airy Forest

This hike explores the south side of Cincinnati's historic Mount Airy Forest. Depart the stately Oval Shelter and descend a steep hollow centered by a rocky drainage. You will drop over 300 feet. Your climb back out includes using the Stone Steps, hand-placed limestone footings that help you negotiate your way directly up the nose of a ridge. The balance of the hike curves around rib ridges and into rocky drainages sloping off the side of Mount Airy. Numerous trail junctions add a navigational challenge to this rewarding hike that will leave you coming back to this trail-filled park.

Start: Oval Shelter
Distance: 2.8-mile loop
Hiking time: About 1.5 to 2.5 hours
Difficulty: Moderate, does have significant elevation changes
Trail surface: Natural surface path in forested woods
Best season: Year-round; seasonal trail closures Nov through Feb
Other trail users: None
Canine compatibility: Leashed dogs permitted

Land status: City park
Fees and permits: No fees or permits required
Schedule: Open daily year-round sunrise to sunset
Maps: Mount Airy Forest; USGS Cincinnati West
Trail contacts: Mount Airy Forest, 5083 Colerain Ave., Cincinnati, OH 45223; (513) 352-4080; www.cincinnatiparks.com

Finding the trailhead: From exit 18 on I-74 northwest of downtown, emerge from the interstate to reach the intersection of West Fork and Colerain Avenue, US 27. Take Colerain Avenue, US 27, north for 1.4 miles to enter Mount Airy Forest. Turn left into the forest then immediately turn left onto Trail Ridge Road and reach the Oval at 0.4 mile. Circle ¾ the way around the oval to reach the Red Oak Trail, on the outside of the road. Pick up the Red Oak Trail as it descends into woodland. Trailhead GPS: N39 10.370' / W84 34.071'

The Hike

This hike takes place at the city of Cincinnati's largest park, Mount Airy Forest, now officially listed on the National Register of Historic Places. A century ago, the park-to-be was an assimilation of small farms on a big hill off Colerain Avenue. Poor agricultural practices turned the hill into naked ground eroding at an alarming rate. The city began purchasing the farms and replanted over 1.2 million trees! They also stabilized the soil, preserving Mount Airy. And by 1914, the *Cincinnati Times Star* boasted, "It is no exaggeration to say that Mount Airy Forest comprises the most picturesque assortment of hills, valleys, streams, woods, lawns, and wild scenery that we have within the city limits." During the 1930s the Civilian Conservation Corps built most of the rustic park structures we see today, which added structural splendor to the literally growing natural scenery as the planted trees blossomed into the gorgeous forest we see today. Nearly all Cincinnatians—even non-park visitors—have seen the stone walls along Colerain Avenue built by the CCC.

The CCC also built the Stone Steps that are one of the highlights of this hike. The vein-like trail network on the 1,459-acre park (40 percent of the total Cincinnati park acreage) is big enough that you definitely need a map; otherwise, you may find yourself hiking in circles. However, trail junctions are well marked, but you will need the map to confirm your position. Download a complete park trail map from the above listed Cincinnati Parks website before starting your trek. During fall and early winter, check the park website for seasonal trail closures. The park, in an attempt to manage the unsustainable deer population, allows bowhunting in the park. A decade

THE CIVILIAN CONSERVATION CORPS

The Great Depression hit the United States in 1929 following a devastating stock market crash. At the time, no one knew how long the economic hard times would go on. In 1933, with the country still in the throes of economic malaise, President Franklin Delano Roosevelt initiated a government work program, the Civilian Conservation Corps, commonly known as the CCC. In it, men were hired on various projects throughout the United States, including transforming Mount Airy into the park we see today. To qualify for the Civilian Conservation Corps, recruits had to be between the ages of eighteen and twenty-eight, be out of school and unemployed. Eligible enrollees were often shipped far from homes to prevent desertion. They earned $30 per month through their efforts, of which $25 went back home. They built hiking trails, scenic roads, cabins, dams, fish hatcheries, improved wildlife habitat, planted trees, and more, at over 800 parks in the United States. They also practiced fire management, making fire roads and also erecting over 3,400 fire watchtowers!

The CCC was organized into camps, generally of 100 to 300 men, using a military structure with an emphasis on discipline. Each camp had its specialists, from cooks to officers. Over 2,600 camps containing a half-million men were spread across all forty-eight states. Camp life was routine. The men generally rose around 6 a.m., ate a filling breakfast then worked until 4:30 in the afternoon, with a lunch break in the middle. Back at camp, the men could do as they pleased, often writing letters home. These descriptive letters to loved ones helped build a historical record of life in the CCC camps.

Whether the CCC helped or hurt the nation's economy remains under debate. The CCC program continued until 1942, when potential enrollees instead entered the military to fight World War II. The CCC was never abolished, only defunded to extinction. Most of the CCC boys have passed away, but their legacy lives on in the Stone Steps of Mount Airy and in the parks we still enjoy today.

Limestone steps placed by the CCC provide a vertical challenge for hikers.

back, the deer population at Mount Airy Park had reached eighty-five animals per square mile, over four times the sustainable desired fifteen to twenty deep per square mile. Deer were eating everything in sight, reducing biodiversity. This hunting has allowed the park's plant life—and wildflowers such as trillium—to recover as well as reduce sick and starved deer.

Stone Steps Loop at Mount Airy Forest

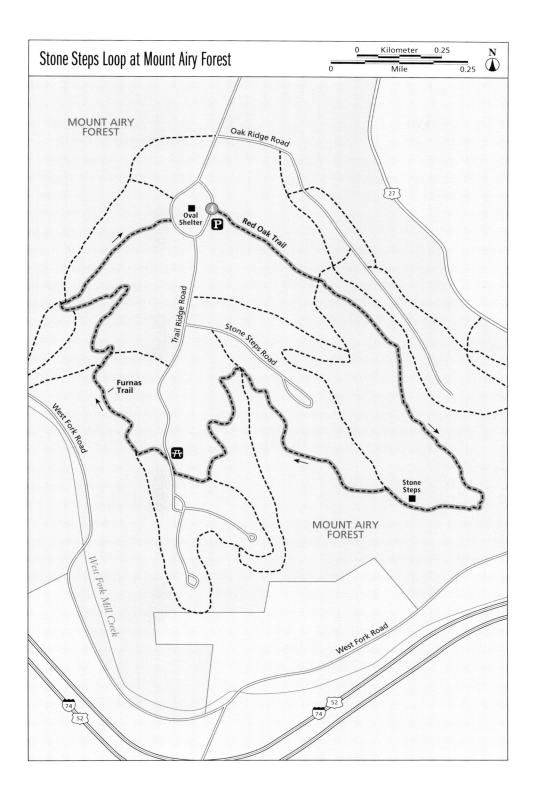

N

0   Kilometer   0.25

0   Mile   0.25

MOUNT AIRY
FOREST

Oak Ridge Road

27

Oval
Shelter

P

4

Red Oak Trail

Trail Ridge Road

Stone Steps Road

Furnas
Trail

West Fork Road

West Fork Mill Creek

Stone
Steps

MOUNT AIRY
FOREST

West Fork Road

74

52

52

74

The single-track Red Oak Trail takes you from the Oval down to the bottom of Mount Airy. The hollow to your right increases in size as you drop. Sounds of the city drift into the woods, but your visual perceptions will be nothing but nature. Your way back up is via the historic Stone Steps. As you ascend, reflect that these footings were laid eight decades past, when this area was on the edge of town, where farms still hung on. From there, you will navigate a plethora of junctions, but you are never far from the Oval (where you parked) in case you get discombobulated. Even at that, you will see the allure of the locale and return to Mount Airy Forest to create loops of your own. A final note: Since Mount Airy is now an urban forest, have your phone with you if hiking solo and keep your guard up.

Miles and Directions

0.0 Leave the Oval Shelter, southbound on the Red Oak Trail.

0.2 Keep straight at the first trail intersection. Continue downhill and step over a streambed. And keep straight at the next junction just ahead.

0.8 Descend to cross a bridge over the hollow you have been paralleling, then open onto a field not far from West Fork Road. Look right for the Ponderosa Trail and begin regaining the elevation you lost.

0.9 Reach the Stone Steps. Make the lung-busting climb straight up the nose of a ridge on limestone steps, one foot at a time.

1.0 Stay left at a three-way junction shortly after the Stone Steps, now on a level track.

1.4 Make a four-way junction. Keep straight.

1.8 Turn right at a three-way junction. Shortly meet Trail Ridge Road. Cross the road and veer right, passing through a picnic area with a water spigot to slake your thirst. Join a spur leading downhill to the Furnas Trail. Just downhill, meet the Furnas Trail and turn right, northbound.

2.1 Pass a narrow trail coming up from West Fork Road.

2.2 Pass a trail leaving right, uphill, to Trail Ridge Road. Ahead, curve around a hollow. Watch for hemlock trees, rare in these parts.

2.5 Pass a trail leading left and downhill. Stay right with the Furnas Trail. Circle around a big sinkhole and pass two more junctions; stay right, avoiding the trail to the Treehouse and taking the trail toward the Oval.

2.8 Emerge on the west side of the Oval, away from your starting point. Head toward the shelter in the middle of the Oval and walk a few feet to the trail's beginning.

GREEN TIP

Never feed wild animals under any circumstances. This includes everything from birds to chipmunks to raccoons to deer. You may damage their health and expose yourself (and them) to danger.

5 Glenwood Gardens

This destination will undoubtedly surprise first-time hikers. Beyond the attractive landscaped gardens, you will enjoy an overlook before looping into the West Fork Mill Creek watershed. The hike will take you into the "back 40" of the gardens, where you will observe the flora and fauna associated with wetlands of not only West Fork Mill Creek but also several ponds and wet meadows. The lesser-used trail system has enough hills to give exercise value as well as scenic beauty that will have you making return trips in different seasons.

Start: Cotswold Visitor Center
Distance: 2.7-mile double loop
Hiking time: About 1.5 to 2 hours
Difficulty: Moderate
Trail surface: Asphalt, gravel
Best season: Year-round
Other trail users: None
Canine compatibility: Dogs not permitted
Land status: County park

Fees and permits: Parking fee required
Schedule: Open dawn to dusk year-round; other gardens within the park have specific hours, call ahead if visiting them
Maps: Glenwood Gardens; USGS Glendale
Trail contacts: Glenwood Gardens, 10397 Springfield Pike, Woodlawn, OH 45215; (513) 771-8733; www.greatparks.org

Finding the trailhead: From exit 14 on I-75 north of downtown Cincinnati, take Glendale-Milford Road west for 1.4 miles to Springfield Pike/OH 4 and a traffic light. Keep straight through the light and veer left into the gardens (If you veer right after the light, you will enter a shopping center). Curve around a traffic circle to reach the parking area and visitor center. Trailhead GPS: N39 15.533' / W84 28.345'

The Hike

Glenwood Gardens is a much-underutilized hiking destination. Perhaps it is even unrecognized as a hiking destination. Once a 360-acre working farm outside Cincinnati way back when, what was the country became city. The heirs of the farm donated land along the banks of West Fork Mill Creek to the Hamilton County parks system in 1993. Later, more acreage was added. The house and surrounding gardens were preserved and expanded. Thus, most area residents think of the gardens only when they think of this park. And it does have alluring gardens, as well as a special garden for children to learn about nature—Highfield Discovery Garden.

But there is more to Glenwood Gardens than what first meets the eye, for Hamilton County has developed a trail system that includes a paved loop connecting to a nature trail network that explores the bottomlands of West Fork Mill Creek and the woods, prairie, wetlands, and meadows along it. The parks system has systematically improved the wetland complex, resulting in a natural area with impressive summer

Glenwood Gardens presents both sculpted and natural flora to visitors to enjoy.

wildflowers and an everywhere-you-look beauty that makes Glenwood Gardens an undiscovered gem of a hike in an area amidst the heart of the greater Cincinnati. That being said, take some time to amble through the gardens while you are here, before or after your hike.

You may never find a more elaborate beginning to a hike, as you pass through an archway and through scenic gardens to an overlook, where the West Fork Mill Creek Valley opens before your eyes. Attractive meadows along West Fork Mill Creek are visible, as well as part of the paved trail. The overlook reveals the lay of the land. You can see where the trails lead. Pass the Legacy Garden, then descend, leaving the developed gardens area to make a trail junction.

Ninety-nine percent of all park visitors have now been left behind. Now hard to imagine, what is scenic park terrain was once cattle country. Enjoy the level path bordered by shade trees in a mix of meadow and woodland. You will soon join the Wetland Loop, a more primitive gravel track that explores numerous ecosystems.

After bridging West Fork Mill Creek, you climb a hill then enter an area of managed wetlands. Birds and birders who watch the avian set thrive in these diverse habitats. The wet meadow area will have a dizzying midsummer array of wildflowers. The lotus blooms in one pond display appealing color. Returning to the stream, you will pass through more mixed habitats before completing the walk. Make sure to explore

WHAT IS A WETLAND?

Parts of this hike travel through wetlands along and near West Fork Mill Creek. We all hear the term "wetland" and then think of our own images of what exactly is a wetland. You might conjure up a swamp, with eerie trees hanging over dark waters, with snakes swimming in the water. Or you might imagine a large open body of water, with waterweeds growing on its surface and waterfowl grouped together. Or you may visualize somewhere like the Florida Everglades, a vast expanse of sawgrass, under which flows an inches-deep sheet of water.

Any one of these images is not entirely incorrect. According to the US Environmental Protection Agency, wetlands are "lands where saturation with water is the dominant factor determining the nature of soil development and the types of plant and animal communities living in the soil and on its surface." To translate the government garble, it means an ecosystem in which water is the key ingredient. One more part of the definition also states, "Wetlands generally include swamps, marshes, bogs, and similar areas." So wetlands can take varied forms.

Wetlands don't have to be under water or even wet year-round to be wetlands. Some wetland plant communities in fact depend on a cyclical flooding and drying out of their terrain. The Everglades is a prime example. So when you hike Glenwood Gardens, look around and see what you define as wetlands.

the developed gardens before or after your visit. The Cotswold Garden includes aesthetically appealing plants from near and far. See the Legacy Garden, where visitors purchase trees in honor of loved ones.

Also, consider bringing some younger future hikers and conservationists to explore Highfield Discovery Garden. It's a fun way for kids to learn about nature hands on, rather than watching a program on a computer screen. Let them see, feel, hear, and touch the real world. Special programs are designed for kids and families. Learn about Ohio's animal and bird life, and how nature changes with the seasons. If you appreciate nature, there's something for you here at Glenwood Gardens.

Miles and Directions

0.0 From the large parking area, walk toward the main gardens, passing through a stone archway. The Cotswold Visitor Center is to your left, but you stay right following signs to the Walking Trails. Shortly reach an overlook.

0.2 Pass an Indian burial mound while descending from the developed gardens. Reach a trail junction. Stay right, northbound on the asphalt trail. West Fork Mill Creek is to your left.

0.4 Pass a park access road. Keep straight.

Glenwood Gardens

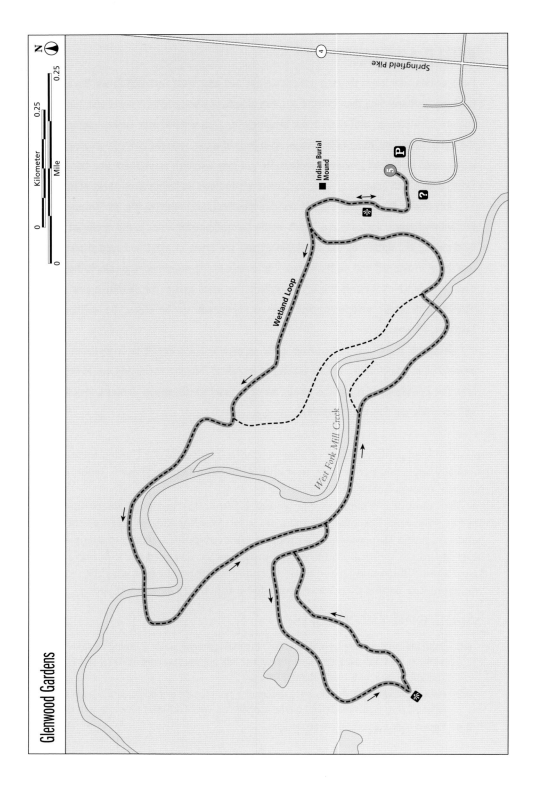

Indian Burial Mound

Wetland Loop

West Fork Mill Creek

Springfield Pike

N

Kilometer
0   0.25

Mile
0   0.25

Lotus blooms are a great reward for a warm summertime hike.

0.5 Reach a trail junction. Here, the main paved loop leaves left. Turn right with the Wetland Loop, also paved. The Wetland Loop shortly bridges a stream and becomes a gravel path. Pass another park access road to the right of the trail. The main route is obvious.

0.8 Cross over West Fork Mill Creek on an elaborate concrete and iron bridge in sycamore-dominated bottomland. Ascend from the stream.

0.9 Pass a four-trunked sycamore on trail right.

1.1 Take a right on a sub-loop of the Wetland Loop. Enjoy wet meadow, pond, and prairie environments.

1.2 Stay right as the trail splits on the loop proper. Ascend to pass small ponds with views from the trail.

1.5 Reach a hilltop vista and contemplation bench. Begin ambling back to West Fork Mill Creek bottoms.

1.8 Finish the mini-loop.

1.9 Stay right at an intersection, cruising down West Fork Mill Creek Valley.

2.2 Bridge West Fork Mill Creek. Enjoy open views of the stream. Next bridge a tributary on a rustic old bridge left over from the farm days. Shortly meet the paved trail and keep right, curving below the main house and gardens.

2.5 Finish the paved loop. Backtrack uphill to the developed gardens.

2.7 Complete the hike after passing back through the developed gardens.

6 French Park Hike

Many Cincinnati hikers believe the stream flowing through French Park to be the most scenic in the city. They cite its numerous cascades, its frozen winter beauty, and the wildflowers that spring forth from its banks. The trail along French Creek may be described as a "water walk," as you must step over the stream several times. The "water walk" is only part of the trek. First, you will hike along another tributary, then circle the park's highland perimeter, saving your "water walk" for last.

Start: Sierra Trail trailhead
Distance: 3.3-mile lollipop
Hiking time: About 2 hours
Difficulty: Moderate, has hills
Trail surface: Natural surface path
Best season: Year-round
Other trail users: None
Canine compatibility: Leashed dogs permitted

Land status: City park
Fees and permits: No fees or permits required
Schedule: Open daily year-round sunrise to sunset
Maps: French Park; USGS Cincinnati East
Trail contacts: Cincinnati Parks, 950 Eden Park Dr., Cincinnati, OH 45202; (513) 352-4080; www.cincinnatiparks.com

Finding the trailhead: From exit 12 on I-71 northeast of downtown, take Montgomery Road/US 22/OH 3 south for 1.6 miles to Ohio Avenue and a traffic light. Turn right onto Ohio Avenue and travel just a short distance to Section Road. Turn left onto Section Road and follow it west for 1.1 miles. Turn right into French Park, passing a parking area. Continue up the main park road, circling behind the French House. At 0.2 mile, just beyond the manor, turn right onto the one-way exit road, following it downhill to a parking area on your left, just before returning to Section Road. Trailhead GPS: N39 11.749' / W84 25.480'

The Hike

French Park was originally an estate centered with the large redbrick manor you see today. Built in the early 1900s and remodeled numerous times since then, the dwelling is now available for event rental from the city of Cincinnati. The house and grounds were donated to the city in 1943. The mostly forested park is groomed around the house but also includes a section of restored prairie. During this hike you will find woodland also occupies a sizeable portion of the park. A picnic shelter at the top of a hill offers a far-reaching view to the west. As you will come near it on your hike, it is very worth checking out.

▶ When choosing trail snacks, consider making homemade healthy goodies like granola bars. Or simply bring fruit—it tastes great with no preparation.

Most of the time you will be circling the perimeter of the 275-acre preserve, though the water walk also travels through the heart of French Park. The trails themselves are in pretty fair shape though the numerous trail junctions combined with a few user-created paths can make things slightly

The French House complements the park scenery and hosts many a social engagement.
COURTESY OF THE CINCINNATI PARK BOARD

confusing for first-time hikers. However, the close proximity of the park border, which is surrounded by houses, and also the park roads and other nearby roads make being lost for very long an unlikely proposition.

You first join the Sierra Trail, named for the Sierra Club, which constructed it in 1992. A prairie to your left offers large and colorful wildflowers in summer. Soon enter woodland, traveling easterly along a streamlet. This watercourse is a tributary of French Creek, which is a tributary of Mill Creek, which is a tributary of the Ohio

A MAN WITHIN A VILLAGE WITHIN A CITY

French Park is owned and run by the city of Cincinnati, but it is actually located in Amberely Village, Ohio, an incorporated hamlet enveloped in urbanity. More than 1,400 households stand within the 3.5-square-mile village, founded in 1940. They have their own police and fire departments, but its schools are part of the Cincinnati public system.

French Park is a recreational centerpiece of Amberely Village. While the home of art collector Herbert Greer French, it was known as Reachmont Farm. French passed away in 1942, after which the farm was given over to the city. Many works of art formerly owned by French now hang in the Cincinnati Art Museum. French was indeed a generous benefactor to this city on the Ohio River.

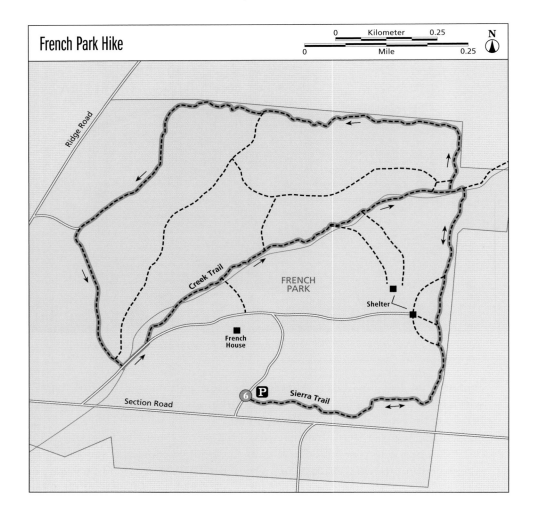

Ridge Road

Creek Trail

FRENCH
PARK

Shelter

French
House

6 P   Sierra Trail

Section Road

River. Soon climb the park's big hill. Note the planted evergreens in the woods. Ahead, pass side trails leading to the shelter atop the hill. Go visit the shelter and take in the westerly view, where you can perhaps see all the way to Indiana on a clear fall or winter day.

Then get your first taste of French Creek, spanning it on a bridge before you resume your circumnavigation of the park grounds. Enjoy traipsing through a meadow, which presents blackberries in summertime. Next you'll join the Creek Trail, which parallels French Creek, with its small cascades dropping over layer after layer of limestone rock strata. You will have numerous crossings, but most of them can be rock-hopped with dry feet except after heavy rains and occasional wet periods in winter and spring. If the crossings seem too difficult, simply follow the main park road behind the French House and walk to your vehicle.

Miles and Directions

0.0   From the parking area near Section Road at the end of the one-way road after passing the French House, take the Sierra Trail, heading east.

0.3   Turn left, curving uphill along the park border, gaining 100 feet in elevation in a short distance.

0.5   Pass the first of three spur trails leading left to the park shelter. A big view opens near the shelter. Keep north along the park boundary.

0.8   Descend to reach French Creek. A bridge spans this upper part of the creek. Begin the loop portion of the hike. Take a few steps downstream then curve right, away from the creek heading uphill on wood-and-earth steps. Just ahead, pass a trail leading left—stay right.

1.0   The main outside loop turns west.

1.2   Reach a trail junction in an open brushy area. The trail leading left heads to the lower parking area. Keep straight, but now on a grassy track.

1.4   Meet a cell tower service road. Turn right, tracing the service road.

1.6   Leave left from the service road, back on trail. Soon enter an open meadow in the process of becoming reforested. Watch for blackberries in summer.

1.9   Reach the lower parking area. Turn left onto the park road, bridging French Creek. Leave the road left, passing through a shady picnic area to pick up the Creek Trail. Immediately rock-hop French Creek. Enjoy the clear stream as it flows over a limestone bed in numerous shoals divided by pools.

2.1   A spur trail leaves right and uphill to the French House.

2.2   A spur trail leads left; keep straight.

2.3   A spur trail leads right uphill toward the picnic shelter. Ahead, a second spur leads toward the picnic shelter.

2.5   Complete the loop portion of the hike. Cross the bridge over French Creek then backtrack on the Sierra Trail to the trailhead.

3.3   Arrive back at the trailhead, completing the hike.

GREEN TIP

Stay on the trail. Cutting through from one part of a switchback to another can destroy fragile plant life.

7 Stanbery Park Hike

Located in the Mount Washington area of greater Cincinnati, Stanbery Park presents 125 acres of hilly wooded respite from the city. Leave the busy traditional park area and take the Schoop Trail, descending to a rocky picturesque stream, on its way to meet the Little Miami River. The steep scenic valley will be rife with wildflowers in spring. Descend the deep hollow, following it to the park's western edge. You will backtrack up the hollow, then pick up a loop trail, crossing several bridges on your return trip.

Start: Oxford Avenue trailhead
Distance: 2.5-mile lollipop
Hiking time: About 1.5 hours
Difficulty: Moderate, has hills
Trail surface: Natural surface path
Best season: Spring for wildflowers
Other trail users: None
Canine compatibility: Leashed dogs permitted

Land status: City park
Fees and permits: No fees or permits required
Schedule: Open daily year-round sunrise to sunset
Maps: Stanbery Park; USGS Newport
Trail contacts: Stanbery Park, 2221 Oxford Ave., Cincinnati, OH 45230; (513) 352-4080; www.cincinnatiparks.com

Finding the trailhead: From exit 69 on I-275, east of downtown Cincinnati, take Five Mile Road north for 1.0 mile to Beechmont Avenue. Turn left onto Beechmont and follow it 2.5 miles to a traffic light and Corbly Road. Take a left onto Corbly, then immediately turn right onto Oxford Avenue and the entrance to Stanbery Park will be on your left. Trailhead GPS: N39 5.672' / W84 23.352'

The Hike

Stanbery Park, home of the Mount Washington Farmers Market and the fall pumpkin chuck, is a fun gathering place with a lively spirit created by local residents who flock to its 125 acres. The park is also enhanced with great trails that take advantage of the vertical variation in terrain and the flora that rises from it. The easternmost part of the park, where the parking area and developed areas are located, can be a beehive of activity on nice days.

The park is known for its statue of a reading boy. The metal edifice was moved here in 1940 from its previous spot at Campus Lane Park in the Mount Washington Community, after Stanbery Park was dedicated. The statue was erected as a World War I memorial.

The park is also known for its prolific wildflower displays. I have seen them first-hand along the trails, and they are astonishing. Legend has it that Albert Schoop, for whom the hiking trail you will be walking is named, planted the wildflowers. However, wildflowers are very difficult to transplant, so either Schoop knew what he was doing,

Trout lilies color the slops of Stanbery Park.

the area already had a profusion of spring color, or it was a combination of both. No matter the origin, the result is masses of trout lilies, trilliums, spring beauties, violets, and more. You will be surprised at the numbers of wildflowers and should make an annual April pilgrimage to Stanbery Park to enjoy the floral Cincinnati treasure.

The pumpkin chuck is a post-Halloween event held each November. Stanbery Park has a large, open, grassy hill (which you climb during your hike). In winter, when the snows carpet the park, sledders come out in droves, sliding down that grassy hill. However, in fall, revelers set up at the top of the hill and fling their pumpkins as far as they can, using a medieval catapult known as a trebuchet. The event is a fund-raiser for the Stanbery Park Advisory Council, a private citizens group advocating for the historic preserve. The pumpkin chuck also is a great way to compost your jack-o-lantern!

This hike has almost 300 feet of elevation change, pretty hefty for an urban park. Join the Schoop Trail, leaving the casual park visitors behind. You step into a wooded world of towering hardwoods, drifting deep into a hollow. Visually it looks like the back of beyond, but the sounds of the city drift into the forest. A trickling branch flowing over limestone rock is cutting a hollow that you enter. Steps aid in your descent.

Official spur trails lead up to the park shelter, but also watch out for user-created paths connecting to adjacent neighborhoods. As the stream cuts deeper, sheer bluffs

SANFORD B. STANBERY, WORLD WAR I—AND LOCAL PARK—HERO

The park is named for Brigadier General Sanford B. Stanbery. He is noted for being the highest ranking officer from this area during World War I. Stanbery was awarded the Army Distinguished Service Medal. In November 1918, Stanbery successfully and heroically led the 155th Infantry Bridge, 78th Division, fighting their way toward Sedan, during the Meuse-Argonne Offensive. After the war, the Millersburg, Ohio, native built his home on the site of what is now Stanbery Park. The city bought the land from the general's widow in 1938. She graciously sold their home and the adjoining property for less than what it cost to build the Tudor-style house alone. The city then converted their grounds into a park, and the house was later demolished.

rise on the far side of this tributary of Clough Creek, which is a tributary of the Little Miami River.

Eventually, you reach a low point and Elstun Road. Your backtrack is all uphill, then you loop around another hollow rising up the north side of the park. A final climb up the ol' sledding hill takes you to the main part of the park and the trailhead.

Miles and Directions

0.0 From the parking area on the east side of Stanbery Park, walk west, away from the park entrance, joining the natural surface Schoop Trail at the edge of the woods. A wooden post marks the path's beginning. An asphalt trail leads left to Corbly Road.

0.2 An impressive white oak rises beside the trail. Keep descending. Watch for previous park incarnations, such as the remains of an old dam on the creek and forgotten concrete picnic tables across the stream.

0.3 Reach a trail intersection. Here, a path leads right, up to the park's circular shelter. Keep straight, heading deeper into the unnamed stream's valley.

0.4 Reach another spur trail leading right, steeply uphill with wooden steps, toward the park.

0.5 The Schoop Trail crisscrosses the stream the first of several times.

0.6 Another spur trail leaves right and rises to the main shelter. Look for a little 2-foot waterfall in the vicinity.

0.7 Just before crossing over to the left bank of the creek, the loop portion of the hike leaves right. You will return here later. For now, cross over to the left bank of the stream and continue westerly. The trail rises well above the creek in rich woods with buckeye as a heavy understory tree.

1.0 Come very near a house just outside the park boundary.

1.1 Cross the creek within vicinity of a second house. You are now on the right-hand bank of the stream. The trail corridor narrows. This is, in fact, still part of Stanbery Park.

1.2 Reach the trail's end at Elstun Road. This is also the low point of the hike. Backtrack uphill.

1.7 Leave left after crossing the creek the second time since Elstun Road. Pick up the loop trail, curving up another hollow centered with a streambed. The path crosses several

bridges over sometimes-dry streambeds. Hardwoods rise overhead. Continue to gain elevation. The hollow narrows.

2.2 Open onto a grassy hill. This is the aforementioned sledding and pumpkin tossing hill. Clamber straight up the grass. Once atop the hill, turn left, joining a concrete path aiming for the trailhead. Continue on the little sub-loop within sight of the parking area. Pass restrooms and iron benches, as well as the historic statue of the reading boy.

2.5 Complete the hike.

GREEN TIP
When hiking with your dog, stay in the center of the path and keep Fido leashed and close by. Dogs that run loose can harm fragile soils and spread pesky plants by carrying their seeds.

8 Woodland Mound Hike

This trek explores just about every foot of every trail at Woodland Mound, a safe and family-friendly Hamilton County park perched high on a bluff above the Ohio River. First you will take the Hedgeapple Trail to visit three ponds. Return to the trailhead and follow the Fitness Trail, a gravel path with exercise stations that heads to an old homesite. The main trail, a paved track by the name of Shared Use Trail, makes a loop through the heart of the park. On your way back to the trailhead, take a detour on the Seasongood Trail, which runs atop a steep wooded ridge. On the way back enjoy some rewarding views of the Ohio River and its boat traffic down below.

Start: Hedgeapple/Fitness trailhead
Distance: 2.9 miles
Hiking time: About 1.5 to 2.5 hours
Difficulty: Moderate
Trail surface: Gravel and asphalt
Best season: Year-round
Other trail users: Joggers
Canine compatibility: Leashed dogs permitted

Land status: County park
Fees and permits: Parking fee required
Schedule: Open daily year-round sunrise to sunset
Maps: Woodland Mound; USGS Withamsville
Trail contacts: Woodland Mound Park, 8250 Old Kellogg Rd., Cincinnati, OH 45255; (513) 474-0580; www.greatparks.org

Finding the trailhead: From exit 71 on I-275, take US 52 east for 3.6 miles, then turn left onto Eight Mile Road. Follow Eight Mile Road just a short distance, then turn right onto Kellogg Road. Follow Kellogg Road for 1.5 miles to the entrance to Woodland Mound Park. Drive past the entrance station, then turn right and follow the park road to a hilltop parking area. The Hedgeapple and Fitness Trails start in the southeast corner of the lot, near the Weston Shelter. Trailhead GPS: N39 2.184' / W84 19.455'

The Hike

Woodland Mound sports over 1,000 acres of bluff-top woods, fields, prairies, and developed areas overlooking the Ohio River, southeast of downtown Cincinnati. The scenic setting is overlain with a connected network of trails. Hike them all and you can cobble together a nice little hike. The park has a manned entrance station and is very family friendly. Therefore, if you are a woman hiking alone, or dragging your kids along to the park, this is a nice and safe place to get a little exercise.

From the parking area, a short paved track leads to a great view of the Ohio River. You may be tempted to walk out and grab your vista before starting the trek. Either way, pick up the Hedgeapple Trail. The gravel track meanders through woods, dropping off the hillside. Interpretive information signs are scattered along the path. The trail splits, adding a little loop to the trek. Pass a couple of ponds in a successional forest. This area was likely pasture a century back, and the ponds were to water cattle. A

Virginia Bluebells signal the onset of spring in Cincinnati.

contemplation bench awaits at the trail's end, where a small, still body of water reflects the forest around it. After returning to the trailhead, you will then tackle the Fitness Trail, a combination hiking and fitness path. There are twenty designed stops along the way. If you did them all along with this entire hike, you'd get a serious dose of daily exercise and probably be too tired to finish the trek. Not all the people will be stopping

ABOUT WOODLAND MOUND PARK

Within its 1,000-plus acres, Woodland Mound has lots of park facilities and activities. The preserve offers several picnic shelters for rent, one of which is on the Ohio River. You pass a couple of other shelters on this hike. The park also has an 18-hole disc golf course, Badger Bluff. The Vineyard is an 18-hole golf course rolling over the northeast side of the park. For kids, Woodland Mound offers Parky's Wet Adventure. It's a wet playground with wet slides, fountains, and sprayers that present a cool respite from a hot summer day. They also have standard playgrounds. Check out the nature center and learn more about the wildlife of Woodland Mound. If you are hungry, stop by the Breezy Point snack bar or go all out and rent the Sweetwine Banquet Center. RVers can enjoy Steamboat Bend Campground, along the river, featuring river-view campsites for recreational vehicles only. There's even a boat launch for those who want to fish or sightsee on the Ohio. Like most other Hamilton County parks, it's a place where you can do a lot, in addition to getting in touch with nature on the trails.

at the stations. Actually many of them will be doing what this hike does: walking all the trails at Woodland Mound back to back.

After returning to the parking area a second time, you will break off, heading on the Shared Use Trail in a big loop. The trailside vegetation is a mix of trees and grass. Bring a hat if you are prone to sunburn. The path travels through a small restored prairie, then by a ball field before curving back toward the Ohio River. Make a little detour on the Seasongood Trail, a natural surface path, before rejoining the Shared Use Trail. Pass an open view of the Ohio River. Developed facilities such as the visitor center are but a short detour distant. It isn't long at all before you have completed the hike.

Miles and Directions

0.0 Start on the Hedgeapple Trail, picking up a gravel path heading downhill toward the Ohio River. The path travels among Osage orange trees. Their nickname is hedge apple. The trail splits; stay with the Hedgeapple Trail, continuing downhill to pass a pond.

0.3 Reach the far end of the Hedgeapple Trail at a pond. Backtrack. On your return trip, stay right at the upper loop and pass a third pond.

0.6 Emerge back at the trailhead. This time, turn right, picking up the Fitness Trail. It offers twenty fitness stations with exercise bars and the like, along with interpretive information and instructions for working out at each station. The wide gravel track undulates along a hillside. It separates along the way, then comes together.

1.0 Make the small loop at the far end of the Fitness Trail. This was an old homesite. Note the planted bushes and flowers. Ignore the gravel path spurring off the loop. Backtrack toward the trailhead.

1.5 Complete the Fitness Trail. Now pick up the Paved Trail, heading counterclockwise. A yellow line divides the path and keeps the traffic flowing in both directions.

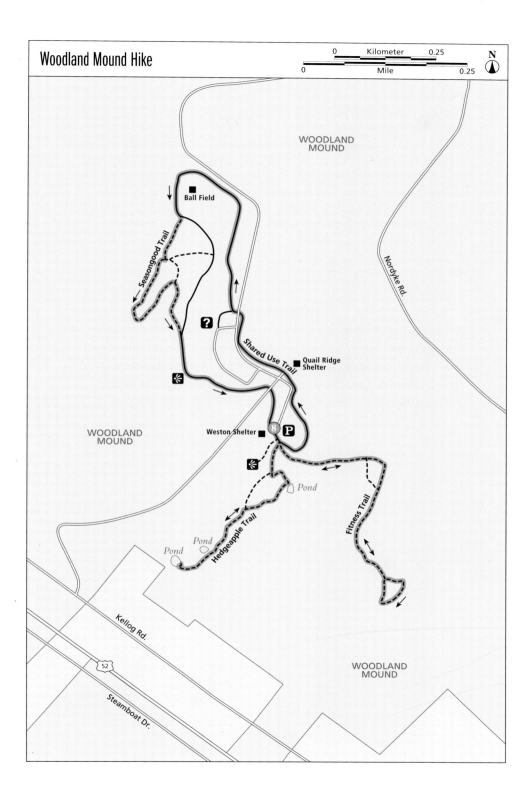

Woodland Mound Hike

0   Kilometer   0.25

0   Mile   0.25

N

WOODLAND
MOUND

■ Ball Field

Seasongood Trail

?

Shared Use Trail

■ Quail Ridge
Shelter

WOODLAND
MOUND

Weston Shelter ■

8 P

Pond

Fitness Trail

Hedgeapple Trail

Pond

Pond

Nordyke Rd.

Kellog Rd.

52

Steamboat Dr.

WOODLAND
MOUND

1.7 Pass the Quail Ridge shelter, then the entrance station. The large parking area for the developed part of the park is across the road to the left.

1.8 Cross the main park road, then stay right to complete the loop. You are close to the visitor center.

2.2 Start turning back south after looping around a ball field. Ahead, split right with the Seasongood Trail. Undulate through prairie.

2.3 Stay right at the actual loop portion of the Seasongood Trail. Look how far the ridge drops off on your right—nearly 300 feet down to Eight Mile Creek! You continue along a ridge. Winter views open of the Ohio River.

2.4 Stay right at the next junction, heading toward the visitor center.

2.6 Stay right, rejoining the Shared Use Trail. Views open of the Ohio River. Watch for barges plying the river. A kids' playground is to your left, as well as the visitor center.

2.8 Cross the park entrance road.

2.9 Complete the hike.

GREEN TIP

While hiking, help keep trails clear. Toss aside manageable fallen debris such as fallen limbs, keeping the path open so hikers can stay on designated trails. After returning to the trailhead, report large fallen trees, missing trail signs, and other problems to the appropriate trail managers.

9 Redwing Loop

This hike travels through the southern portion of the Rowe Woods at Cincinnati Nature Center, exploring the aquatic and land scenery of the preserve. You will first visit Powel Crosley Lake before leaving the beaten path on the Whitetail Trace, visiting meadows, prairies, woods, and ponds. Wander into the upper valley of East Branch Avey's Run, where you can see first-hand stream and wetland restoration. The final part of the hike climbs over hills before returning to East Branch Avey's Run, where a waterfall spills over a limestone lip. Make a final climb, returning to Powel Crosley Lake and completing the circuit.

Start: Rowe Visitor Center
Distance: 4.1-mile loop
Hiking time: About 2.5 to 3 hours
Difficulty: Moderate to difficult, lots of hills
Trail surface: Some gravel, mostly natural surface path
Best season: Sept through May
Other trail users: None
Canine compatibility: Dogs must be registered online before hike; dogs must be leashed at all times on property

Land status: Cincinnati Nature Center property
Fees and permits: Entrance fee or membership required
Schedule: Open daily year-round during daylight hours
Maps: Rowe Woods Trails; USGS Goshen, Batavia, Withamsville
Trail contacts: Cincinnati Nature Center, 4949 Tealtown Rd., Milford, OH 45150; (513) 831-1711; www.cincynature.org

Finding the trailhead: From exit 59 on I-275, east of downtown Cincinnati, take OH 450 east just a short distance to US 50. Turn right and take US 50 east for 2.0 miles to Round Bottom Road. Turn right onto Round Bottom Road and follow it for 0.5 mile, then turn left on Tealtown Road. Follow Tealtown Road for 0.6 mile then turn right into the Rowe Woods Tract of the Cincinnati Nature Center. Follow the entrance road past the attendant gate and veer left to reach the parking area and visitor center. Trailhead GPS: N39 7.526' / W84 14.746'

The Hike

This hike starts at the Rowe Visitor Center, the hub of Rowe Woods at Cincinnati Nature Center. Before or after your hike, make sure to check out the informative kiosks, displays, and library. Nature center staff members are on hand to answer your questions. You can also get a trail map at the center or online. The land and water adventure first circles around Powel Crosley Lake, a small impoundment where you may see waterfowl. There is also a bird blind here with feeders nearby for observing songbirds up close. A small marsh pond near the main lake presents yet another aquatic attraction. A boardwalk allows for close-ups of this wetland. The hike then heads south on the Whitetail Trace. A blend of open meadows and woods makes for ideal deer habitat. I have personally seen deer on this stretch of trail. Visit another

RESTORING A STREAM

Along this hike you settle into a valley that was once a farm. This subsistence farm was first cleared in the 1800s. The winding tributary of Avey's Run had rich soils, deposited over time during floods. The farmer cleared the trees from the vale, making it arable. To maximize the yield in the valley, the farmer used primitive tools to straighten out the stream, allowing more land to be farmed. Less land was flooded, too. Over time, the soils were exhausted, especially without being replenished by nutrients during high-water events. The straightened-out stream also cut a deep channel. Floods scoured the stream more and more when the rains came. Over time, the life in the stream was degraded, since the stream was changed from a watery wetland to a silt-free rock bed that rapidly rose and fell with precipitation, rather than rising and lowering gradually. When suburbia arrived upstream (it encircles the Cincinnati Nature Center), runoff from roads and other impermeable surfaces contributed to the torrential runoff that further degraded the watercourse.

In 2007, with a grant from the Ohio Environmental Protection Agency, the Cincinnati Nature Center, along with interested partners, decided to restore the stream. First, they re-dug the channel, replicating its original shallow, meandering curves instead of the altered straight and deep channel. This way, high waters would slow down, cruising around the curves instead of surging straight downstream. The banks were stabilized with rocks, logs, and root balls. Burlap was laid over the banks to keep soils from washing away. Small rocks were spread on the stream bottom, creating riffles, which adds oxygen to the stream and more evenly deposits sediment during floods. V-shaped spillovers were built to deepen the channel in spots, for a variety of stream widths and depths adds to the variety of life within. Lastly the Redwing Trail was rerouted along the stream. Today you can appreciate for yourself the watery improvements along this tributary of East Branch Avey's Run. So can the people downstream, for this creek flows into Avey's Run, which flows into Stonelick Creek, which flows into the East Fork Miami River, which . . . well, we all live downstream, so natural flood control is a good thing for man and the world in which we live.

GREEN TIP

If you're driving to or from the trailhead, don't let any passenger throw garbage out the window. Keep a small bag in the car that you can empty properly at home.

A fall sky reflects off Powel Crosley Lake.

pond before joining the longest path at Rowe Woods, the Redwing Trail. It heads into the farthest recesses of the preserve, meandering throughout the upper watershed of Avey's Run.

At one point you will drop to an isolated valley, crossing a tributary of Avey's Run. Here, you can see first-hand the restorative work of returning a channelized stream to its original course. The nature center hopes to rehab still more waterways within the nature center property down the line. A century and a half ago, a farmer of yesteryear altered the watercourse to make more room for crops and to better drain what is now a hill-ringed, meadowy wetland. From there you will leave the restored tributary to roam through fields and woods, through habitat favorable for the trail's namesake, the redwing blackbird.

Your travel through the upland ends when you join the Geology Trail. It drops to East Branch Avey's Run, spanning the watercourse on a high bridge, which allows good looks at the stream. Your best view will be upstream, as you can enjoy a wide, low limestone waterfall. Be apprised this stream may all but dry up in late summer and fall. Your best bet for seeing the cataract is winter and spring. The time of rebirth will also have the added benefit of wildflowers, of which there are plenty along this circuit.

Redwing Loop

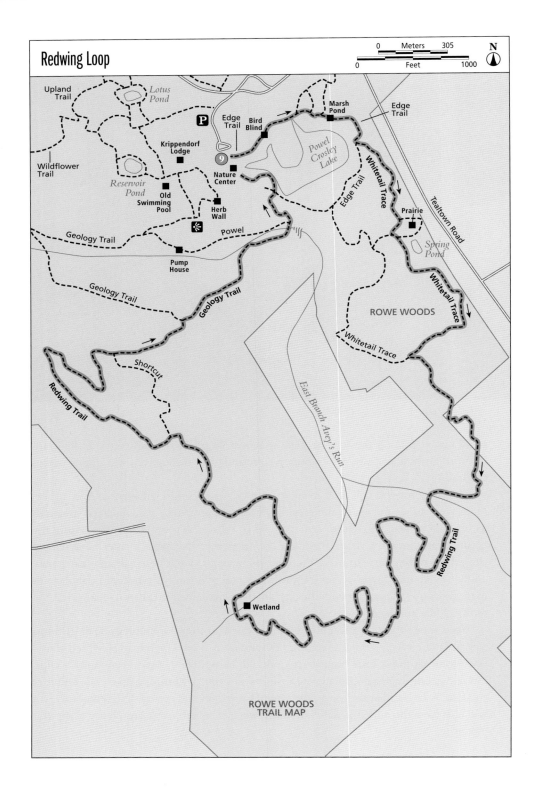

Meters 0 — 305
Feet 0 — 1000

N

Upland Trail

Lotus Pond

Edge Trail

Marsh Pond

Edge Trail

P

Krippendorf Lodge

Edge Trail

Bird Blind

9

Powel Crosley Lake

Whitetail Trace

Wildflower Trail

Reservoir Pond

Nature Center

Old Swimming Pool

Herb Wall

Edge Trail

Tealtown Road

Prairie

Geology Trail

Powel

Spring Pond

Pump House

Whitetail Trace

Geology Trail

Geology Trail

ROWE WOODS

Shortcut

Whitetail Trace

Whitetail Trace

Redwing Trail

East Branch Avey's Run

Redwing Trail

Wetland

ROWE WOODS
TRAIL MAP

Miles and Directions

0.0 Start at the Rowe Visitor Center. As you face the visitor center, leave left on the green-blazed Edge Trail. Walk a gravel track, shortly passing a bird blind to your left. Powel Crosley Lake lies off to your right. The path crosses an arm of the small impoundment. Stay right as the Lookout Trail leaves left. Come to the Marsh Pond, following the wooden boardwalk along the water's edge. Turn south in upland woods.

0.3 Meet the Whitetail Trace. The Edge Trail keeps straight—you can see a lakeside shelter within sight. Turn left, joining the Whitetail Trace. Enter maturing hardwoods, heavy with maple.

0.5 Open onto a prairie, where native grasses are being restored. A short trail circles the prairie perimeter. Shortly pass a spur trail leading right. It shortcuts the Whitetail Trace.

0.6 Walk over the dam of the Spring Pond. The trail remains level in upland woods.

0.9 Intersect the Redwing Trail. Turn left here, still in mixed field and forest. Head southerly then cross a dirt right-of-way connecting to private land. Keep south, still in Cincinnati Nature Center property, descending to some hollows near the park boundary. Wood and earth steps aid your ascents and descents.

1.3 Rock-hop the uppermost part of East Branch Avey's Run. Begin winding westerly, working around hollows and on ridges, in younger woods. Watch for deer trails crisscrossing the Redwing Trail.

2.1 Pass a contemplation bench overlooking a wooded ravine.

2.4 Rock-hop a tributary of East Branch Avey's Run and enter restored stream and wetland. The trail crosses the wetland on an elevated berm then circles downstream, passing interpretive signage explaining the wetland and stream restoration, as well as the replanting of native plants.

2.5 Turn away from the stream, ascending to a large meadow. Circle around the edge of the opening.

3.0 A shortcut leaves right after leaving the meadow. Enter mature woods of cherry, sugar maple, and oaks. Bridge a steep ravine.

3.5 The other end of the shortcut comes in on the right. Keep straight on the Redwing Trail. Climb.

3.6 The Redwing Trail ends. Meet the Geology Trail. Stay right, winding downward to East Branch Avey's Run.

3.9 Bridge East Branch Avey's Run and intersect the other end of the Geology Trail. Look upstream for a good view of a waterfall. The cascade descends about 5 feet over a horseshoe-shaped limestone rim. Stay with the part of the Geology Trail that climbs steeply on wood-and-earth steps.

4.0 Return to the Edge Trail. Turn left, then jog right, picking up a boardwalk along Powel Crosley Lake. Enjoy more aquatic scenery, looking for waterfowl, too.

4.1 Reach the back door of the nature center, ending the hike.

10 Far Ridge Loop

If you like ups and downs, this hike is for you. Start up high, at the Cincinnati Nature Center's hilltop visitor building. Visit Powel Crosley Lake. From that impoundment, drop to East Branch Avey's Run and find a waterfall. Follow the creek downstream and a few rock hops later reach the wide flat along Avey's Run. But you climb back toward the visitor center on the aptly named Wildflower Trail. Old-growth trees tower over this path, which takes you back down to Avey's Run. This time, rock-hop Avey's Run and climb again, now on the Far Ridge Trail. Wander in solitude through backwoods before dropping to Avey's Run once again. Climb a breathtaking set of steps to make interesting Fox Rock on the Geology Trail. One more descent leads to East Branch Avey's Run. A final climb returns you to the trailhead and a deserved rest.

Start: Rowe Visitor Center
Distance: 4.0-mile loop
Hiking time: About 2.5 to 3 hours
Difficulty: Difficult, lots of hills
Trail surface: Some gravel, mostly natural surface path
Best season: Sept through May
Other trail users: None
Canine compatibility: Dogs must be registered online before hike; dogs must be leashed at all times while on property

Land status: Cincinnati Nature Center property
Fees and permits: Entrance fee or membership required
Schedule: Open daily year-round during daylight hours
Maps: Rowe Woods Trail map; USGS Batavia, Withamsville, Madeira, Goshen
Trail contacts: Cincinnati Nature Center, 4949 Tealtown Rd., Milford, OH 45150; (513) 831-1711; www.cincynature.org

Finding the trailhead: From exit 59 on I-275, east of downtown Cincinnati, take OH 450 east just a short distance to US 50. Turn right and take US 50 east for 2.0 miles to Round Bottom Road. Turn right onto Round Bottom Road and follow it for 0.5 mile, then turn left onto Tealtown Road. Follow Tealtown Road for 0.6 mile then turn right into the Rowe Woods Tract of the Cincinnati Nature Center. Follow the entrance road past the attendant gate and veer left to reach the parking area and visitor center. Trailhead GPS: N39 7.526' / W84 14.746'

The Hike

Though this trek is only 4 miles long, it packs a lot of highlights and even more hills into a figure-eight loop. The Rowe Visitor Center makes for a great starting point, since it offers a building full of resources to help you further appreciate the human and natural history of the 1,000-plus-acre swath of Clermont County, on the eastern flank of greater Cincinnati. The Cincinnati Nature Center is a nonprofit, environmental education organization of which you can be a member or just a paying visitor. It has been in operation for decades. The nature center's current mission statement is "inspiring passion for nature and promoting environmentally responsible choices

These jonquils were planted way back when Carl Krippendorf owned what is now the Cincinnati Nature Center.

through experience, education, and stewardship to ensure a sustainable future." The Rowe Woods Tract is but one of two tracts that comprise the greater nature center. The other tract is Long Branch Farm and Trails. It is 9 miles northeast of Milford, in Goshen, Ohio. The 582-acre onetime working farm has paths as well.

Not only can you get involved as a member, but the Cincinnati Nature Center presents numerous programs for kids and adults, from nature camp and school programs for kids to adult lecture series and more. They also have rental facilities for groups, which benefit the Cincinnati Nature Center and offer a great setting for weddings, meetings, and such. To learn more visit their website, www.cincynature.org.

You can see some of the facilities firsthand on this hike. Start this trek after walking through the Rowe Visitor Center. Stop and mull around the library or see the displays. Grab a souvenir at the gift shop. Just make sure to knock the dirt off your shoes before you enter. The hike explores a boardwalk along Powel Crosley Lake. The still water of the impoundment will contrast with East Branch Avey's Run, cutting a deep valley through glacial soils, reaching limestone and spilling down, down, down, deeper to meet West Branch Avey's Run. Come to the waterfall on East Branch, dropping in horseshoe fashion over a 5-foot lip.

You will head deeper in this valley, passing an old pump house, left over from when Carl Krippendorf lived here in his hilltop abode. The pump house was built in 1911, running water from the once dammed creek up to the house, using gasoline and electrical power. Krippendorf began constructing his house in 1898. After completing it in 1901, he acquired this property on Avey's Run in order to get a reliable water supply to his swimming pool, located near the house.

Beyond the pump house, the trail crosses East Branch Avey's Run. Large stepping-stones have been stretched across the creek at the crossings. If the water is excessively high, you may have to abandon the hike and try some hilltop trails instead. At other times, the stream may be but a trickle, or even dry, allowing the easiest of passages.

Then you meet the Wildflower Trail, easily one of the most scenic paths in Rowe Woods. The trail ascends a steep slope, which may leave you looking head down, panting. But this approach will reward you with lots of wildflower sightings in spring—toothwort, mayapple, trillium, trout lilies, and more. You may miss what's overhead—big trees—beeches, oaks, and maples.

What goes up will go down on this hike. A couple of trail connections takes you back down the other end of the Wildflower Trail and into a sizeable bottomland along lower Avey's Run. Here, big sycamores reign over another wildflower haven. Then you join the only track on the west side of Avey's Run—the Far Ridge Trail. Reaching it can be challenging if the streams are running, as it requires a rock hop of lower Avey's Run. Once across, take on the steepest section of the entire hike. The loop then levels off and you roam in solitude before looping back down to Avey's Run, crossing at the same spot a second time.

The hike then cruises through a flat meadow with hiking as easy as it gets. Next, wood steps stretch sharply up to Fox Rock. Here, a deck leads to a geologically interesting cliff face. This overhanging outcrop hosts site specific vegetation, such as walking fern and purple cliffbrake. A shelter here makes for an ideal relaxing location, where you can peer down on East Branch Avey's Run atop Fox Rock.

A return trip to the waterfall on East Branch is the next order. This time you can view it from a bridge and from the stream bluff. The final climb of the trek leads back to the visitor center, ending the hike.

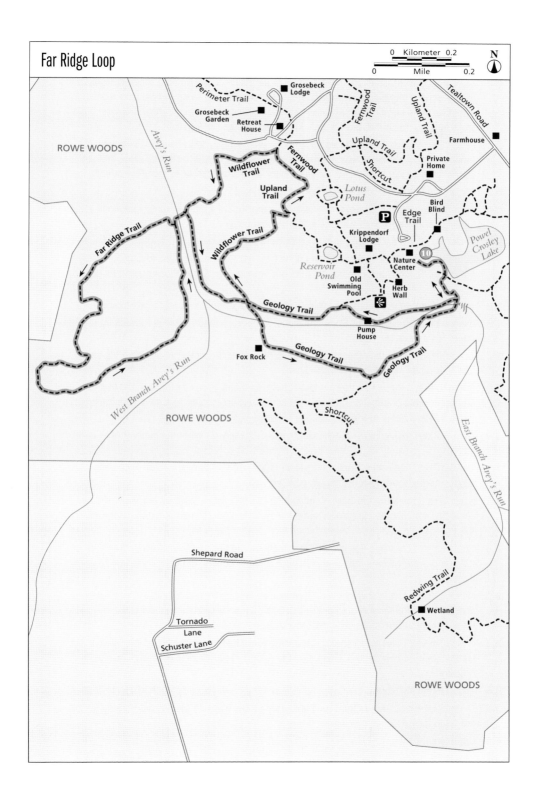

Far Ridge Loop

0   Kilometer   0.2

0   Mile   0.2

N

Perimeter Trail

Grosebeck Lodge

Fernwood Trail

Upland Trail

Tealtown Road

Grosebeck Garden

Retreat House

Fernwood Trail

Upland Trail

Farmhouse

ROWE WOODS

Avey's Run

Wildflower Trail

Upland Trail

Shortcut

Private Home

Lotus Pond

P

Edge Trail

Bird Blind

Far Ridge Trail

Wildflower Trail

Krippendorf Lodge

Nature Center

Powel Crosley Lake

Reservoir Pond

Old Swimming Pool

Herb Wall

10

Geology Trail

West Branch Avey's Run

Fox Rock

Pump House

Geology Trail

Geology Trail

East Branch Avey's Run

ROWE WOODS

Shortcut

Shepard Road

Redwing Trail

Tornado Lane

Wetland

Schuster Lane

ROWE WOODS

Miles and Directions

0.0 Start at the Rowe Visitor Center. Walk through the visitor center and out the back door, then pick up a trail that shortly turns into a boardwalk along Powel Crosley Lake. Look for waterfowl while cruising the shoreline boardwalk. Shortly run into the Edge Trail. Take a few steps left then meet the Geology Trail. Turn right onto the Geology Trail.

0.2 Reach East Branch Avey's Run and a waterfall after steeply descending on wood steps. Turn right and continue downstream. Pass a bridge over East Branch Avey's Run that you will be walking over later. Watch for gravel bars, rocks, and cascades along the stream.

0.3 Steps lead left a short distance to access the stream.

0.4 Pass the stone pump house. Curve away from the stream a bit then reach limestone steps leading up to the gardens astride the Krippendorf Lodge.

0.5 Rock-hop East Branch Avey's Run twice in rapid succession.

0.7 Come to a four-way intersection. You will be here again later. Stay right, joining the Wild-flower Trail. Climb sharply on natural path and wooden steps. Try to look around for large trees.

1.0 Take a left onto the Upland Trail, which has more old-growth trees, and more climbing.

1.1 Intersect the Fernwood Trail. Congratulations, you just climbed 200 feet. Stay left, north-bound on a more level track.

1.2 Turn left, picking up the other end of the Wildflower Trail. Descend among more big trees and thousands of daffodil blooms in April.

1.5 Come to Avey's Run and a trail junction. Congratulations, you just dropped 200 feet and are now in wide bottomland. Admire several massive sycamores. Turn right toward the Far Ridge Trail and come to a wide rock hop of Avey's Run.

1.6 The Far Ridge Trail splits. Stay right, climbing very steeply on a slender footpath with wood steps.

1.8 The Far Ridge Trail eases. Continue a slight ridgetop incline through mature woodland. Begin cruising southwesterly through quiet woods.

2.1 Open onto a meadow and travel through it for 0.1 mile. You should be enjoying solitude, since this loop has no intersections and it is isolated from the rest of the trail network. After reaching a high point, begin circling back toward Avey's Run.

2.9 Complete the Far Ridge Trail circuit. Cross back over to the east side of Avey's Run and turn right onto the Wildflower Trail. Cruise through a partly wooded flat with Avey's Run to your right.

3.1 Come to the four-way trail junction. Stay right, picking up the Geology Trail. Cross East Branch Avey's Run on rocks when flowing. Take on a wooden staircase climbing toward Fox Rock. I counted 196 steps. Count for yourself.

3.3 Reach Fox Rock and a trail shelter. Make sure to explore the underside of the outcrop via the elevated boardwalk. Continue on the Geology Trail, heading east atop a wooded ridgeline.

3.5 The Redwing Trail comes in on your right. Stay left, now descending on the Geology Trail.

3.8 Bridge East Branch Avey's Run. Look upstream for the waterfall. Begin backtracking toward the visitor center.

4.0 Complete the hike.

11 Lookout Loop

This trek in the wooded hills of Cincinnati Nature Center explores the northern part of the preserve. It leaves the buildings and short nature trails around the nature center for outlying terrain, where streams cut wildflower-laden north-facing valleys to a view looking north. The hike then heads for a second hillside, which has more pronounced ups and downs, also passing by some of the historic buildings on the property known as Rowe Woods.

Start: Rowe Visitor Center
Distance: 4.1-mile loop
Hiking time: About 2.5 to 3 hours
Difficulty: Moderate, but does have hills aplenty
Trail surface: Natural surface path in forested woods
Best season: Sept through May
Other trail users: None
Canine compatibility: Dogs must be registered online before hike; dogs must be leashed at all times while on property

Land status: Cincinnati Nature Center property
Fees and permits: Entrance fee or membership required
Schedule: Open daily year-round during daylight hours
Maps: Rowe Woods Trail map; USGS Goshen, Madeira, Batavia
Trail contacts: Cincinnati Nature Center, 4949 Tealtown Rd., Milford, OH 45150; (513) 831-1711; www.cincynature.org

Finding the trailhead: From exit 59 on I-275, east of downtown Cincinnati, take OH 450 east just a short distance to US 50. Turn right and take US 50 east for 2.0 miles to Round Bottom Road. Turn right onto Round Bottom Road and follow it for 0.5 mile then turn left onto Tealtown Road. Follow Tealtown Road for 0.6 mile then turn right into the Rowe Woods Tract of the Cincinnati Nature Center. Follow the entrance road past the attendant gate and veer left to reach the parking area and visitor center. Trailhead GPS: N39 7.526' / W84 14.746'

The Hike

Cincinnati Nature Preserve covers rolling hilly terrain on the south side of Stonelick Creek near Milford. The tract is centered on the 175-acre former hilltop estate of Carl Krippendorf, located off Tealtown Road. It is from this collection of buildings and gardens that the impressively extensive trail network emanates. This particular hike leaves the nature center pulse of the park and crosses Tealtown Road, passing the farmhouse located where Carl Krippendorf first came to this neck of the woods, ostensibly to regain his health, for he was a sickly youth. The farmhouse you see was built in 1890 and was called Edge Hill Farm. The tract where Krippendorf later built his lodge was culled from Edge Hill Farm. You will pass near the wood frame house, exploring a mix of field and wood. Reach the first of two warm-up vistas overlooking Stonelick Creek Valley. Circle into tiny tributaries of Stonelick

The Cincinnati Nature Center is known for wildflower displays like this.

Creek, sometimes flowing—more often not—to reach a ridge extending toward the brow above Stonelick Creek. Here, you will find a spur path extending out the ridge leading to a shelter, and a fine view overlooking the Stonelick Creek Valley. This is a good place to relax and appreciate the preserved 1,025 acres that comprise the Rowe Woods portion of the Cincinnati Nature Center.

The trek leaves the vista and crosses back over Tealtown Road, then works its way to the Fernwood Trail. This path also explores hills falling toward Stonelick Creek and the creeks that drain it. The hills here are a little steeper and the climbs a little tougher. On your return, you will pass near historic gardens and old buildings part of the Groesbeck Lodge, built in the early 1900s. It was constructed using native limestone. The slate roof adds to the building's rustic country impression. A smaller stone garden structure, along with columns arranged in a Stonehenge-like fashion around a formal garden, offers a glimpse into monied country living when this locale was beyond the bounds of greater Cincinnati.

You will gain a better understanding of this life on the final part of the hike, as well as an appreciation of huge hardwoods towering overhead. Pick up the Upland Trail, passing through old-growth woods before coming to a swimming pool and the gardens and the impressive Krippendorf Lodge. The large, attractive structure fairly beckons with its wraparound porch. Carl and his wife, Mary, resided there part-time until central heat was added in the 1930s. Before then, the house was heated only by fireplaces. You will likely gain a greater—at least up close—appreciation of the gardens. A plethora of plants grow along walkways and stone terraces. The decorative array of blooming greenery complements the unimproved naturally occurring flora on the "back 40" of the property. Your trip ends at the Rowe Visitor Center, which is certainly worth a visit with its natural history information and demonstrations.

The trail system itself is in stellar shape. The paths are graveled or mulched near the nature center and are otherwise well kept. Trail intersections are clearly marked. Even the most novice hiker with the nature center trail map can find their way through the numerous intersections. The area immediately around the nature center and gardens can be a maze, but it would be impossible to get truly lost here, just briefly discombobulated.

Miles and Directions

0.0 Start at the Rowe Visitor Center. As you face the visitor center, leave left on the green-blazed Edge Trail. Walk a gravel track, shortly passing a bird blind to your left. It has feeders to attract the avian set. Powel Crosley Lake lies off to your right. The path crosses an arm of the small impoundment.

0.1 Turn left, joining the Lookout Trail. Pass two alternate paths that connect the Edge Trail to the Lookout Trail. Walk under cherry, maple, and oaks.

0.3 Reach the nature center entrance road. Thousands of planted daffodils arise here in spring. Turn right, briefly following the entrance road, then carefully cross Tealtown Road, still on the Lookout Trail. Pass the farmhouse and barn on the location where Carl Krippendorf first came to this property. The path travels open fields.

0.5 Pass a shortcut path bisecting the Lookout Trail. Keep straight, still in a meadow. Come near the Willow Pond. Limited views open to the north.

0.8 Come to a cleared overlook stretching east across the Stonelick Creek Valley. Just ahead, another shortcut leads left along a tree line. The path now curves into stony watersheds feeding Stonelick Creek. Bridges span many of these streambeds, which normally flow only after rains.

1.1 Pass another cleared overlook. Continue hiking westerly under hardwoods and cedars.

1.2 Come to a three-way trail junction. Keep straight as a shortcut comes in on your left. Just ahead, split right, heading toward the trail shelter and the best vista.

1.3 Pass by the spur leading back to the main loop. Keep straight toward the shelter.

1.4 Come to the open-sided shelter. A cleared view stretches north across the Stonelick Creek Valley. Backtrack and stay right.

1.5 Stay right after rejoining the Lookout Trail.

1.6 Bisect Tealtown Road and reenter woods, shortly bridging a tributary of Stonelick Creek. The north-facing vale will be rich with spring wildflowers.

1.9 Turn right, joining the Upland Trail. Meander west in hardwoods in the upper hollows and pass a shortcut leading left back to the trailhead parking area.

2.1 Meet the Fernwood Trail. Turn right here, northbound in decidedly bigger trees.

2.2 Pass a spur path leading left to the nature center amphitheater.

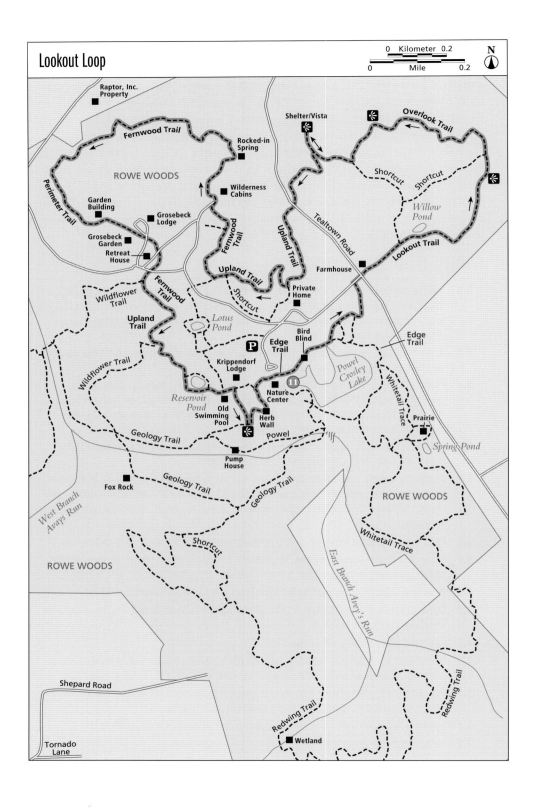

Lookout Loop

Raptor, Inc.
Property

Fernwood Trail

Shelter/Vista

Overlook Trail

0   Kilometer   0.2
0   Mile   0.2

N

ROWE WOODS

Rocked-in
Spring

Shortcut

Shortcut

Willow
Pond

Perimeter Trail

Garden
Building

Grosebeck
Lodge

Wilderness
Cabins

Fernwood
Trail

Upland Trail

Tealtown Road

Lookout Trail

Grosebeck
Garden

Retreat
House

Fernwood
Trail

Upland Trail

Shortcut

Private
Home

Farmhouse

Wildflower
Trail

Upland
Trail

Lotus
Pond

Edge
Trail

Bird
Blind

Edge
Trail

Wildflower Trail

P

Krippendorf
Lodge

Nature
Center

Powel
Crosley
Lake

11

Whitetail Trace

Reservoir
Pond

Old
Swimming
Pool

Herb
Wall

Powel

Prairie

Spring Pond

Geology Trail

Pump
House

Fox Rock

Geology Trail

Geology Trail

ROWE WOODS

West Branch
Avays Run

ROWE WOODS

Whitetail Trace

Shortcut

East Branch Avey's Run

Shepard Road

Redwing Trail

Redwing Trail

Tornado
Lane

Wetland

2.3 Briefly follow the wider track going toward the Wilderness Cabins. Turn left before reaching the Wilderness Cabins, back on foot trail. Descend steeply in a wildflower area and viney woods.

2.5 Come to a rocked-in spring. This was used for the nearby homesite. The house's fallen remains can be seen down trail. This house was built for John Rosenberger, who farmed this acreage from the 1920s through the 1940s. Begin westerly on a north-facing slope. Look for old fence posts and other remnants of Rosenberger's farm. Pass near the Raptor, Inc. property on Barg Salt Run Road.

3.0 The Fernwood Trail turns south and climbs steeply.

3.2 Open onto a meadow, reaching the stone garden building of the Groesbeck Lodge. Travel along a wide track, passing the Groesbeck Lodge on your left and the stone pillars of the Groesbeck's formal garden. The columns are laid out in a circular fashion, recalling Stonehenge. Look for large beech trees in the area. The Fernwood Trail crosses the road to the Groesbeck Lodge and passes near the Retreat House. Bisect two more roads.

3.4 Stay straight as the Wildflower Trail drops sharply right off a slope. Old-growth hardwoods tower over the path.

3.5 Meet the Upland Trail again as the Fernwood Trail ends. Turn right, rejoining the Upland Trail. Soon pass a second intersection with the Wildflower Trail. Watch for huge oaks in this area.

3.7 Reach the Reservoir Pond after meeting a spur trail leading left toward the Lotus Pond. The Reservoir Pond was dug to hold water for the Krippendorfs, to fight potential house fires. Look for turtles sunning in the still pond. Pass the other end of a loop around the Reservoir Pond. Ahead, come to the now-empty swimming pool. This keyhole-shaped outdoor pool was a rarity in its day and was a big hit with visitors to the Krippendorf home. It later developed a leak and was turned into a leaf bin.

3.9 Pass near the Krippendorf home after bridging a stream on a rustic stone bridge. Turn right near the home, heading south in gardens under old-growth hardwoods. A spur path keeps straight near the house.

4.0 Limestone steps lead down to East Branch Avey's Run. Come near the herb wall in a mini-maze of short garden paths. The Rowe Visitor Center is within sight. Turn back north toward the Krippendorf house, passing under a metal arched gate. Come within sight of the house, then turn right.

4.1 Return to the Rowe Visitor Center, completing the hike. Now that you have escaped the garden maze, consider heading back to leisurely explore the gardens.

GREEN TIP

Pack out what you pack in, even food scraps, because they can attract wild animals.

Southwest Ohio

This section contains the most hikes of any section in this guide. It covers all the great Southwest Ohio outdoor destinations outside of metro Cincinnati. Ohio state parks play a starring role. Here, find the right hike for you among these state getaways, from the lakeside, riverside, and hillside paths of East Fork State Park, deep-woods treks at Hueston Woods, and other, lesser visited destinations, such as Stonelick Creek State Park. Soak in the lotus blooms at Cowan Lake State Park. Check out waterfalls tumbling into Caesar Creek Lake. Step back in time at Fort Ancient. The area also includes hikes in Miami University's intriguing trails system, along with a few other surprises.

Water, woods, and hills come together to make Southwest Ohio a hiking paradise.

12 East Fork Loop

This 5-mile circuit explores rolling terrain, much of it along the south shore of East Fork Lake at East Fork State Park. Using a combination of the park's Backpack Trail and the Newman Trail, hikers will be impressed with the variety of flora and landscapes through which you stroll. Be apprised you will be sharing part of the trail at the beginning with mountain bikers and at the very end with equestrians. The balance of the trek is hiker only.

Start: South Trailhead
Distance: 5.0-mile loop
Hiking time: About 2.5 to 3.5 hours
Difficulty: Moderately difficult
Trail surface: Natural surface path in forested woods
Best season: Late Sept through mid-May
Other trail users: Mountain bikers, equestrians
Canine compatibility: Leashed dogs permitted

Land status: State park
Fees and permits: No fees required, permit required for overnight camping
Schedule: Open year-round 6 a.m. to 11 p.m.
Maps: East Fork State Park Trails, available online and at park office; USGS Batavia
Trail contacts: East Fork State Park, 3294 Elklick Rd., Bethel, OH 45106; (513) 734-4323; http://parks.ohiodnr.gov/eastfork

Finding the trailhead: From exit 65 on I-275 east of downtown, take OH 125 east for 10 miles to Bantam Road and a traffic light. Turn left onto Bantam Road and follow it 0.2 mile, then turn left into the state park on Park Road 1. Follow Park Road 1 for 0.5 mile, passing the park office on your right, to the left turn for Mountain Bike Trail, Backpack Trail Access. This is known as the south trailhead. Turn left and follow the gravel road just a short distance to dead end. Trailhead GPS: N39 0.403' / W84 8.514'

The Hike

This hike takes place at big East Fork State Park, which offers a plethora of trails whether you are a mountain biker, equestrian, backpacker, or day hiker. The park also offers camping, boating, fishing, and swimming. This hike combines portions of two of its longest trails, the 8-mile Backpack Trail and the 32-mile Steven Newman Worldwalker Perimeter Trail, commonly known as the Newman Trail or the Perimeter Trail.

During its 5-mile trek, this hike travels through a multiplicity of environments with a great assortment of trees, making it a great fall color hike. The trek begins in flatwoods, then dips to a stream. This rocky watercourse with steep bluffs can run from a torrent to a trickle, depending upon the season. Curve in and out of hollows that feed it, shaded by sugar maples galore. Later you will enjoy some lakeside terrain. Parts of the hike travel a high bluff overlooking the old riverbed of

▶ **If possible, keep your group small. This way you will not disturb other hikers. You will also stand a better chance of seeing wildlife.**

MORE ABOUT EAST FORK STATE PARK

East Fork State Park is one of the largest preserves in the greater Cincinnati area. The park is also rich in trails, with paths both short and long, from quiet nature trails to the Steve Newman Perimeter Trail. The state park presents a varied landscape, from wide flat floodplains grown up in woodlands, high bluffs above East Fork, prairie and grassland, and lots of land transitioning to forest from farm use. This topographical diversity combined with the large trail network adds up to a lot of hiking potential in addition to the hike presented above.

Many of the hiker-only paths extend but a couple of miles or less, exploring interesting parts of the park. Of special note is the 1.4-mile Fern Hill Trail. This woodsy ramble meanders through hills above the north shore of East Fork Lake. The narrow footpath crosses a rocky stream cutting a deep hollow, which you ascend. Pass a big white oak tree and skirt around the head of the hollow before passing near the park campground. The final part travels through former farm country before returning to the trailhead. Equestrians have over 25 miles of bridle paths to ride. Most of them are also open to hikers. They are also primarily located on the lake's north shore.

The park also offers other recreation activities. A lot of outdoor fun is focused on 2,160-acre East Fork Lake. In summer, swimmers cool off at the large swim beach, complete with restrooms, changing areas, and showers. Anglers use one of the six park boat launches to scour the lake for smallmouth and largemouth bass, as well as panfish. Boaters tool around the lake, enjoying the scenery, and can be seen pulling skiers and tubers across watery flats.

State park campers can choose from over 350 campsites with electric hookups. There's even a separate camping area for equestrians. The campgrounds have hot showers, flush toilets, and water taps. Don't want to camp? How about staying in one of the eight park cabins? They make roughing it easy.

Hiking is a year-round activity. And when the chill sets in and the snow falls, the park offers additional winter activities. Park visitors sled the white hills, ice skate, and even ice fish. Skiers travel cross-country on the park trails. So keep East Fork State Park in mind, whether you are hiking or not, in all seasons.

East Fork Little Miami River, the watercourse impounded by East Fork Lake. The trail also ambles through former farmland that is now becoming reforested since it is out of use. However, the vast majority of the hike is under a tree canopy.

The trails are well marked, and you will also benefit from bridges spanning many streambeds. Along the way you will come to a designated backcountry campsite. This loop would be a great beginner's backpack for those who want to expand beyond day

The streams of East Fork are typically low during summer.

hiking and get a feel for camping out while on the trail. The campsite has a pit toilet, fire ring, trail shelter, and tent sites. Bring your own water, which you could cache on one of the road crossings.

Miles and Directions

0.0 From the South Trailhead join the red-blazed Backpack Trail heading north into spindly straight flatwoods. This part of the hike is shared with the Mountain Bike Trail.

0.2 The trail forks. The main portion of the yellow-blazed Mountain Bike Trail leaves left. Stay right with the Backpack Trail as it dips into a hollow.

0.5 Step over the rocky stream cutting through the hollow. Begin roughly tracing the stream you just crossed toward East Fork Lake. Wander in and out of small hollows.

1.3 Come near East Fork Lake with views. It is but a short downhill walk to reach the water.

2.0 The Technical Trail, another mountain bike path, keeps straight while the Backpack Trail curves left to bridge a small drainage. For the next couple of miles the loop is hiker only.

2.4 Cross Park Road 3. Winter views open up of the main body of East Fork Lake. Hike in a harbor of hickories. Come alongside the edge of a steep drainage.

2.9 Pass an old homesite to the left of the trail before crossing Park Road 2. Come alongside a picnic area.

3.1 Saddle up to a high bluff above the lake. Trace the curve of the bluff. Spur trails lead right, uphill to the picnic area.

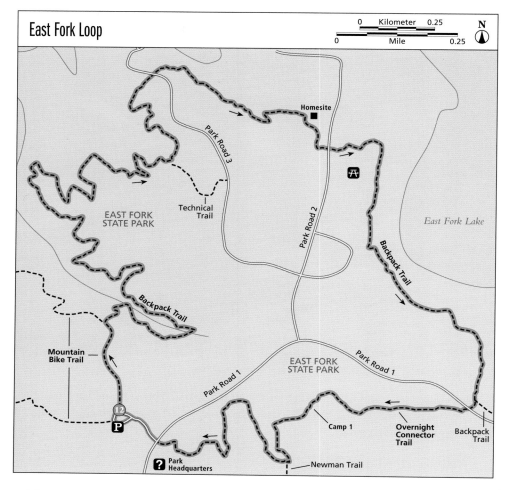

0   Kilometer   0.25

0   Mile   0.25

N

Homesite

EAST FORK
STATE PARK

Technical
Trail

Park Road 3

Park Road 2

East Fork Lake

Backpack Trail

Backpack Trail

Mountain
Bike Trail

Park Road 1

EAST FORK
STATE PARK

Park Road 1

Camp 1

Overnight
Connector
Trail

Backpack
Trail

Park Road 1

12

P

Park
Headquarters

Newman Trail

3.2   A spur trail drops left, very sharply downhill to a picnic table, and on to the lake. Stay with the red-blazed Backpack Trail.

3.8   Reach a trail junction. Here, the Backpack Trail leaves left. You turn right with the Overnight Connector Trail. Immediately cross Park Road 1. Begin cruising westerly in flatwoods on an old roadbed.

4.2   Reach the backcountry campsite, Camp 1. After leaving the campsite, join a spur of the Newman Trail, which is open to equestrians and hikers.

4.3   Cross a stony streambed then join the Newman Trail. Turn right, westbound. Enter old farmland in various stages of succession.

4.8   Curve behind the park headquarters.

4.9   Cross Park Road 1. Follow the gravel road toward the South Trailhead.

5.0   Reach the South Trailhead, completing the loop.

13 Poplar Loop at East Fork State Park

It is hard to find a relatively long hike in greater Cincinnati that doesn't cross a road, but this hike accomplishes that. The trek, using the Steve Newman Worldwalker Perimeter Trail, meanders hilly shores of East Fork Lake, crossing numerous drainages, including big Poplar Creek. Eventually, it meets the Backpack Loop, then makes a circuit amid high wooded bluffs and returns in deep forest. A backpacker campsite and shelter add overnighting possibilities to the hike.

Start: Bethel Boat Ramp
Distance: 8.4-mile lollipop
Hiking time: About 4 to 5 hours
Difficulty: More difficult due to distance and elevation changes
Trail surface: Natural surface path in forested woods
Best season: Late Sept through mid-May
Other trail users: Equestrians and mountain bikers for first 2.8 miles
Canine compatibility: Leashed dogs permitted

Land status: State park
Fees and permits: No fees required; permit required for overnight camping
Schedule: Open daily year-round 6 a.m. to 11 p.m.
Maps: East Fork State Park Trails, available online and at park office; USGS Bethel, Williamsburg
Trail contacts: East Fork State Park, 3294 Elklick Rd., Bethel, OH 45106; (513) 734-4323; http://parks.ohiodnr.gov/eastfork

Finding the trailhead: From exit 65 on I-275 east of downtown Cincinnati, take OH 125 east, passing the Bantam Road entrance to East Fork State Park at 10.0 miles, continuing for 4.7 more miles to Main Street in Bethel. Turn left onto Main Street/OH 133 north and follow it for 0.4 mile to Bethel Concord Road. Turn left onto Bethel Concord Road and follow it for 1.2 miles to Macedonia Road. Turn left onto Macedonia Road and follow it for 0.4 mile, then turn right onto Reisinger Road. Follow it 0.8 mile to dead-end at Bethel Boat Ramp. Park at the boat ramp. The actual trailhead is 0.1 mile back up Reisinger Road, but there is no parking there. Please do not park at the trail crossing. Trailhead GPS: N38 59.921' / W84 5.425'

The Hike

This hike combines two of the longer trails in the entire greater Cincinnati area. First, you will start on the Steve Newman Worldwalker Perimeter Trail, which makes a 32-mile circuit around East Fork Lake. Our hike then picks up the 8-mile Backpack Trail. Just to further confuse you, the two aforementioned trails are also part of the greater North Country National Scenic Trail (NCT), a multistate, long-distance path that runs in conjunction with several park trails. The light blue blazes indicate the NCT, which traverses much of the Buckeye State. The trail's moniker is "Exploring America's Northwoods." Ironically, this is about as far south as the NCT goes. It is not anywhere near complete, but disconnected sections aspire to link New York State to North Dakota. In many places the North Country Trail runs in conjunction with

The blue blaze on this hickory indicates this path is also part of the greater North Woods Trail.

other trails, such as here. Here in the Buckeye State, the NCT uses the same path as the Buckeye Trail.

Much of Southwest Ohio is field and cropland, but woodlands reign inside the borders of East Fork State Park. The boundaries of the state park often run close to the shoreline around Harsha Lake, which impounds East Fork Little Miami River.

Harsha Lake is more commonly known as East Fork Lake. This sometimes-narrow corridor between the lake and the park boundary forces the trail to occasionally go up or down steep hills and also make it turn where you think it won't or shouldn't go. However, this is not a bad thing, as it adds a challenge to the trek.

A rich, viney forest of tulip trees, sugar maple, and cherry shade the trail as it courses westerly from Bethel Boat Ramp. Wind in and out of stony hollows, sometimes coming directly alongside the park boundary where you can see fields and houses. The ultimate goal is Poplar Creek, a major tributary of Harsha Lake. Poplar Creek creates a surprisingly steep gorge with limestone bluffs. You will be standing atop these bluffs before you drop to meet Poplar Creek proper.

Poplar Creek creates a long arm of Harsha Lake. Enjoy hilltop views as you circle around Poplar Creek embayment. Take note there is no bridge over Poplar Creek. In fall, the stream may be dry. During late winter and spring, it may be flowing boldly. Turn around if the fairly wide creek crossing looks iffy. If you are turned back by a high Poplar Creek, simply take the Steve Newman Worldwalker Perimeter Trail the other direction from Bethel Boat Ramp.

The hike shortly reaches Backcountry Camp 2, an overnighting site with a trail shelter. It is located in a sugar maple grove on a high flat well above Harsha Lake. A backcountry permit is required for overnighting at the site. Call the park office well ahead of your scheduled backpack to make arrangements. Ahead, you begin the loop portion of the hike, now on the hiker-only Backpack Trail. The path stays on a high bluff cut with steep rocky ravines. Nearly pure cedar thickets crowd the track.

After reaching the loop of the Backpack Trail, you turn south, wandering hills well back from the lake. The single-track path occasionally bisects old and faded

WHO IS STEVE NEWMAN?

Part of your hike travels the Steve Newman Worldwalker Perimeter Trail. The trail was named for the local resident after he walked around the world—literally. From April 1, 1983, to April 1, 1987, Steve Newman used his feet to span five continents and cover 15,000-plus miles. Along the way he had many adventures and encounters with people and places. Newman battled heat, cold, insects, wild pigs, and more. He often felt the urge to quit, but somehow kept putting one foot in front of the other. Things we take for granted, like eating, sleeping, and communicating, became challenges as he passed through twenty-one countries. His return journey to his hometown of nearby Bethel, Ohio, became quite a spectacle. And for his final trek, Newman walked the perimeter of East Fork State Park—his coup de grace on his worldwide walk. This perimeter trek became the trail you use, and is the park's longest at 32 miles. And for him to add this final loop to an around-the-world hike is a compliment indeed, coming from a man who states, "Walking is a way of life."

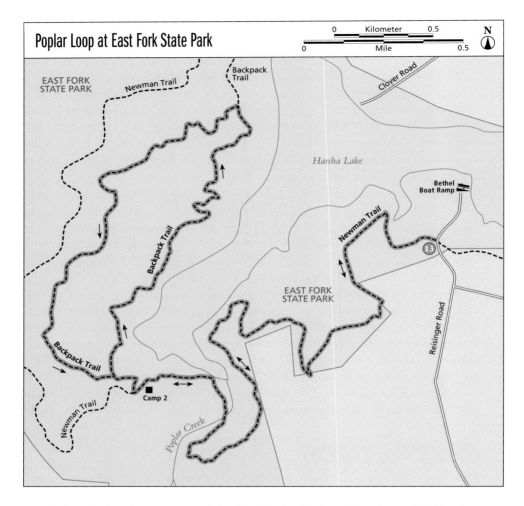

Poplar Loop at East Fork State Park

EAST FORK
STATE PARK

Newman Trail

Backpack
Trail

Clover Road

Harsha Lake

Bethel
Boat Ramp

Newman Trail

Backpack Trail

EAST FORK
STATE PARK

13

Reisinger Road

Backpack Trail

Camp 2

Newman Trail

Poplar Creek

wooded roads, but the correct trail is clear. Look also for other signs of civilization, such as straight lines of trees, indicating former fence rows and farm fields, left over from pre-park days. A sharp dive precludes your completion of the loop. From there, it is 2.9 miles back to the trailhead, with nary a road crossed.

Miles and Directions

0.0 Start from the Bethel Boat Ramp, walking back up Reisinger Road. Pick up the Steve Newman Worldwalker Perimeter Trail. Turn right, westbound, wandering through hilly forest.

0.1 Bridge a streambed by culvert, then pick up an old roadbed. Feel the crumbly asphalt beneath your feet. Shortly leave the roadbed left, climbing a steep hill. This is a good example of the trail having to stay within the confines of the park boundary and lake.

0.5 Cross under a large power line, then come along a pasture fence line. Soon turn away from the fence line.

0.9 Step over a large rocky tributary then near the park boundary again.

1.4 Cross back under the large power line, then begin circling around Poplar Creek embay-ment. Soon rise to a high wooded bluff atop the embayment.

2.2 Cross stony Poplar Creek after descending into sycamores. Briefly continue downstream before turning away. Look for limestone bluffs above the water.

2.7 Reach Camp 2 backcountry campsite after passing through an old homestead. The camp offers a pair of shelters, a privy, and fire ring. Spur trails lead to streams. However, you may have to get water from the lake during dry times. Come to a trail junction just beyond the camp. Here, the Steve Newman Worldwalker Perimeter Trail leaves left, you turn acutely right, down a draw, joining the red-blazed hiker-only Backpacker Loop, spanning an inter-mittent stream on a bridge.

2.9 The Backpacker Loop splits at the bottom of a hollow. Turn right here, steeply climbing out of the hollow to join a high ridge above Harsha Lake. Views of Harsha Lake open through the trees.

3.1 Cross under the power line again. Continue working north, bisecting steep drainages.

4.1 Reach a trail junction. Here, the Backpack Loop splits. To the right, the trail leads to the South Trailhead. However, this loop turns left, southwesterly, over rolling hills of sugar maple.

4.5 Bisect an open grassy roadbed.

4.7 Dip to a major streambed. Climb back onto level terrain in pawpaws.

4.8 Pass through a noticeable cedar thicket.

5.2 Cross back under the power line. Ahead, turn into a steeply cut drainage.

5.5 Complete the loop portion of the hike. From here, begin backtracking for Bethel Boat Ramp.

5.7 Return to Backcountry Camp 2.

6.2 Re-cross Poplar Creek.

7.0 Cross under the power line.

7.9 Cross under the power line a final time.

8.4 Reach Reisinger Road. The Bethel Boat Ramp parking area is downhill to the left.

14 Cloverlick Creek Hike

This out-and-back endeavor heads to the embayment of Cloverlick Creek, on East Fork Lake, at big East Fork State Park. You will be hiking the Perimeter Trail, which runs in conjunction here. First you will tackle many a hill, working your way east toward Cloverlick Creek, also dropping into pretty little hollows. High bluffs overlook the lake scenery. Eventually, you will make Cloverlick Creek, a little above where its flow ceases and the creek becomes part of East Fork Lake. Here you can enjoy both still and moving waters. This is a good turnaround point.

Start: Bethel Boat Ramp
Distance: 3.8-mile out-and-back
Hiking time: About 2 to 3 hours
Difficulty: Moderate but has continual elevation changes
Trail surface: Natural surface path in forested woods
Best season: Late Sept through mid-May
Other trail users: Equestrians
Canine compatibility: Leashed dogs permitted

Land status: State park
Fees and permits: No fees required
Schedule: Open daily year-round 6 a.m. to 11 p.m.
Maps: East Fork State Park Trails, available online and at park office; USGS Bethel
Trail contacts: East Fork State Park, 3294 Elklick Rd., Bethel, OH 45106; (513) 734-4323; http://parks.ohiodnr.gov/eastfork

Finding the trailhead: From exit 65 on I-275 east of downtown Cincinnati, take OH 125 east, passing the Bantam Road entrance to East Fork State Park at 10.0 miles, continuing for 4.7 more miles to Main Street in Bethel. Turn left onto Main Street/OH 133 north and follow it for 0.4 mile to Bethel Concord Road. Turn left onto Bethel Concord Road and follow it for 1.2 miles to Macedonia Road. Turn left onto Macedonia Road and follow it for 0.4 mile, then turn right onto Reisinger Road. Follow it 0.8 mile to dead-end at Bethel Boat Ramp. Park at the boat ramp. The actual trailhead is 0.1 mile back up Reisinger Road, but there is no parking there. Please do not park at the trail crossing. Trailhead GPS: N38 59.921' / W84 5.425'

The Hike

It's a wonder this part of the Steve Newman Worldwalker Perimeter Trail isn't walked more often. The path has good parking and travels one of the prettiest parts of East Fork Lake and the lands that surround it. The trail has excellent spring wildflowers and vibrant fall colors as it travels through varied habitats. It is a notch more rugged and primitive than your average Cincinnati path if you are looking to add more challenge to your trek.

A singletrack path makes an inauspicious beginning, first leading under a power line. The North Country National Scenic Trail runs in conjunction with the Perimeter Trail at this juncture. The power line cut ends. You can leave the trail and look out over the Cloverlick Creek embayment of East Fork Lake where the Perimeter Trail enters

Bloodroot is an early wildflower popping up in the woods around Cloverlick Creek.

full-blown woods. At times the trail will be hemmed in by the bluff to your left and the Army Corps of Engineers property boundary to the right.

Overhead, younger hardwoods of beech, locust, cherry, and tulip trees are fighting to grow tallest in what once was a field several decades back, before the lake came to be. Watch for fence posts and barbed wire from pre-dam days. Also look for drainages, now wooded, heading directly downhill, vestiges of erosive farming practices. The forest

NORTH COUNTRY NATIONAL SCENIC TRAIL

It all started with the National Trails System Act of 1968. The US Congress officially established what came to be known as "national scenic trails." Part of the law funded a study to develop other potential national scenic trails in addition to the Appalachian Trail and the Pacific Crest Trail. Out of this the North Country Scenic Trail (NCT) continues to evolve. From North Dakota in the west to New York in the east and Ohio in the middle, the NCT remains a work in progress. It enters Ohio at the Michigan boundary then heads south to southwest Ohio, where this segment passes through East Fork State Park. It then curves east, passing through the Wayne National Forest, then travels northeast to the Pennsylvania border. In Ohio, the NCT mostly runs in conjunction with the Buckeye Trail. The 4,600-mile route remains unfinished, but Ohio is lucky to have this resource running through the state. If you want to get involved with the NCT, check out www.northcountrytrail.org.

keeps this in check, and the drainages continue to fill with leaves and other forest debris. Buckeye is a major understory tree in this woodland.

You will come to another change wrought by the establishment of East Fork Lake—the crumbling continuation of Bethel Concord Road. You drove in on the still-used part of the road on the way to the trailhead. Bethel Concord Road used to continue north, crossing Cloverlick Creek, but was flooded by the lake. A disjunct section of the road is still in use north of Cloverlick Creek.

The Perimeter Trail continues weaving in and out of hollows. Watch for private property signs in places. You won't miss the steep in-and-out of a hollow where three small streams converge bordered by precipitous hills. I think it is one of the prettiest spots in the region. In spring, the wildflowers will be blooming by the thousands and the streams will be running. In fall, dry creekbeds and autumn colors paint a different picture. This is a place to linger.

Cloverlick Creek is just ahead. Here, the stream may be running bold and brown in spring, or trickling in summer or not at all in fall. At normal flows it can be rock-hopped in spring. But use your good judgment as to whether to cross. Winter and high water don't mix. If you get cold and wet, bad things can happen. If that is the case, just turn around and call it a day.

Once you cross Cloverlick Creek, the habitat changes. The trail is level and you hike bottomland. If you continue on, be vigilant as old roads and user-created equestrian paths spur off the main trail. Stick with the green and light blue blazes and you will be fine. Curve around the embayment of Cloverlick Creek, saddling alongside a bluff overlooking the water below. Depending on lake levels, you may be looking at flowing stream or placid impoundment. The hike rambles farther around the lake for 20-plus miles from here. Bring your backpacking gear if you want to make the whole loop.

Cloverlick Creek Hike

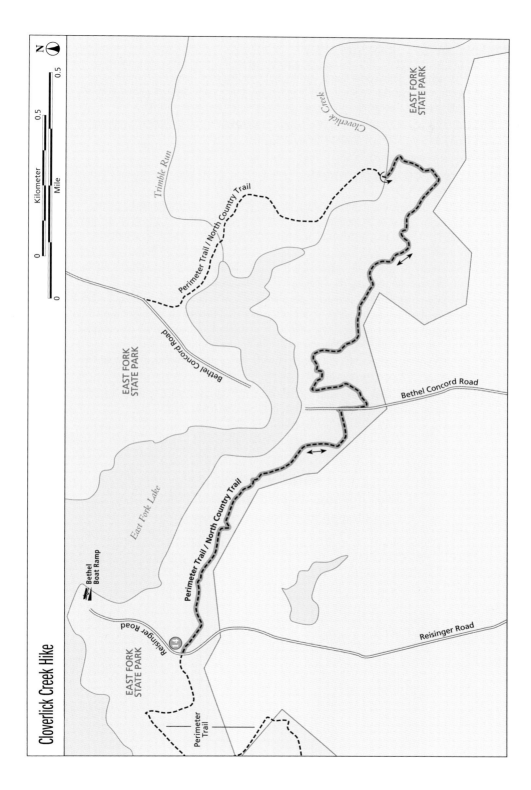

N

Kilometer

0   0.5   0.5

Mile

0   0.5

EAST FORK STATE PARK

Cloverlick Creek

Trimble Run

Perimeter Trail / North Country Trail

Bethel Concord Road

EAST FORK STATE PARK

Bethel Concord Road

East Fork Lake

Perimeter Trail / North Country Trail

Bethel Boat Ramp

Reisinger Road

EAST FORK STATE PARK

Perimeter Trail

Reisinger Road

Miles and Directions

0.0 Start from the Bethel Boat Ramp, walking back up Reisinger Road. Pick up the Steve Newman Worldwalker Perimeter Trail. Turn left, eastbound, passing over a streambed while walking under a power line. This area may be muddy in winter and spring.

0.2 Leave the power line clearing near a view of the lake below. You are traveling the edge of a bluff dropping 150 feet down to the water's edge.

0.3 Bisect an old roadbed.

0.5 Come along the edge of a nearly sheer bluff above East Fork Lake. Winter views open to the northeast.

0.8 Come to the remains of the old Bethel Concord Road. Turn right here, walking up the crumbling asphalt to the current dead end of the road (the old road also goes left into the lake). From the current road's end at some guardrails, leave left, back on standard single-track trail.

1.3 Come to the "9" mile mark. This indicates the mileage if you were starting the entire Perimeter Trail from the trailhead near the state park headquarters.

1.5 After steeply descending, reach an unnamed stream, with two other branches all coming together. The north-facing hollow is one of the better wildflowers spots in southwest Ohio. The biggest branch has a small wet-weather waterfall just upstream of the trail crossing. Rock-hop the stream then climb steeply back out.

1.7 Begin dropping into the flats of Cloverlick Creek. After a steep descent, turn left, downstream, in oft-flooded bottomland.

1.9 Cross Cloverlick Creek. Open onto a grassy area. This is a good place to relax. From here, begin backtracking for Bethel Boat Ramp, or explore on a bit.

3.8 Arrive back at Reisinger Road, ending the hike.

GREEN TIP
Even if it says it's biodegradable, don't put soap into streams or lakes.

15 Beechtree Loop at Stonelick State Park

You will understand the term "flatwoods" after taking this trek that travels forest and shore of 200-acre Stonelick Lake. The hike starts near the popular state park campground, meandering under rich hardwoods that rise from level terrain. Join the Beechtree Trail, named for impressive smooth-trunked gray giants that shade the way. A little road walk takes you to the aptly named Lakeview Trail, where watery vistas await. The hiking remains easy due to the flat terra firma. Consider combining your hike with other activities at this fine Ohio state park.

Start: Campground check-in station
Distance: 3.8-mile lollipop
Hiking time: About 1.5 to 2 hours
Difficulty: Easy due to flat terrain
Trail surface: Forested natural surface
Best season: Sept through June
Other trail users: None
Canine compatibility: Leashed dogs permitted
Land status: State park

Fees and permits: No fees required
Schedule: Open daily year-round 6 a.m. to 11 p.m.
Maps: Stonelick State Park, available online and at park office; USGS Newtonsville
Trail contacts: Stonelick State Park, 2895 Lake Dr., Pleasant Plain, OH 45162; (513) 734-4323; http://parks.ohiodnr.gov/stonelick

Finding the trailhead: From exit 59A on I-275, east of downtown Cincinnati, take Milford Parkway north 1.0 mile to meet US 50 and OH 131 at a light. Keep straight through the light to join OH 131 east for 8.5 miles to OH 727. Veer left onto OH 727 and follow it for 3.1 miles to Lake Drive. Turn right onto Lake Drive and follow it toward Camping, Beach, Picnic Area, Boat Rental. Enter the park after 0.3 mile. Keep straight, following Lake Drive 2.0 miles toward the campground. The Southwoods Trail starts on your left, within sight of the campground check-in station. To park, pass the check-in station and turn left into a parking area. Trailhead GPS: N39 13.007' / W84 3.417'

The Hike

Stonelick State Park is a water-centric state-run recreation entity located east of Cincinnati. It offers fishing, boating, camping, swimming, and more. Its trail system, while not elaborate, seems underutilized. Maybe that is because it travels through such flat terrain, contrasting with most Tri-State hiking destinations that are found where vertical variation is the norm. But variety is the spice of life, and a walk in flatwoods amid surprisingly large trees may be just the getaway you're looking for. Face it, sometimes we need a little exercise but don't want to kill ourselves. This loop may just do the trick.

Unlike some other lake-oriented parks, Stonelick's boundaries extend well away from the impoundment created by damming Stonelick Creek. This allows you to travel along both aquatic and non-aquatic environments, in deep woods where you

Carved upon beech trees like this give the trail a name.

are among nothing but tall trees, many of them impressive in size, especially the sturdy gray beeches found on the Beechtree Trail.

Your hike starts on the Southwoods Trail, and the well-shaded track actually undulates a bit as it descends toward a tributary of Stonelick Creek. After joining the Beechtree Trail, you will understand the meaning of flatwoods. Literally the ground is so level that in spring and after heavy rains water can pool and take a while to drain. Therefore you may want to avoid this hike after a downpour. Fall is the best time to enjoy this hike, for you will have dry ground and colorful yellows and golds courtesy of the sugar maples and beeches. Sweet gums are an unusual component of the Stonelick flatwoods. You will find their star-shaped leaves and "gumball" seedpods easy to identify. And in fall their leaves turn a deep maroon.

The paths are well blazed, but old roads leading to a defunct water tower may confuse while hiking the Beechtree Trail. And part of being in flatwoods is the lack of landmarks such as valleys or hilltops to help orient you. While navigating you may notice the large number of bat houses in the park and along the trails. This is a modern nonchemical response to keeping mosquitoes at bay. (The pesky bloodsuckers love standing water.)

LET'S GO TO THE BEECH

Beech trees are a focal point of this Ohio state park hike. The gray-trunked tree ranges throughout the Buckeye State. Perhaps it should've been called the Beech State. Interestingly, the beech grows best in the northeast of Ohio and down this way in the southwest, where bottomlands and well-drained glacial soils create ideal conditions for the trees.

Beech trees are among the easiest trees to identify in southwest Ohio. First, the smooth gray trunk makes it stand out in the forest, as the carved trees along this trail testify. Many woodland walkers simply can't resist the flat surface of the beech—it seems a tablet for a handy pocketknife. The smooth trunks contrast greatly with the knobby and fissured oaks and hickories that thrive in this region. Pick up a beech leaf from the forest floor. The sunlight absorbing leaves are generally 2 to 4 inches long. Note the sharply toothed edges of the leaves. They are a dark green on top and lighter underneath. In fall, they turn a yellowish golden brown. Under ideal conditions, beech trees can reach 120 feet in height. However, the average mature trees, like those you will see along the trail, reach 60 to 80 feet from the ground.

After the leaves fall from the beech, you will notice the buds of next year's leaves. They are but 0.5 inch in length but resemble a mini cigar. Come spring, these buds will unfurl to once again convert sunlight for the tree as it resumes growing during the warm season.

Beechnuts are an important food for wildlife, from mice to deer, and birds from ducks to blue jays. Critters break apart the burr-covered shell to reach the nutrient-rich treat. Beechnuts are about the size of your thumbnail. For man, the wood of beech trees is used for everything from flooring to railroad ties to charcoal. And of course, many people think it is used as a carving tablet.

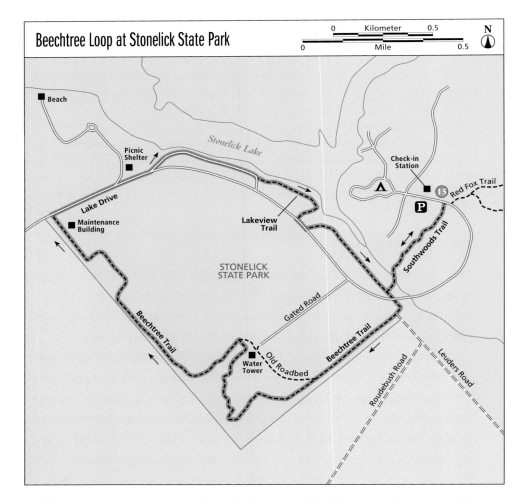

Beechtree Loop at Stonelick State Park

Kilometer
Mile
N

Beach

Stonelick Lake

Picnic Shelter

Check-in Station

Red Fox Trail

Lake Drive

Maintenance Building

Lakeview Trail

STONELICK STATE PARK

Southwoods Trail

Beechtree Trail

Gated Road

Beechtree Trail

Water Tower

Old Roadbed

Roudebush Road

Leuders Road

There are so many beeches along the Beechtree Trail that even the most prolific carver can't initial every one of these gray giants, standing impressively like a silent army. Of course, no one should be defacing these trees in the first place. The stately dark woods will contrast with the fields, which you come near before reaching Lake Drive.

A little road walk is necessary to meet the Lakeview Trail. Take advantage of the picnic facilities you'll see before resuming a footpath. Views will open of the lake. The Lakeview Trail is well used by anglers. You will likely see a bank angler patiently waiting for a line. All too soon you are backtracking to the trailhead, perhaps wishing you'd brought your own line.

Miles and Directions

0.0 Start near the campground check-in station. Pick up the Southwoods Trail, located away from the campground on Lake Drive. The Red Fox Trail leaves northbound from the same trailhead. Bridge several streamlets while heading southwest.

0.3 Bridge an unnamed tributary of Stonelick Creek then rise to reach a trail junction. Here, your return route, the Lakeview Trail, leaves right. Keep straight, rising to Lake Drive. Turn left onto Lake Drive, walk a few feet, then cross the road to pick up Beechtree Trail.

0.8 Watch as the official trail leaves left while the old roadbed you have been following curves right. If you stay with the old roadbed, it will lead to a defunct water tower. Stay left with the hiking trail. The correct path keeps southwest, then turns back northwest and comes within sight of the water tower. Stay with the blue paint blazes. If you find yourself at the tower, a path reconnects to the Beechtree Trail. Do not take the grassy road leading northeast from the water tower back to the main paved park road.

1.3 The Beechtree Trail comes within sight of the old water tower then turns southwest.

1.5 The path comes along the park boundary, across from a field. Turn northwest.

1.7 Cross a particularly wet area that has had a bridge over it in the past.

1.8 Temporarily curve away from the boundary into deep woods.

2.2 The Beechtree Trail ends. Turn right onto Lake Drive after passing the maintenance building. Follow Lake Drive northeasterly. This part is a road walk.

2.4 A road leaves left to the park swim beach. Note the inviting shaded picnic shelter.

2.5 Lake Drive splits again. Stay left, following the paved road into the main park picnic area. Come directly alongside Stonelick Lake.

2.9 Pick up the Lakeview Trail as the picnic area road curves right to rejoin Lake Drive. This is where the road walk ends. The Lakeview Trail meanders along the shoreline in lush forest.

3.1 Briefly return to Lake Drive as the trail uses Lake Drive to bridge a stream. Turn left back into forestland along the lake on a rocky trail.

3.5 Meet the Southwoods Trail. Turn left, backtracking.

3.8 Reach the trailhead, completing the balloon loop.

GREEN TIP

Remember that great care and resources (from nature as well as from your tax dollars) have gone into creating these trails. Don't deface trail signs or trees. It takes a long time for trees to grow big enough to be carved into. There's no need to let passersby know that you were there.

16 Cowan Lake State Park Hike

Have you ever seen a mass of floating lotus blooms? That is one highlight from this relatively short hike that combines two nature trails at Cowan Lake State Park, east of Cincinnati. While most other park visitors are on the lake, you can be one of the few traveling through hilly woods to reach a high bluff overlooking upper Cowan Creek embayment. Enjoy views of the slender still water before heading down to the lake itself, where water plants stretch along Cowan Creek. Your return route takes you into more hilly woods, enhanced by a multilevel wooden staircase.

Start: Near the park office
Distance: 1.7-mile double loop
Hiking time: About 1 hour
Difficulty: Easy due to distance
Trail surface: Natural surface path
Best season: Year-round, mid- to late summer for lotus blooms
Other trail users: None
Canine compatibility: Leashed dogs permitted
Land status: State park

Fees and permits: No fees required
Schedule: Open daily year-round 6 a.m. to 11 p.m.
Maps: Cowan Lake State Park, available online and at park office; USGS Clarksville
Trail contacts: Cowan Lake State Park, 1750 Osborn Rd., Wilmington, OH 45177; (937) 382-1096; http://parks.ohiodnr.gov/cowanlake

Finding the trailhead: From exit 32 on I-71 northeast of downtown Cincinnati, take OH 350 east to OH 730. Turn left onto OH 730 north and follow it 3.3 miles toward Wilmington to Osborn Road. Turn right onto Osborn Road and follow it 1.6 miles to the entrance to Cowan Lake State Park. Turn right into the park and immediately turn right to park at the office, on your right. The Oldfield Trail starts across the road from the park office, near some white pines. Trailhead GPS: N39 23.317' / W83 53.047'

The Hike

This hike is a little on the short side, but it is rewarding nonetheless. Should you desire to hike more, the park offers more nature trails, though the ones between the campground and park office can be a confusing, intertwined network of official and user-created trails. So be prepared to do a little rambling and perhaps backtracking should you jump into that network.

The hike described here is easier to follow and much less confusing. Your first path is the Oldfield Trail. Farms used to occupy the stream bottoms and adjacent hills of Cowan Creek. These bottoms, now flooded, were the richest, most arable terrain. Cowan Lake was created by the US Army Corps of Engineers, primarily for flood control and water storage. Losing this verdant cropland was a negative offset to flood prevention and providing reliable drinking water. Farmers were bought out, moving away, yet their imprint on the land remains on lands bought by the corps yet not flooded, whether it is old fields now growing up in sumacs and tulip trees, ponds, faint tractor tracks, or a rusty plow.

The single-track path descends toward a quiet, small lake bay joining the Lotus Cove Nature Trail. A small stream lazily ambles toward Cowan Lake. You join a wooded peninsula, then come along a bluff. The uppermost part of Cowan Lake opens before you, a serpentine aquatic meander, its edges overflowing with lotus. Off to the side a wide wetland is filled with the water plants, growing so dense as to seem a single mat of life on the lake surface. The views from the bluff and from the water's edge are a highlight of this hike.

Beyond the Lotus Cove Nature Trail, your hike returns to the Oldfield Trail. Enter a forest of sycamores and pawpaws before rising to some former fields for which the trail is named. All too soon you are emerging near the park office.

The park office is a good jumping-off place for other hiking opportunities at Cowan Lake State Park. You can pick up the Dogwood Trail, Indian Trail, Beechnut Loop, and Lakeview Trail behind the park office. Just have time, an open mind, a compass, and your smartphone. You will work toward the park campground, crossing stream drainages flowing toward Cowan Lake and surmounting hills between the drainages. And if you get turned around, simply take the campground access road

EXPLORE COWAN LAKE STATE PARK

Cowan Lake is a reservoir created by the Army Corps of Engineers in 1950. Nearly 700 acres in size, it is the centerpiece of the state park that borders much of it. The state park offers more than hiking trails. Boaters, while limited to 10 horsepower motors, enjoy the lake, and the low horsepower motor limit creates a more tranquil atmosphere and leaves the lake to anglers searching for finned underwater creatures, paddlers who stroke their way around the lake, and sailors who ride the winds. Bass, crappie, and catfish, as well as muskie, are sought after. Even if you are boatless, you can still enjoy Cowan Lake. A fishing pier provides a venue for shore-bound anglers. For water lovers who aren't fishing, the park has a big swim beach, complete with a bathhouse, showers, and even a snack bar. Landlubbers can ride bikes or play volleyball and basketball at park-provided courts. Compete on the miniature golf course.

With so much to do here, you may want to consider overnighting it at 1,075-acre Cowan Lake State Park. The park features a large campground with over 250 campsites. Most of them have electricity. Hot showers add a civilized touch to the experience. Campers even have their own swim beach and boat ramp. If you don't feel like roughing it, consider renting a park cabin. Nearly thirty cabins are available; some even have fireplaces. Therefore, when you bring your hiking shoes to this state park, you might also want to pack your tent and make an overnight adventure out of it.

This boardwalk helps preserve the natural features at Cowan Lake State Park.

GREEN TIP

Don't take souvenirs home with you. This means natural
materials such as lotus blooms, rocks, shells, and driftwood
as well as historic artifacts such as fossils and arrowheads.

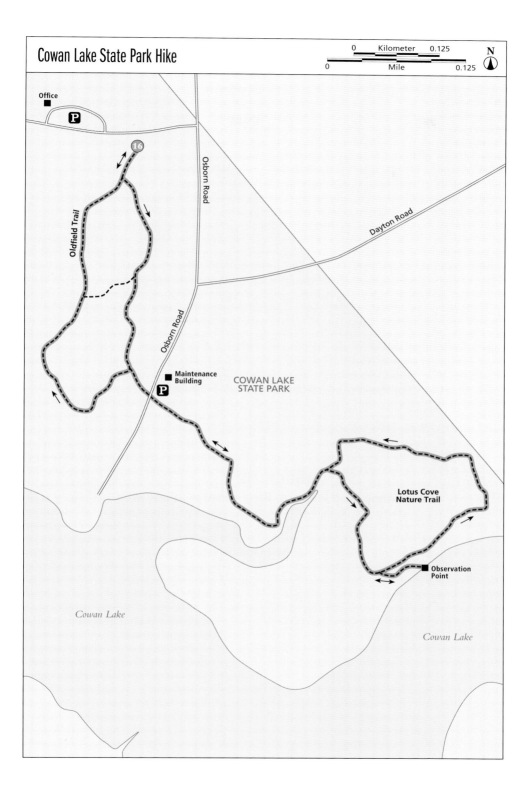

Cowan Lake State Park Hike

0   Kilometer   0.125
0   Mile   0.125

N

Office
P

16

Oldfield Trail

Osborn Road

Dayton Road

Osborn Road

Maintenance
Building
P

COWAN LAKE
STATE PARK

Lotus Cove
Nature Trail

Observation
Point

Cowan Lake

Cowan Lake

back to the park office. It's better than asking for directions, especially if you are a man.

Miles and Directions

0.0 Start across from the park office, joining the Oldfield Trail as it leaves a grove of white pines to enter hardwoods. The trail immediately splits; head left, descending into sugar maple woods.

0.1 The trail splits again; stay left to quickly reach a pair of wooden bridges spanning a deep drainage. The trail leading right shortcuts the Oldfield Trail.

0.2 Intersect a spur trail leading left to the Lotus Cove Trail. Head left to cross a park road then bisect a grassy area to meet the Lotus Cove Nature Trail.

0.4 Make a sharp left after descending to reach bottomland. Bridge the tributary creating the small valley.

0.5 Reach the loop portion of the Lotus Cove Nature Trail. Split right.

0.6 Come to a spur trail leading right, downhill from an oak bluff to a waterside observation deck. User-created trails lead along the bluff to good vistas of upper Cowan Lake. Backtrack to the main loop, passing abandoned wood and earth steps leading to the lake. Watch for numerous cherry trees.

1.1 Complete the loop portion of the Lotus Cove Nature Trail after leaving the bluff above Cowan Lake and passing an observation fence above a stream. Backtrack to the intersection with Oldfield Trail.

1.4 Split left on the Oldfield Trail. Descend a set of wooden multitier steps.

1.6 The Oldfield shortcut trail leaves right. Stay left toward the trailhead.

1.7 Reach the white pine grove and the end of the hike.

GREEN TIP
Be a happy land steward. Pick up after others who have left trash behind, so that those who come after you will enjoy a more natural hiking experience.

17 Trails of Fort Ancient

Come tour this hilltop circular earthwork built by pre-Columbian Ohioans. The trail system explores the boundaries of this enclosure from its perch high above the Little Miami River. So impressive is the site that it was made Ohio's first state park back in 1891. Fort Ancient, apparently built for ceremonial purposes, was once thought to be a defensive stronghold. You can tour the grounds and decide for yourself. First you will walk inside the grounds, then come to a perch overlooking the Little Miami Valley. Drop to meet the Little Miami Scenic Trail, then return to a second over-look. Wind more along the hand-built walls, trying to understand Ohio's past at this national natural landmark. By the way, a tour of the nearby museum is very worth your time, and helps you not only comprehend Fort Ancient but also additional Ohio Indian history.

Start: Fort Ancient Picnic Area
Distance: 1.6-mile loop
Hiking time: About 1 to 1.5 hours
Difficulty: Easy due to distance
Trail surface: Some mulch, mostly natural surface path
Best season: Year-round
Other trail users: None
Canine compatibility: Pets must be leashed at all times
Land status: State of Ohio property

Fees and permits: Entrance fee or membership required
Schedule: Apr through Nov: Tues through Sat 10 a.m. to 5 p.m., Sun: noon to 5 p.m.; Dec through Mar: Sat 10 a.m. to 5 p.m., Sun: noon to 5 p.m.; Closed on Mon.
Maps: Fort Ancient; USGS Oregonia
Trail contacts: Fort Ancient, 6123 State Route 350, Oregonia, OH 45054; (513) 932-4421; www.fortancient.org

Finding the trailhead: From exit 32 on I-71, northeast of downtown Cincinnati, take OH 123 south just a short distance to OH 350. Turn left and take OH 350 east, bridging the Little Miami River, driving for a total of 3.6 miles to the Fort Ancient. Turn right into the property, passing the left turn into the museum parking area. Keep straight and reach a parking area on your left before the road takes a hard right. Trailhead GPS: N39 23.985' / W84 5.647'

The Hike

I recommend touring the museum before your hike, but you may just not want to go inside on a gorgeous day. The site itself is amazing when you think about it—over 18,000 feet of hand-dug linear earthworks. That is 3.5 miles! The mounds were built over a period of 500 years by the Hopewell Indians, starting around the time of Christ. The irregular-shaped enclosure, resembling a bone with knots at both ends, spreads over a 100-or-so-acre site on a flat about 300 feet above the Little Miami River (the entire Fort Ancient property today encompasses 768 acres). Interestingly, the walls were built with over seventy gateways, or passages, through the mounds.

Leafless days will reveal the full extent of Fort Ancient.

These passages negate the theory of the earthworks as defensive. Also, moats were built inside the walls of the fort, which is also counter to sensible defensive earthwork building. Interior mounds further debunk the fort as defensive.

So the fort was likely built for ceremonial purposes, but exactly what for we don't know. Archaeological studies are ongoing at Fort Ancient. Other Hopewell earthworks appear in Ohio and Indiana. For other unknown reasons, the Indian culture we call Hopewell fell apart around a century after Fort Ancient was completed. The earthworks remain as a fascinating monument to their way of life.

The hike leaves Fort Ancient's picnic area, then travels astride a line of mounds. Today the mounds are covered in grasses and trees. The trees—hickory, oak, and cherry—are surprisingly large atop the earthworks. You are walking westerly, and this segment of the "wall" is oriented east–west. What once were "moats" on the inside walls are now silted in, but water still pools there in wet times.

Your first stopping point is the North Overlook. It will give you a sense of perspective as to the depth of the Little Ohio valley. Next, the hike takes you down a steep draw to the Little Miami River. Watch for wildflowers in spring. It's a 220-foot descent to reach the Little Miami Trail, the rail trail that extends through the valley of the Little Miami River. If you want to extend this relatively short hike, the rail trail provides miles of paved track for you to enjoy. Otherwise, head back up to the Terrace Trail. This path runs below the earthworks. You can gain a bottom-up view of Fort Ancient while tooling along the bluff slope, broken by streamlets descending toward the Little Miami.

A pass-over allows you to safely scale the fragile wall, and you rejoin the Earthworks Trail. The walls range from 4 to 23 feet in height. You can again walk along the mounds, amazed by the amount of labor using very primitive hand tools—bones of animals for digging, woven baskets for moving dirt, mostly simple human muscle—from a

OHIO'S NATIVE PAST

Ohio's Hopewell Indians are credited with building what is known as Fort Ancient. But aboriginals reached the Buckeye State well before then. After crossing from Asia, the earliest North Americans slowly spread across the continent, including Ohio. These hunter-gatherers were loosely organized and moved in small bands, following game and wild growing foods. Later, groups settled into home territories, the easing climate expanded growth of nut-bearing trees, but aboriginals also hunted smaller game and fished with nets. Tools such as axes came into greater use. Limited trading occurred among native peoples of North America.

Then we come to what is known as the Woodland Period. The change defining this period was the establishment of plant cultivation—farming if you will, of making pottery and building structures for ceremonial rather than purely practical purposes. An important aspect was also what is known as complex burials. Highly respected individuals were buried in mounds and sometimes buried with objects used in life on earth.

The Hopewell people, who built the walls of Fort Ancient, rose during the Middle Woodland Period. The elaborate walls reflect their advanced culture, as well as more permanent home structures. Their artwork was advanced, too, but the impressive mounds here and at other Ohio sites were their trademark.

For whatever reason, the next period of time saw a cultural decline. Natives used local resources, rather than trading, for tools and other goods. Also, rock shelters became common living sites. Eventually, peoples began grouping in villages containing upwards of 500 people. Agriculture became a mainstay. After, coming into contact with Europeans, everything changed. Trading brought in new goods, new ways—and disease. Eventually, the upheaval ended their lifeways in Ohio and beyond.

Fort Ancient rises high above the Little Miami River.

group of peoples whose average lifespan was thirty to thirty-five years. It is easy to see with the short life spans and primitive tools why it took nearly half a millennium to complete Fort Ancient!

It isn't long before you reach the South Overlook, which gives another perspective of the Little Miami as it curves around the south side of the site. Continue following the curves of the walls, returning to the trailhead near a large parking area.

Miles and Directions

0.0 Start at Fort Ancient Picnic Area on the Earthworks Trail. Walk a mulched path westerly, with a park road to your left. Mounds and the earthen wall rise to your right.

0.2 Come to the elevated North Overlook after passing a short spur trail connecting to the access road's end. Enjoy a westerly view across the Little Miami River Valley. Join a connector trail, which leaves downhill from the North Overlook. The Earthworks Trail goes left.

0.3 Reach a trail junction. Turn right, descending on the River Trail. The Terrace Trail goes left. You will pick that up later. Continue descending steeply down a wildflower-filled hollow.

0.5 Intersect the Little Miami Scenic Trail. The river is just a few feet ahead. The scenic trail heads up and down river, availing an opportunity to extend your hike. For a short destination, turn right and head upriver to the Fort Ancient canoe/kayak launch at the OH 350 bridge, then turn around. Otherwise, backtrack up the River Trail.

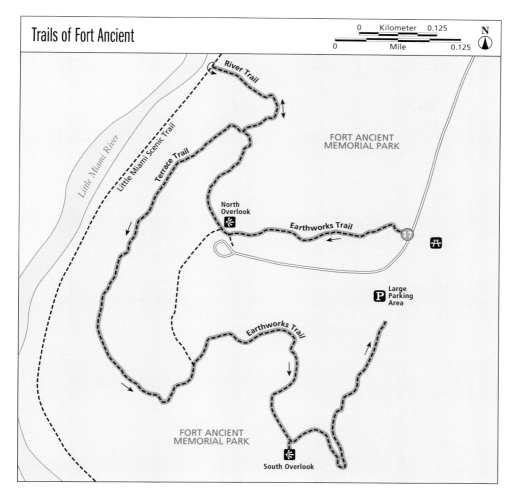

Trails of Fort Ancient

0   Kilometer   0.125

0   Mile   0.125

N

River Trail

FORT ANCIENT
MEMORIAL PARK

Little Miami Scenic Trail

Terrace Trail

Little Miami River

North
Overlook

Earthworks Trail

17

Large
Parking
Area

Earthworks Trail

FORT ANCIENT
MEMORIAL PARK

South Overlook

0.7   Join the Terrace Trail. This slender footpath runs parallel to the earthworks above and the river way below.

1.0   A boardwalk takes you over the earthworks to meet the Earthworks Trail. Turn right here, traveling once again inside the walls of Fort Ancient. Cut across some steep hollows, noting the periwinkle planted by the Civilian Conservation Corps to stabilize the earthen walls. Open onto a field, but stay right on the edge of field and forest.

1.3   Reach the South Overlook, where you can peer across the wooded Little Miami Valley. Though the parking area is visible across a large field, continue along the walls, heading southeast. Check out more large mounds and surprisingly large trees.

1.6   Arrive back at the parking area, completing the hike.

18 Caesar Creek Gorge State Nature Preserve

This loop hike explores a preserved slice of the Buckeye State, where cliffs and tall hills rise from clear Caesar Creek. Everywhere-you-look beauty surrounds the trail, including the creek itself, where rocky rapids divide silent pools, where bass forage on abundant aquatic life and logs provide perches for turtles. The hike leaves the gorge bottom, and climbs onto wooded hills, availing yet another environment in this botanically rich park. Before you dismiss this walk as too short, the paved Little Miami Scenic Trail passes directly by the trailhead, offering mile upon mile of pathway for hikers and bikers.

Start: Caesar Creek Gorge State Nature Preserve parking area
Distance: 1.9-mile balloon loop
Hiking time: About 1 hour
Difficulty: Easy, does have a hill climb
Trail surface: Natural surface path in forested woods
Best season: Year-round
Other trail users: None
Canine compatibility: No dogs allowed

Land status: State nature preserve
Fees and permits: No fees or permits required
Schedule: Open daily year-round dawn to dusk
Maps: Caesar Creek Gorge State Nature Preserve; USGS Oregonia
Trail contacts: Caesar Creek Gorge State Nature Preserve, 4080 Corwin Rd., Oregonia, OH 45054; (513) 897-3055; http://naturepreserves.ohiodnr.gov/caesarcreekgorge

Finding the trailhead: From exit 36 on I-71 northeast of downtown Cincinnati, take Wilmington Road west for 1.4 miles. Intersect Corwin Road and stay with Corwin Road as it twists and turns for 4.6 miles. The Caesar Creek Gorge State Nature Preserve will be on your right. Trailhead GPS: N39 29.506' / W84 6.087'

The Hike

The state of Ohio has a program whereby they purchase and preserve special natural areas that represent important biodiversity of the Buckeye State. The program originated with the Ohio Natural Areas Act of 1970. Specifically, areas must "contain scientifically and educationally valuable examples of Ohio's native plant and animal communities, geological features, or the habitats of rare or endangered species." Today, it is funded by the Natural Areas Income Tax Refund Checkoff, a program whereby citizens designate monies used solely for the acquisition of lands to be placed in the natural areas program.

Caesar Creek Gorge has been a designated state natural area since 1975. The nearly 500-acre parcel is cut by a 200-feet-deep gorge. Glacial meltwater rushed through the valley, cutting deeper and deeper, creating bluffs and exposing walls pocked with

Caesar Creek flows crystalline through its protected gorge.

ancient fossils. The preserve protects nearly 2 miles of the gorge, from just below Caesar Creek Lake Dam to Caesar Creek's confluence with the Little Miami River.

The Little Miami and its tributaries such as Caesar Creek were home to aboriginal Ohioans who sowed the rich bottoms for squash, beans, and corn. Sycamores and other moisture-loving species thrive in the bottoms today. The hills and bluffs were

LITTLE MIAMI SCENIC TRAIL—AND RIVER

The Little Miami Scenic Trail brushes by Caesar Creek Gorge preserve and presents an ideal opportunity to expand your adventure while here. The scenic trail corridor is actually a linear state park, a concept being utilized all over the nation, as railroad right-of-ways become trail passages. The approximately 75-mile path is enjoyed by more than hikers—cross-country skiers, roller bladers, bicyclers, and equestrians use the state trail. Interestingly, since this path runs along the Little Miami River, canoeists and kayakers use the trail for shuttles. Paddlers will find more than 80 miles of aquatic enjoyment on the Little Miami, a federally and state designated scenic river. Numerous outfitters, who rent canoes and kayaks while providing shuttles, are situated along the river and make a paddle trip easy, even for those without a boat. Anglers vie for smallmouth bass, which grow big and feisty in such clear, clean waters.

The Little Miami was Ohio's first designated state scenic river, receiving this special status back in 1969. The river has many faces from its beginning as a mere babbling brook in Clark County. It next cuts through hard dolomite, creating the Clifton Gorge, another must-see Ohio treasure, that presents a floral habitat resembling areas farther north, in addition to the crashing whitewater that cut the gorge in the first place. Bluffs rise beyond Clifton Gorge, as the Little Miami works south toward the East Fork Miami River. Here, cliffs tower above the stream, adding more scenic beauty. It is not only the river itself that is protected but also all the life within it. After five decades of protection, the health of the river has made a great comeback, including mussels, which need clear, clean water to survive. Development continues to creep upstream from the Little Miami's mouth, making this protected corridor all the more valuable.

The paved Little Miami State Trail runs from the outskirts of Cincinnati all the way up to Springfield. Accesses can be found all along the path, including the same trailhead used for Caesar Creek Gorge State Nature Preserve. It is 3.0 miles down to Oregonia and 4.6 miles down to Mathers Mill. It is 6.3 miles to Fort Ancient and 11.3 miles to Morrow access. Northbound it is 7.0 miles to Spring Valley Lake and 13.5 miles to the Hedges Road access.

The Caesar Creek Gorge trail access is also a state paddler access. The paddling distances are roughly the same as the trail distances. Just think: You could go for an outdoor triple play here—hike Caesar Creek Gorge, bicycle the Little Miami Scenic Trail, and paddle the Little Miami River. Now that's making the most of the area's wonderful outdoor natural resources.

0   Kilometer   0.25

0   Mile   0.25

N

Middletown Road

Caesar Creek

Corwin Road

18

P

Little Miami
Scenic Trail

Caesars Trace

CAESAR CREEK GORGE
STATE NATURE PRESERVE

CAESAR CREEK GORGE
STATE NATURE PRESERVE

mostly left alone, even when settlers pushed into the Little Miami valley. It was during this time that Caesar Creek got its name. Shawnees attacked a party of settlers on
the Ohio River, capturing a black slave named Caesar, who joined the natives and
became quite a hunter. This creek was one of his favorite hunting haunts, and he
named it for himself. Interestingly, the Shawnee of what became southwest Ohio had
another prisoner for a time—the famed backwoodsman Daniel Boone.

Thick forests of maple thrive in the preserve. Distinguishing between sugar maples
and red maples is easy. Look at the leaf of a sugar maple. The curves between lobes of
the sugar maple are U shaped, whereas the curves between lobes of the red maple are
at right angles. Beech, oak, and other hardwoods help safeguard the superior water
quality for which Caesar Creek is known. Their root systems help keep saturated soil
in place after heavy rains, minimizing erosion. As you hike, the ultra–clear water con-
firms such an assessment. The bottomlands are rich wildflower habitat, and the gorge

bluffs harbor relic prairie plant species. It all adds up to a wild atmosphere and natural getaway that Caesar himself may still appreciate.

Miles and Directions

0.0   Start from the parking area off Corwin Road. Join Caesars Trace as it heads uphill on a wide track.

0.1   Reach a trail junction and kiosk. A trail goes left to meet the Little Miami Scenic Trail near the confluence of Caesar Creek and the Little Miami River. Turn right, away from the river, climbing, still on a wide track. White-trunked sycamores rise from the river valley below.

0.2   Reach the loop portion of the hike. Take the footpath leading left, downhill, and away from the roadbed you've been following. Soon dip into bottomland, after crossing wet-weather stream braids of Caesar Creek.

0.4   Come alongside Caesar Creek. Under normal conditions the water clarity will amaze. Lazy pools accumulate where the current slackens. Watch for slender needle rush in the wetter trailside margins.

0.7   Impressive gray bluffs rise across Caesar Creek. Continue meandering in rich bottomland.

0.9   The flat through which you are walking becomes pinched in by a large hill. Leave the bottom, turn back downstream, and ascend into hickories and oaks. Leave the river altogether.

1.2   Level off, joining a wide grassy track. A spur trail leads acutely left and forms another small loop of its own. Travel amid hardwoods and cedar, as well as through small grassy clearings. Other former fields are being overtaken by locust trees.

1.5   Reach the other end of the small loop. Turn right here, heading downhill, still on a wide track, roughly following a power line.

1.8   Complete the loop portion of the hike. Begin backtracking.

1.9   Arrive back at the trailhead, completing the hike.

19 Crawdad Falls/Peninsula Loop

This balloon loop hike starts at Caesar Creek State Park's Pioneer Village, a re-created community of yesteryear that's worth a visit itself. For the hike you pick up the Perimeter Loop Trail rolling through woodlands before coming to Crawdad Falls, a limestone cascade on Jonahs Run. From there, the hike makes its way to a peninsula jutting into Caesar Creek Lake. Make an elongated circuit to the end of the peninsula, enjoying aquatic views and passing picnic shelters that make for ideal stopping spots. After completing the loop, make a return trip on the Perimeter Loop to Pioneer Village.

Start: Pioneer Village Road
Distance: 6.7-mile balloon loop
Hiking time: About 3 to 4 hours
Difficulty: Moderate, primary challenge is distance not elevation changes
Trail surface: Natural surface path in forested woods, short road walk
Best season: Sept through May
Other trail users: None
Canine compatibility: Leashed dogs permitted

Land status: State park
Fees and permits: No fees or permits required
Schedule: Open daily year-round 6 a.m. to 11 p.m.
Maps: Caesar Creek Lake, available online and at corps visitor center; USGS New Burlington
Trail contacts: Caesar Creek State Park, 8570 E. State Route 73, Waynesville, OH 45068-9719; (513) 897-3055; www.caesarcreek statepark.com

Finding the trailhead: From exit 45 on I-71 northeast of downtown Cincinnati, take OH 73 north 4.0 miles to Oregonia Road. Turn left onto Oregonia Road and follow it for 2.0 miles to Pioneer Village Road. Turn right onto Pioneer Village Road and follow it for 0.2 mile, to a parking area on your left, just past a large field parking area, open for special events at the Pioneer Village. Trailhead GPS: N39 29.125' / W84 2.211'

The Hike

This hike leaves east on the yellow-blazed Perimeter Loop Trail from Pioneer Village Road. Pass around a metal gate, working through a field. Shortly enter woods on a grassy track. The forest of maple and oak crowds the path and overhangs the trail. Descend to rock-hop a branch before rising into habitat in transition from field to forest. These areas, where field and forest meld, are ideal habitat for bird and beast. Keep your eyes open for wildlife.

The trail traces seldom-used Lukens Road for a short piece before resuming the foot trail and coming to Crawdad Falls, a limestone cascade on Jonahs Run. A sturdy bridge crosses Jonahs Run just above the 20-foot-wide, 3-foot drop and the trail circles around the fall, all of which allow you to enjoy the watery highlight from different perspectives. Like most area streams, Jonahs Run will flow strong in winter and spring, drying to a trickle by fall, and perhaps entirely dry up.

A single-track path weaves through diverse woods on this circuit.

The hike then cruises along the embayment of Jonahs Run before resuming its northbound ways, aiming for the Fifty Springs Peninsula. A few abandoned nature trails may confuse, but once you get going on the loop portion of the hike, the walk is a piece of cake. Besides, the path runs a narrow corridor with Caesar Creek Lake on one side and the Fifty Springs access road on the other. Stopping places are numerous, as you will pass picnic shelters aplenty on the circuit.

You will drop into moist, beech-filled hollows between drier cedar and brush hills that lead toward the lake, which shimmers in the distance through the trees. The trail also explores numerous environments, from lakeshore to field to woods and even a pond. Sugar maples, sassafras, and sweet gum rise from former fields. The loop then begins circling the arrowhead of the peninsula, approaching a far-reaching shoreline vista.

The hike returns toward the main Perimeter Loop Trail, passing a couple of picnic shelters and joining an old roadbed. The roadbed travels atop a bluff and features lake views. Once you complete the loop part of the hike, it is a 1.7-mile backtrack to the trailhead.

A TRIP BACK IN TIME: THE PIONEER VILLAGE

Caesar Creek's Pioneer Village, located at this hike's trailhead, is a living history museum. It has a mission and it is this: "to preserve our history and promote a better understanding of early life in Southwestern Ohio." The numerous old structures and wooden buildings will lure you toward them, before or after your hike. You can take a self-guided tour of the grounds any day. However, the cabins are only open during weekends when events are held. The buildings replicate everything from an old-time inn to a country store to a pioneer house to a blacksmith shop.

The buildings were brought together from all over the region. For example, the Amos Hawkins House came from the banks of Caesar's Creek in Massie Township. Hawkins erected this house in the 1820s. The two-story structure was built from tulip trees. The house was dismantled and moved here in 1974, including the original stone foundation.

Some buildings were erected even earlier. The Samuel Heighway Cabin is believed to have been built in the late 1700s along the old road between Cincinnati and Columbus, near present-day Waynesville. Until it was partly burned by fire in 1971, the structure had been continuously lived in, believed to be the oldest continuously inhabited structure in the state.

The Furnas House, built in the 1820s, was moved here after the Caesar Creek Lake project was under way. The homestead would've been flooded by the lake but was instead moved here and is in its original condition. Many more structures can be enjoyed at Pioneer Village and each has its own story.

Themed special weekend events are held throughout the year at Pioneer Village, ranging from gospel music to old-time cooking to Civil War reenactments, harvest festivals, and more. These are great times to not only see the structures from the outside but also see the inside of the buildings with interpretation by event staff. It really adds to the experience, creating more than a hike from this trailhead.

You can be more than a visitor at Pioneer Village. Become a member of Caesar Creek Pioneer Village. Your dues help keep up the historic area. Furthermore, you can volunteer to host or work on projects, keeping this treasure of Southwest Ohio open for Ohioans to come.

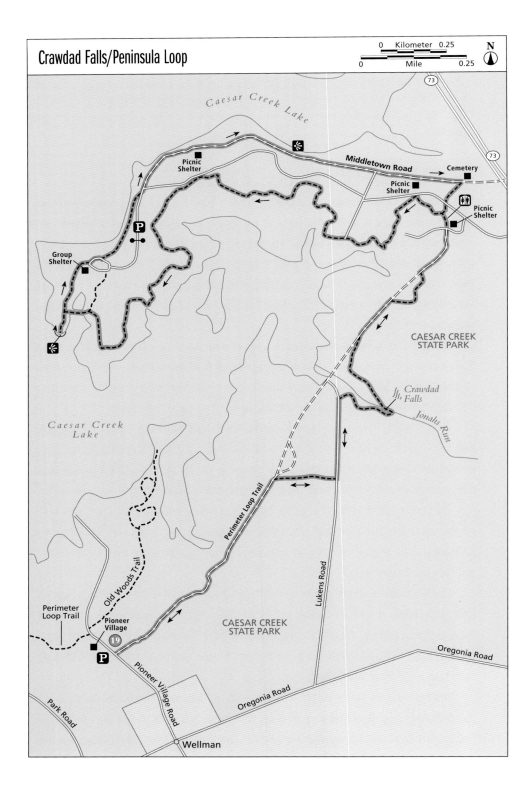

Crawdad Falls/Peninsula Loop

0   Kilometer   0.25

0   Mile   0.25

N

Caesar Creek Lake

Middletown Road

73

73

Picnic Shelter

Cemetery

Picnic Shelter

Picnic Shelter

P

Group Shelter

CAESAR CREEK STATE PARK

Caesar Creek Lake

Crawdad Falls

Jonahs Run

Perimeter Loop Trail

Old Woods Trail

Lukens Road

Perimeter Loop Trail

Pioneer Village

19

P

CAESAR CREEK STATE PARK

Oregonia Road

Pioneer Village Road

Oregonia Road

Park Road

Wellman

Miles and Directions

0.0 Start east from Pioneer Village Road, on the Perimeter Loop Trail. Enter a field.

0.3 Dip to cross a rock branch. Keep northeasterly.

0.5 Bridge a small branch.

0.7 Emerge at Lukens Road. Turn left onto the paved but lightly traveled, crumbly asphalt track.

0.9 Leave right from Lukens Road, near a gate. Enter woods with the Jonahs Run arm of Caesar Creek Lake to your left. Note the lotus blooms on the upper end of the embayment. You may also see waterfowl here.

▶ **Leave old farm and home relics for others to discover and enjoy for themselves.**

1.1 Reach Crawdad Falls. Span Jonahs Run on a sturdy bridge.

1.5 Drop steeply to a branch.

1.7 Emerge in a grassy area with a picnic shelter in sight, as well as the Fifty Springs access road. Walk to the picnic shelter, then toward a restroom building. Look for a grassy path leaving left near the restrooms and the Fifty Springs access road. Join the grassy path as it becomes a natural surface forested trail. Ahead, a few abandoned nature trails may briefly confuse, but the main loop is easily the most beaten down track.

2.1 The trail makes an abrupt right. Stay with the most used path where faint junctions remain.

2.2 Bisect a closed, abandoned paved road.

2.8 Come within sight of a picnic shelter across the road. You are on one of the narrowest parts of the peninsula. Enter a meadow.

2.9 A spur trail leads right to a parking area. You can shortcut the loop here.

3.6 Reach a trail junction near a pond. Stay left, crossing the pond dam.

3.7 Come to another junction. Turn left for an out-and-back trek to a point and lake vista. Backtrack from the vista.

3.9 Emerge at the group camp, with a large picnic shelter, fire ring, and restrooms. As you look out from the shelter, look left, walking the paved loop for a foot trail entering woods.

4.0 Come to the narrow part of the peninsula, briefly join the main road then veer left, as the road turns back right.

4.3 Pass through a grassy picnic area with a shelter. The trail reenters woods on the far side of the shelter. Pick up an old roadbed and walk an easterly track on a bluff above Caesar Creek Lake.

4.6 Enjoy bluff-top views.

4.8 Pass by another picnic shelter.

4.9 The trail emerges onto a paved road. You can see a cemetery to your left. Turn right and walk the paved road, shortly emerging onto the main Fifty Springs Road. You can see the very first picnic shelter you accessed. Head toward the shelter, completing the loop portion of the hike, then begin backtracking.

5.8 Reach Lukens Road beyond Crawdad Falls. Turn left and leave right from Lukens Road after 0.2 mile.

6.7 Arrive back at Pioneer Village Road, completing the hike.

20 Horseshoe Falls Hike

This hike offers numerous trailside highlights—fossils, bluff views, a stream, a waterfall, lake views, a historic mill site, lakeside trail, and some extra loops that add to the trail mileage. Start at a well-maintained recreation area, crossing Caesar Creek Dam spillway, viewing fossils, then turn up Flat Fork, where Horseshoe Falls awaits. Circle around the Flat Fork Valley and cruise the shore of Caesar Creek Lake, looping back from Wellman Boat Ramp.

Start: Flat Fork trailhead near Caesar Creek Lake Dam
Distance: 4.9-mile multiple loop
Hiking time: About 2.5 to 3 hours
Difficulty: Moderate
Trail surface: Mostly natural surface track, some gravel
Best season: Sept through May, spring for boldest waterfall
Other trail users: None
Canine compatibility: Leashed dogs permitted

Land status: Army Corps of Engineers, comanaged by state park
Fees and permits: No fees or permits required
Schedule: Open daily year-round
Maps: Caesar Creek Lake, available online and at corps visitor center; USGS Oregonia
Trail contacts: Caesar Creek State Park, 8570 E. State Route 73, Waynesville, OH 45068-9719; (513) 897-3055; www.caesarcreek statepark.com. US Army Corps of Engineers, 4020 N. Clarksville Rd., Waynesville, OH 45068; (513) 897-1050.

Finding the trailhead: From exit 45 on I-71 northeast of downtown Cincinnati, take OH 73 north 4.0 miles to Oregonia Road. Turn left onto Oregonia Road and follow it for 3.3 miles to Clarksville Road and a sign for the Caesar Lake visitor center. Turn right toward the visitor center on Clarksville Road and follow it 0.9 mile to the right turn to Flat Fork Recreation Area, just before crossing the Caesar Creek Lake Dam. Enter the recreation area, staying in the upper parking area, and look right for a hiker trail sign near some steps. GPS Trailhead: N39 29.005' / W84 3.427'

The Hike

I wish all trailheads were as nice as Flat Fork trailhead. It has a well-spaced parking area, shaded picnic tables, a picnic shelter, and restrooms. The area is immaculate and well cared for. US Army Corps of Engineers facilities are known for being well-funded, high-quality projects. The lake is co-managed with Caesar Creek Lake State Park. The Perimeter Loop Trail is your ticket on this hike. The first-rate track was laid out to explore numerous trailside features. You will initially leave the forest and open onto the man-made dam spillway. Though obviously created with heavy machinery, the level spillway exposes fossils from the Ordovician Period. In the exposed rock, you can see life from an ancient seabed. Look for outlines of corals and seashells and unidentifiable critters. The seashells were created millions of years ago, when animals such as trilobites along with vegetation and mud matter sank to the seafloor,

Trailside hardwoods color the path in autumn.

eventually drying out and turning into stone. These animals retained their outlines while fossilizing. When the spillway was dug, the prehistoric world was exposed in a rock mosaic. Visitors come from distant places to go fossiling here. However, collecting fossils is not allowed unless you get a permit from the rangers at the nearby visitor center.

Don't forget autumn wildflowers when considering fall hikes.

Beyond the spillway, the trail begins circling around Flat Fork. You can see the streamshed evolve from embayment to full-fledged creek. A view opens from a limestone cliff down to Horseshoe Falls, a wide, ledge-type cataract. After circling around to Horseshoe Falls, you will reverse your vantage point—looking from the water's edge upward at the limestone cliff atop which you stood earlier. Note the limestone layering revealed in the cliff. Follow Flat Fork down to the site of an old water-powered mill site, long since reverted to its natural state by periodic and certain flooding from Flat Fork. The loop curves back to Caesar Creek Lake. The waterside track presents multiple lake vantages, including one from a spur trail leading to a peninsular point. Here you can view the dam spillway, the dam itself, and the stump-filled Flat Fork embayment.

Rewarding vantage points are constant as you parallel the shoreline, turning into the main body of the impoundment. The dam continues standing out clearly along the opposite shoreline. Finally, make the big Wellman Boat Ramp parking area. A short period of road walking reconnects you to the main trail system. The hike reenters woods and shortly begins circling back around Flat Fork embayment. On your return trip there are a couple of short loops that you can finish off in order to pick up as much new trail as possible.

In addition to this hike, a shorter all-access spur trail also leaves from the same parking area. Nearby you can also explore the fossils of the spillway beyond where the trail crosses it. Furthermore, check out the tailwater recreation area just below the dam, where a short path explores the upper end of the Caesar Creek Gorge.

Miles and Directions

0.0 Start at the upper parking lot of Flat Fork Recreation Area, joining the Perimeter Loop Trail as it descends wood and gravel steps to pass a picnic shelter. Begin cruising beside Caesar Creek Lake. Spur trails lead to the water's edge. You can see the peninsular point where you will be later.

0.2 Cross the dam spillway, where exposed fossils delight hikers and aspiring geologists. On the far side of the spillway the trail splits; stay right, heading up wood steps into a sugar maple forest.

0.6 Intersect the other end of the first small loop, which is used by bank anglers. Begin circling around the cove of Flat Fork.

0.8 Reach the cliff top and vista of Horseshoe Falls. It isn't evident from this point, but you're standing on an overhanging bluff.

1.0 Reach Flat Fork. There has been a bridge here in the past and there might be again in the future. If the water is excessively high, endangering your safety in crossing, turn back. Most often it will be an easy rock hop. Cross Flat Fork and turn downstream.

ORDOVICIAN FOSSILS

The reason the greater Cincinnati area is home to so many ancient fossils is due to what is known as the Cincinnati Arch. The feature, entirely underground, is a massive fold of rock that brought the record of ancient times toward the earth's surface. You will see a huge number of fossils when crossing the dam spillway and also near Horseshoe Falls. During the Ordovician Period a great sea covered this area and was full of what we think of today as strange-looking life forms.

Simple invertebrate creatures, the precursors of today's underwater life, comprise many fossils. But the kingpin of that day was the trilobite, and you can see its imprint. Thousands of species roamed the waters of planet Earth. A general description reveals the trilobite as flattish with an outer skeleton and its soft parts on the inside, the opposite of us humans. Though they weren't big, they were not the prettiest creature. Suffice it to say if a trilobite was crawling on your neck, you'd knock it off real quick. When walking across the spillway, or along its walls, see if you can spot some of the wildlife roaming this area long ago—including the prolific and ubiquitous trilobite.

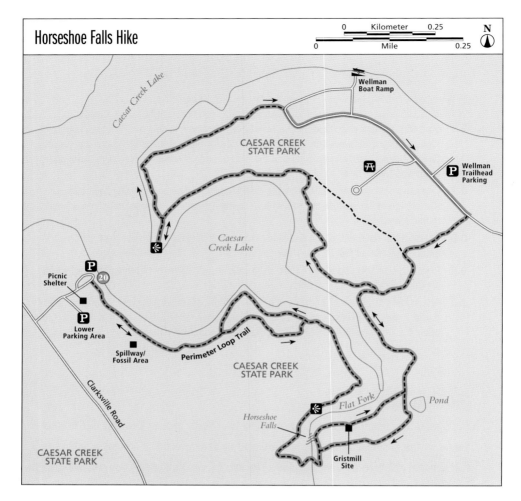

0   Kilometer   0.25

0   Mile   0.25

N

1.1 Reach another mini-loop junction. Stay left, soon passing Horseshoe Falls, a wide, 4-foot ledge dropping into a pool that can be completely dry in late summer and fall. Continue downstream along Flat Fork. As you walk beyond the falls, look for spur trails leading left to the water's edge, including one that reaches the base of the cliff you were standing atop earlier. Shortly pass the site of the old mill. Climb steps away from the mill site.

1.3 Come to a trail intersection. Stay left, working around the Flat Fork embayment.

1.5 Make another trail junction after turning away from Caesar Creek Lake. The most heavily used trail keeps straight, easterly. You, however, turn left, bridging a streamlet, then curve back out to the shoreline, cruising atop a ridge with elevated vistas.

1.8 Stay left at a trail intersection, still along the shore.

2.1 Reach a path leading left to a peninsular point, descending through cedars. Two-hundred-seventy-degree views open of Caesar Creek Lake.

2.5 Come to a four-way intersection in a grassy area. Keep straight for Wellman Boat Ramp, as a spur goes left to the lake and right to the Wellman Boat Ramp.

2.6 Reach the Wellman Boat Ramp parking area. Stay right and begin ascending from the lake on the ramp access road.

2.9 A spur road leaves right to a picnic area. Just ahead you will pass the Wellman trailhead parking area, on your left.

3.0 Leave the road and pick up the Perimeter Loop Trail as it leaves right.

3.1 Stay left as a spur leaves right back toward the lake. Turn into the Flat Fork watershed.

3.3 Complete the biggest loop of the hike. Begin backtracking.

3.6 Come to a trail intersection. Stay left, picking up new trail as you pass by a small pond atop a hill.

3.9 Make another trail junction. You are just upstream of Horseshoe Falls on Flat Fork. Stay left, crossing Flat Fork.

4.3 Stay right at a trail intersection, picking up new trail, traveling along the shore to a grass, rock, and cedar point, popular with bank anglers. You can see the main trailhead from the point. After completing this loop, open onto the dam spillway.

4.9 Arrive back at the trailhead, completing the hike.

GREEN TIP
Before you start for home, ask yourself:
Have you left the wilderness as you'd want to see it?

21 Old Sugar Camp Hike

Take a walk along Caesar Creek Lake and surrounding environs. First, you will leave the trailhead for a deep valley rife with mature sugar maples, once a location for tapping maple syrup. After circling this scenic hollow, walk a high bluff above the lake to reach a spur to the shore and a peninsular point with great views. The trek continues to a lakeside beach, which offers remote water access and wide-reaching vistas. The rewards seem to outstrip your effort—the trail has some undulations but isn't hard.

Start: Day Lodge
Distance: 4.2-mile out-and-back with small loop
Hiking time: About 2 to 2.5 hours
Difficulty: Moderate
Trail surface: Natural
Best season: Year-round
Other trail users: None
Canine compatibility: Leashed dogs permitted
Land status: US Army Corps of Engineers, comanaged by state park

Fees and permits: No fees required
Schedule: Open daily year-round
Maps: Caesar Creek Lake, available online and at corps visitor center; USGS Oregonia
Trail contacts: Caesar Creek State Park, 8570 E. State Route 73, Waynesville, OH 45068-9719; (513) 897-3055; www.caesarcreek statepark.com. US Army Corps of Engineers, 4020 N. Clarksville Rd., Waynesville, OH 45068; (513) 897-1050.

Finding the trailhead: From exit 45 on I-71 northeast of downtown Cincinnati, take OH 73 north 4 miles to Oregonia Road. Turn left onto Oregonia Road and follow it for 3.3 miles to Clarksville Road and a sign for the Caesar Lake visitor center. Turn right toward the visitor center on Clarksville Road and follow it 2.4 miles (passing the visitor center at 1.5 miles) to the Hopewell Recreation Area. Turn right and stay straight toward the Hopewell Day Lodge, making a quick left just before dead-ending at the day lodge. The trail starts at the far end of the parking area, to your left as you are looking at the day lodge. Trailhead GPS: N39 30.378' / W84 3.129'

The Hike

If you like big trees, small streams, lake views, and beaches—and trailside solitude, this hike on the Perimeter Loop Trail is for you. Enjoy a little of all the above along the shores of Caesar Creek Lake. The presence of sugar maples was a major factor in the preservation of the large trees along a tributary of Caesar Creek. For while it was profitable to cut timber, especially on level land that could be farmed following the tree clearing, it was also profitable to tap sugar maples for their sap, which could be boiled down into maple syrup, then sold. Part of the hike passes through what is called a "sugar bush," a concentration of sugar maples that could be tapped. Every year, tappers would come to the area and undertake their operations, staying long enough to create a "sugar camp" while at the "sugar bush." Along with the sugar maples, other big trees thrived in Old Sugar Camp Hollow, leaving a rich forest for us today.

Overlooking Caesar Creek Lake

You will see these big woods shortly after beginning the hike. Look for regal oaks with widespread limbs, now surrounded by shagbark hickory and beech among others. You will be crossing the upper edge of ravines that are flowing downhill to your right, toward Caesar Creek Lake. Pawpaws flank together in such moist situations. The forest canopy remains noticeably high as you pass through the hollow of Old Sugar Camp.

CAESAR CREEK LAKE BY THE NUMBERS

The views you will enjoy on this hike are of Caesar Creek Lake. Originally authorized under the Flood Control Act of 1938, the lake was designed to hold back heavy rains and melting snows that would damage the Little Miami River Valley. It would be forty years before the dam was completed and the lake began to fill. Construction actually began in 1971 and was completed in 1978. Caesar Creek drains 237 square miles of land above the lake. At full summer pool the impoundment covers 2,830 acres and stretches 7.5 miles in length. The dam holding this water back is nearly 0.5 mile wide and 265 feet high. The lake project provides monetary benefit to the region in two ways. First, it saves the valley money in unrealized flood damages, since it prevents such catastrophes. Secondly, the lake draws in visitors—including us hikers—who spend our money in the region. But the project was not without cost to some people—New Burlington, Ohio, lies submerged under its waters. The residents were bought out and forced off their land by eminent domain.

Beyond the big trees, the hike rejoins the Perimeter Loop Trail. It travels high above the shoreline of Caesar Creek Lake in a noticeably younger forest. Roll through forestland, gaining occasional views of the lake through the trees. A spur trail leads along a ridgeline to the lake's edge. A bluff makes accessing the water challenging but it does offer a rewarding unobstructed vista.

Back on the Perimeter Loop Trail, you come near park boundary before dropping to Caesar Creek Lake. As you near the shoreline, a spur trail leads to the water's edge and a gray sand beach. In spring, high water may nearly or completely immerse the beach. Conversely, in fall, lower water will expose more beach. Look for deer and other animal tracks in the sand.

On your return trip you can save 0.5 mile by shortcutting the Old Sugar Camp Loop and staying on the Perimeter Loop Trail. After your hike save a little energy to check out the nearby prairie wetland. On your drive into the Hopewell Day Lodge, a signed road diverges right. The parking area is a short piece down that road. You will see a gravel parking area. A grassy trail leads through open prairie to an elevated observation tower above a wetland that is great for observing songbirds and more.

Miles and Directions

0.0 Start at the Day Lodge Parking Area, joining the single-track Perimeter Loop Trail. Enter a mature forest near a huge oak tree. Skirt along the edge of a field. Look for more big oaks in the immediate vicinity.

0.2 Cross the dam spillway, where exposed fossils delight hikers and geologists. On the far side of the spillway the trail splits—stay right, heading up wood steps into a sugar maple forest.

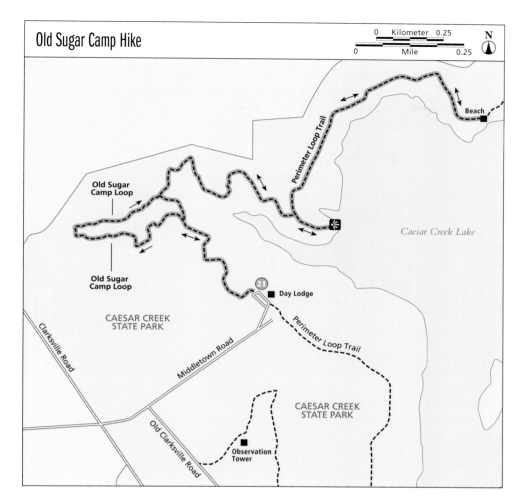

Old Sugar Camp Hike

0   Kilometer   0.25

0   Mile   0.25

N

0.3   Intersect and join the Old Sugar Camp Loop left, as the Perimeter Loop keeps straight. Enter a deep hollow full of tall trees. A sharp drop falls off to your right.

0.4   Dip to cross a side hollow. Note the rocky limestone streambed. Continue westerly up Old Sugar Camp Hollow.

0.7   Cross the primary unnamed streambed creating Old Sugar Camp Hollow. Begin turning back easterly in bottomland. Watch for rock outcrops near the stream and on the hillsides.

0.9   Return to the Perimeter Loop Trail. Turn left, northbound, climbing out of Old Sugar Camp Hollow. Shagbark hickories proliferate in these younger woods.

1.5   Come to a trail intersection. A marked spur trail leads right, along a ridgeline toward Caesar Creek Lake. Pass a huge white oak to the right of the trail.

1.6   Reach the viewpoint on the spur trail. Caesar Creek Lake opens to your east. Since the trail ends on a bluff, accessing the water is difficult. Backtrack to the Perimeter Loop Trail, resuming northbound on a hill well above the water.

2.2   Dip to cross a wet-weather tributary. Shortly descend toward the lake.

2.4 A spur trail leads right a short distance to the lake. A beach lies at the water's edge. A hiker could swim here in the warm season, or just enjoy a water-level vantage of Caesar Creek Lake. Backtrack on the Perimeter Loop Trail.

3.3 Pass the spur to the lake.

3.9 Reach the Old Sugar Camp Loop. Keep straight on the Perimeter Loop Trail, crossing the stream creating Old Sugar Camp Hollow.

4.2 Arrive back at the Day Lodge trailhead, completing the hike.

GREEN TIP

For rest stops, go off-trail so others won't have to walk around you. Head for resilient surfaces without vegetation if possible.

22 Trace Run Double Loop

This challenging hike explores the rugged Trace Run section of the Caesar Creek Lake shoreline. A great training hike, it goes up and down, up and down, through hill and hollow. In addition, the hike also has scenic highlights, including multiple shoreline vistas, streamside overlooks, and occasional old trees. You will share the trail with mountain bikers as you first tackle the Red Loop. It borders a big shoreline peninsula before crossing Trace Run. From there, make a large loop that enjoys both shoreline and streamside beauty. Allow ample time for both distance and the challenging terrain.

Start: Harveysburg Road
Distance: 8.9-mile double loop
Hiking time: About 4 to 6 hours
Difficulty: Most difficult due to distance and elevation changes
Trail surface: Natural surface path in forested woods, short road walk
Best season: Year-round
Other trail users: Mountain bikers
Canine compatibility: Leashed dogs permitted
Land status: Army Corps of Engineers, comanaged by state park

Fees and permits: No fees or permits required
Schedule: Open daily year-round 6 a.m. to 11 p.m.
Maps: Campground to Harveysburg Trails, available online; USGS New Burlington
Trail contacts: Caesar Creek State Park, 8570 E. State Route 73, Waynesville, OH 45068-9719; (513) 897-3055; www.caesarcreek statepark.com. US Army Corps of Engineers, 4020 N. Clarksville Rd., Waynesville, OH 45068; (513) 897-1050.

Finding the trailhead: From exit 45 on I-71 northeast of downtown Cincinnati, take OH 73 north 3.2 miles to Harveysburg Road. Turn right onto Harveysburg Road and follow it 1.1 miles to the trailhead on your right. Trailhead GPS: N39 30.867' / W83 59.377'

The Hike

Don't be dissuaded by the fact that this trail network is used primarily by mountain bikers. For this is arguably the most challenging set of pathways in the greater Caesar Creek Lake area. It certainly is one of the longer networks. You will be along the lake much of the time, as well as deep wooded valleys. Though there is a limit to the undulations simply because there's only so much elevation to go up or down, it is the aggregate total and nearly constant nature of these undulations that will challenge hikers. For the same reason the double loop also serves as a great training hike if you are heading to the Smoky Mountains in Tennessee or the Rockies out West.

The trail system is marked with color-coded plastic posts that correspond to the names of the trails. Unlike some mountain biking trails, this system does not divide into numerous paths that create a spider web of confusion. The system is well marked and maintained with only a few segments where trails diverge and come back

This big tree was likely here before Ohio was a state.

together for no apparent reason. Winter is a great time to hike this trail, especially when the temperatures are hovering just above freezing. Mountain bikers are asked to stay off the trails unless temperatures are 28F or lower during the winter, to avoid creating muddy patches. The trail is never crowded on weekdays. If you are looking for solitude or wanting to avoid the bikers, hike during the above suggested time periods.

Begin a pattern of turning into a hollow then circling around it, heading toward Caesar Creek Lake. Once near the lake you turn back into the next hollow and repeat the process. The Red Loop eventually snakes south along the Trace Run embayment. Once at Trace Run, you begin a big loop on the far side of that creek, now on the Blue Trail. Travel under white-trunked sycamores and lush streamside woods as you peer down on clear pools divided by gurgling shoals.

> Trail etiquette states bikers should yield to hikers. Considerate hikers extend goodwill toward all trail users whether they are on foot, two wheels, or horseback.

Beyond Trace Run, the hike climbs to Ward Road, does a short road walk before reentering public land near a house, and joins the Black Trail. It works down-hill for a tributary of Turkey Run Creek. Crisscross the stream in rich woods before coming to a small nest of interconnected trails. The Yellow Trail begins on the far side of this creek. You won't get lost if you just stay on the west, left, side of the stream. After passing the Ward Road trailhead, the hike picks up the Blue Trail and enjoys inspiring views into the heart of Caesar Creek Lake.

Finally the double loop crosses Trace Run a second time. Your challenge isn't over after rejoining the Red Loop. More undulations lie between you and the home stretch. Have a well-earned cold drink waiting at the trailhead. While chugging away, you will agree not only is this a great training hike for Cincinnati trail treaders but a scenic journey in its own right.

Miles and Directions

0.0 Start from the Harveysburg Road trailhead on the Red Trail, taking a wide track on an old roadbed that soon curves back acutely right.

0.1 Come to the loop portion of the Red Trail. Your return route keeps straight, but you turn left on a single-track path in a mix of white pine and sugar maple. Watch for an abundance of yucca plants.

0.5 Pass a pile of metal junk in a ravine. This erosion-stopping technique used by farmers of old is frowned upon today since it is both unsightly and also allows fluids and other pollutants to wash down the ravines into the water system.

0.7 Cruise directly along the shoreline of Caesar Creek Lake, then turn back into a hollow.

1.2 Enter a cedar grove near the lake. Watery views open. Pass a pond on your right then begin turning into the Trace Run embayment.

1.4 Pass the ruins of a 1950s jalopy.

1.5 Reach a trail junction. Here a sub-loop leaves right and circles around a ravine. The main path keeps straight and dives into and climbs back out of the aforementioned ravine.

1.6 Reach the other end of the sub-loop. Stay left.

1.7 A spur trail leaves right on a wide track back to the trailhead. Stay left and end trail junctions for a while.

2.1 Bridge a fern-filled tributary. Continue the ups and downs as you cut across wet-weather drainages spilling toward Trace Run.

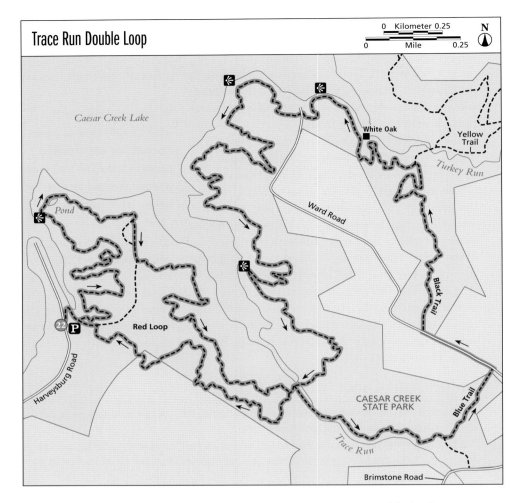

0   Kilometer 0.25

0   Mile   0.25

N

Caesar Creek Lake

Pond

White Oak

Yellow
Trail

Turkey Run

Ward Road

Black Trail

22   P

Red Loop

Harveysburg Road

CAESAR CREEK
STATE PARK

Blue Trail

Trace Run

Brimstone Road

2.7 Reach a trail junction on a hill above Trace Run. Your return route leaves right, but for now, turn left and steeply descend to Trace Run, a perennial stream. Once at the stream, trails run on both sides of it. Cross Trace Run (a potential ford) then turn upstream, joining a single-track path traveling along the edge of the bank. You should be on the left bank.

3.3 Reach a trail junction. Here, a spur trail leads right a short piece to Brimstone Road. Stay left on the Blue Trail, northbound. Climb away from Trace Run.

3.5 Reach paved Ward Road. Turn left, walking the road past houses.

3.7 Leave right from Ward Road, near the driveway of 510 Ward Road, joining the Black Trail, northbound in cedar woods descending to a tributary of Turkey Run. Proceed to cross the stream twice, down a hollow filled with tulip trees and sycamores.

4.2 Ascend from the stream only to turn back.

4.3 Reach a trail junction. An unofficial path leaves left and downhill, while the official path also heads downhill back to the unnamed stream, then turns down to cross the stream and meet the Yellow Trail. Cross back over to the west side of the stream and climb steeply into a piney bluff well above Turkey Creek embayment.

4.9 Pass a massive white oak to the right of the trail.

5.2 Emerge onto the Ward Road trailhead. Pick up the Blue Trail across the road, heading westerly. Shortly open onto the main body of the lake.

5.5 Come to another great lake view. Continue cruising along scenic shoreline before turning up a ravine.

5.9 Come very near Ward Road a final time before returning to the lake.

6.2 Turn south back into the Trace Run embayment. Continue undulating into and out of tributaries.

7.0 Reach the top of a ridge. A spur trail leads right to a view. The main path works toward Trace Run, dipping into bottomland.

7.6 Cross Trace Run and climb steeply to a trail intersection. You have been here before. Now it's time to complete the Red Loop. Keep straight, southwesterly, on untrodden trail.

7.8 Come near a field and the park boundary. Turn westerly. Wander amid hills and hollows.

8.4 Come within sight of a cornfield.

8.7 Reach a trail junction. Here, a wide road-like trail leaves right; you turn left, descending.

8.8 Complete the loop portion of the Red Loop. Backtrack toward the trailhead.

8.9 Finish the hike.

CAN YOU EAT AN OSAGE ORANGE?

Along the way on this hike, you may see an Osage orange tree. It has an unmistakable fruit, a large green ball stretching up to 6 inches in diameter, also known as a hedge apple. Originally native to the Red River, the waterway dividing Texas from Oklahoma, the thorny, strong, and densely wooded tree was transplanted throughout the Midwest and Great Plains as a fence that grew. Plant them in a row and as long as they kept cutting it back, homesteaders could fashion the gnarly trees into fences with which neither man nor beast would want to tangle. The wood of an Osage is nearly rot-proof.

The fruit of an Osage orange recalls the smell of an actual orange when sitting in the sun. Only female trees bear the fruit. The Osage orange is edible by humans. However, it is the seeds that are edible, a complete contrast to real oranges. It is quite a task to pick out the Osage seeds for consumption, though apparently squirrels have plenty of time on their paws to do such a thing. They love Osage oranges.

23 Spring Valley Loop

This is a great wildlife watching hike, especially for waterfowl enthusiasts. Situated on a lake that was once a commercial fur farm in the Little Miami River Valley, Spring Valley Wildlife Area presents open waters and wetlands, a wetland complex, that attract a diversity of creatures. You will leave the trailhead and take a long boardwalk to an elevated observation deck that allows views near and far. After this, a loop trail circles the lake allowing for more aquatic opportunities along an extended shoreline.

Start: Pence Jones Road trailhead
Distance: 2.6-mile loop
Hiking time: About 1.5 to 2.5 hours
Difficulty: Easy, mostly level
Trail surface: Some boardwalk, mostly grassy path
Best season: Year-round
Other trail users: None
Canine compatibility: Pets must be leashed at all times
Land status: Ohio Department of Natural Resources property

Fees and permits: No fees or permits required to hike
Schedule: Open dawn to dusk; call or check website ahead of time during potential hunting seasons
Maps: Spring Valley Wildlife Area Map; USGS Waynesville
Trail contacts: Wildlife District Five Office, 1076 Old Springfield Pike, Xenia, OH 45385; (937) 372-9261; http://wildlife.ohiodnr.gov/springvalley

Finding the trailhead: From the intersection of OH 73 and US 42 in Waynesville, northeast of downtown Cincinnati, take US 42 north for 5.6 miles to Roxanna–New Burlington Road. Turn right onto Roxanna–New Burlington Road and follow it for 1.5 miles to Pence Jones Road. Turn right onto Pence Jones Road and follow it south for 0.3 mile to an unnamed gravel road leading right to the trailhead parking at a dead end. Trailhead GPS: N39 34.355' / W84 0.645'

The Hike

This destination is underutilized as a hiking haven. Sure, Spring Valley Wildlife Area is often used by anglers fishing Spring Valley Lake and hunters in season, but hikers are underrepresented. Actually, the Department of Natural Resources constructed this trail to attract most non-harvesting outdoor enthusiasts, especially birders and hikers. Encompassing 842 acres, the Sinclair Fur Farm initially flooded the valley. It was acquired by the DNR back in the 1950s. Since then they have managed the area for wildlife, including making the lake both open water and marsh. Other areas are sown for wildlife crops, still other areas remain woodland. It is this mix of ecosystems, the overlapping of ecotones, that makes the area viable for aquatic fur-bearing mammals such as mink and muskrat, as well as for land critters like raccoon, deer, and rabbit. The waters are plied by ducks and

▶ **Carry a reusable water container that you fill at the tap.**

Overlooking a wetland in the Spring Valley Wildlife Area

geese. Open fields harbor pheasant and quail. Bass and bluegill swim under the watery surface. The wildlife area extends not only around the lake but also the east bank of the Little Miami River from Roxanna–New Burlington Road down to where the river nears Spring Valley Lake. The Little Miami Scenic Trail travels along the riverbank here, adding more hiking or biking possibilities to a Spring Valley adventure.

Start the trek by dropping off a hill and immediately reaching the loop portion of the hike. This circuit goes counterclockwise and shortly comes to the trail connecting to the 653-foot boardwalk stretching into Spring Valley Lake. From here, you gain a different perspective of the area, culminating in the climb to the top of the 13-foot-high observation tower. Here, Spring Valley Lake and adjacent lands open in all cardinal directions.

Next you will begin circling the clear lake. Some areas will have aquatic grasses; still others will be open water. At times the double-track trail will be hemmed in by trees. In other places an elevated grassy berm is bordered on both sides by open water. This variety of water and land enhances the outing.

ABOUT THE OHIO DEPARTMENT OF NATURAL RESOURCES

It has been almost 150 years since Ohio began managing wildlife in the Buckeye State. After the Civil War, residents became concerned with declining populations of fish in Ohio's waters. The Fish Commission was born, and began not only enforcing fish regulations but also propagating fish to place in waters, as well as improve habitat for the finned creatures. If the management was good enough for fish, then it was good enough for game. In 1949 the Ohio DNR came to be. Even then it was becoming apparent that managing ecosystems as a whole was more productive for all species, rather than trying to enhance conditions for just one life form, say for deer only, or trout only. The best habitats are managed for lots of species, such as is done here at Spring Valley, and the interconnected strands in the web of life are strengthened.

This entire outlook was realized when the DNR's mission was enhanced in 1973. Then, the DNR was charged with managing Ohio's endangered species, both flora and fauna, and making conditions favorable for the perpetuation of the threatened plants and animals. This is reflected in their mission statement: "to conserve and improve fish and wildlife resources and their habitats for sustainable use and appreciation by all."

The DNR has a lot on its plate. For the state's two million anglers they watch over 124,000 acres of inland waters (read: lakes), almost 7,000 miles of flowing streams, Ohio's swath of Lake Erie, and nearly 500 miles of the Ohio River! Landward, they manage 135,000 acres of terra firma for not only hunting but the aforementioned endangered species management. For endangered species, the DNR has to restore habitat to its original pre-Columbian state rather than simply sowing crops for wildlife or otherwise altering the landscape.

The DNR also enforces wildlife regulations and provides environmental education, from safe-hunting seminars to fishing clinics to increasing awareness about the non-game wildlife resources that call Ohio home.

The lower end of the lake is dammed. You will cross this weir by foot and reach an auto-accessible boat ramp and alternate trail access. But in a flash you are back in woods, walking north with the lake just a coin toss away and a hardwood-covered hill rising to your right. All too soon the loop is completed and the hike is over. Consider fishing the lake or biking the Little Miami Trail to stretch out your day. Or you can bring your binoculars and try to identify birds and other critters you encounter.

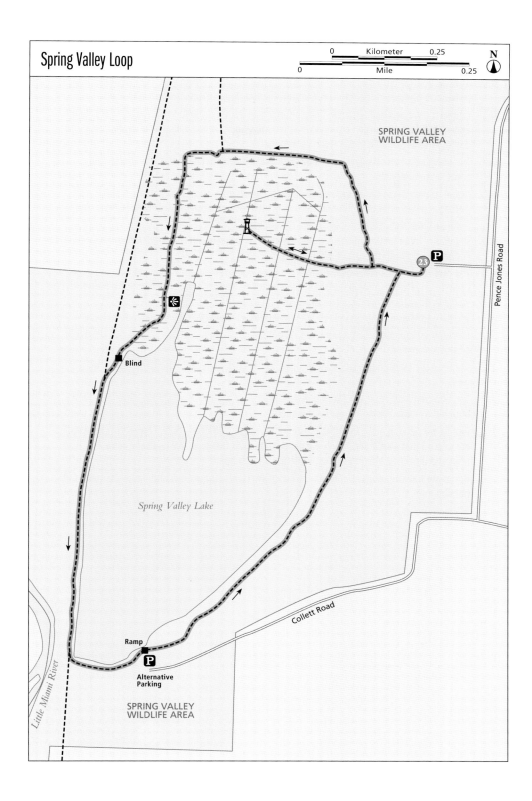

Spring Valley Loop

Kilometer
0   0.25
Mile
0   0.25

N

SPRING VALLEY
WILDLIFE AREA

Pence Jones Road

23

Blind

Spring Valley Lake

Collett Road

Ramp

P

Alternative
Parking

SPRING VALLEY
WILDLIFE AREA

Little Miami River

Miles and Directions

0.0 Start at the trailhead off Pence Jones Road. Pass around a chain gate on a double-track path, dipping to immediately reach a trail junction. Stay right and dip to lake level.

0.1 Intersect the boardwalk access. Split left this time as the main loop leaves right. Follow an elevated land berm, which opens to a marsh portion of Spring Valley Lake. Sycamores and cattails border the track. Watch for waterfowl.

0.2 The elevated berm changes to a boardwalk. The boardwalk crosses grassy marsh and some open channels.

0.3 Come to the end of the boardwalk and the observation tower. Climb the open structure and soak in views of the lake and beyond. Watch for waterfowl in open waters. Note the nonnative cypress trees near the observation tower. Backtrack.

0.5 Rejoin the main loop, heading left, northbound on a grass-and-rock trail. A line of trees separates you from the lake. A hill rises to your right.

0.7 The main loop turns left, westerly, while a fainter path keeps north. Stay left with the main path, now walking an elevated berm. Look south for the observation tower rising from the water. Willows, bald cypress, and sycamore flank the trail.

0.9 A spur trail leaves right, due north, for the wildlife area headquarters. Stay left, westerly, still on the main loop. Just ahead, the loop turns south. This part of the path can be wet in spring and winter.

1.2 Come to the lake's edge. Good views open to the east. A canal borders the trail to the west.

1.3 The trail parallels the open shore of Spring Valley Lake. Water and wildlife views are unobstructed. Wildlife blinds are set on the shore.

1.8 Reach the parking area and boat ramp on the south side of the lake. Follow the shoreline through a grassy area and reach a gate. Pass around the gate and head north on double-track grass path shaded by cherry, white oak, and maple.

2.6 Complete the loop portion of the hike. Turn right, climb a small hill, and reach the trailhead parking area.

24 Bachelor Preserve Loop at Miami University

This hike takes place at the main parcel of Miami University Natural Areas. Take a trek along scenic Harkers Run, traveling beneath verdant woodland. The hike then breaks off for the hills, exploring the greater part of Bachelor Preserve, a tract within the greater natural area. It then crosses a swinging bridge to the east side of Harkers Run. Here you will find quiet Bachelor Pond set in the hills. The circuit then makes its way back to the trailhead, passing big trees along the way.

Start: OH 73 trailhead
Distance: 6.1-mile lollipop
Hiking time: About 3 to 4 hours
Difficulty: Moderate to difficult, numerous hills
Trail surface: Natural surface path
Best season: Year-round
Other trail users: Runners
Canine compatibility: Pets must be leashed at all times
Land status: Miami University property

Fees and permits: No fees or permits required to hike
Schedule: Open dawn to dusk year-round
Maps: Miami University Natural Area Trails; USGS Oxford
Trail contacts: Miami University, 501 E. High St., Oxford, Ohio 45056; (513) 524-2197; http://miamioh.edu/student-life/natural-areas/

Finding the trailhead: From the intersection of OH 73 and OH 177 northwest of Hamilton, northwest of downtown Cincinnati, take OH 73 west for 2.7 miles to the University Natural Areas parking on the right, just before OH 73 bridges Four Mile Creek. Look for a sign indicating the Dewitt Homestead. This natural area is east of the main Miami University campus. Trailhead GPS: N39 30.500' / W84 42.968'

The Hike

Some groups talk the talk and others walk the walk. In this case, back in 1992, Miami University President Paul Pearson saw the sprawl of greater Cincinnati and Dayton heading toward Oxford. He wrote, "We all recognize the rapid rate of loss of natural greenbelt areas in our state and nation as our population increases, causing growing demands for housing, commerce and industry, highways, power lines, and other support services. I am very concerned that the natural greenbelt areas around much of Miami's Oxford campus will fall victim to those demands." This statement springboarded the preservation of over 1,000 acres, set aside as natural sanctuary. Instead of waiting for someone else to preserve a greenbelt, Miami University did it, and today we have a trail network in excess of 15 miles upon which we can hike.

The trails here are well maintained and clearly marked, with a trail map at each major intersection. This keeps you apprised of your whereabouts, allowing you to

This swinging bridge is but one highlight on this hike.

focus on the natural beauty rather than constantly navigating. This particular trek makes a balloon loop through the heart of the natural areas. It first heads up the valley of Harkers Run, which meets Four Mile Creek just downstream of the trailhead. The stream flows over rocks, slows around gravel bars, and deepens in pools where fallen trees slow the current. Wildflowers will flank the path in April. Watch for impressive sycamores in the flats. This trail corridor also serves as a wildlife corridor, where animals can travel in relative security to wild lands south of OH 73.

Leave Harkers Run on the Bachelor Preserve Pine Loop. This 416-acre plot was given to the university in 1947 by faculty member Joseph M. Bachelor, who lived here and farmed the land. It is managed for wildlife, but much of the open land has grown into trees. However, it does harbor old-growth forest. The hike makes its way to Bonham Road and explores the trails north of there, including Kramer Preserve. This 12-acre tract was added in 1987. It features tall hardwoods that tower over a tributary of Harkers Run. Adjacent open fields contrast with the deep woods through which you walk.

Rejoin Harkers Run south of Bonham Road. Absorb the everywhere-you-look streamside beauty. Then come to a highlight—a 45-foot-long swinging bridge over Harkers Run. It connects to the Bachelor Preserve East Loop, where dark and shady evergreens add a new dimension to the hike.

Then you emerge at bright and open Bachelor Pond, where a nexus of trails converge. Pick up the Reinhart Preserve Loop, which explores the 45-acre tract added to the greater natural areas in 1991. This tract offers a little bit of everything from old-growth hardwoods to fields to cedar/grass complexes. The path is rarely level, and undulates in and out of small streamsheds flowing toward Harkers Run. At one point you will stand atop a sheer bluff overlooking the stream below.

The hike circles into high cedars mixed with grasses before visiting Bachelor Pond one more time. It keeps south to make Harkers Run, this time crossing it on big concrete elevated steps. From there, it's a simple downstream backtrack to complete the hike.

Miles and Directions

0.0 Start at the trailhead off OH 73. Take the road bridge over Harkers Run, heading toward the Dewitt Homestead. Just after the bridge, immediately turn right and pick up a natural surface path heading east on the north side of Harkers Run. Woods grow tall above the trail, with fields on either side of Harkers Run.

0.4 Watch for a gigantic sycamore on trail right. Even as large as it is, the tree leans downstream, shaped by the occasional powerful flood that fills Harkers Run.

0.5 Reach a trail junction and the loop portion of your hike. The Bachelor Preserve East Loop leaves right, but you keep straight along Harkers Run then meet another trail junction. Head left on the Bachelor Preserve Pine Loop, leaving bottomland for hilly hardwoods and white pines.

1.0 Keep straight at an intersection, as a trail leaves right back toward Harkers Run. This hike continues northbound toward Bonham Road. Join an old roadbed.

1.1 Veer right as a spur trail heads due north for Bonham Road.

1.3 Emerge on Bonham Road and alternate trailhead parking. Keep straight, reentering woods, now on the Bachelor Preserve North Loop. Stay left as the actual loop goes left and right.

1.6 Reach the north end of the north loop. Keep straight, heading for Kramer Preserve. Cut across steep tributaries.

1.7 Begin the Kramer Preserve Loop. Stay left, wandering beneath impressive mature hardwoods of maple, oak, and beech. Pass a closed forest research area.

2.1 Complete the Kramer Preserve Loop. Backtrack toward the Bachelor Preserve North Loop.

2.2 Stay left on the Bachelor Preserve North Loop, heading southeasterly on new trail, toward Bonham Road. A high bluff on a tributary of Harkers Run adds an elevated view of the surrounding forest.

2.4 Pass the lower end of the Bachelor Preserve North Loop. Stay left.

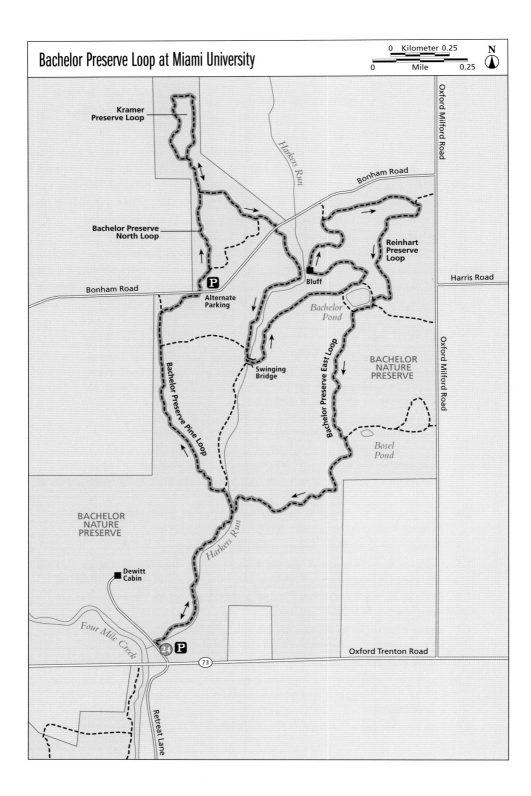

Bachelor Preserve Loop at Miami University

0   Kilometer 0.25

0   Mile   0.25

N

Kramer
Preserve Loop

Harkers Run

Bonham Road

Bachelor Preserve
North Loop

Reinhart
Preserve
Loop

Harris Road

P

Alternate
Parking

Bluff

Bachelor
Pond

Bonham Road

Oxford Milford Road

BACHELOR
NATURE
PRESERVE

Swinging
Bridge

Bachelor Preserve Pine Loop

Bachelor Preserve East Loop

Oxford Milford Road

*Bosel
Pond*

BACHELOR
NATURE
PRESERVE

Harkers Run

Dewitt
Cabin

Four Mile Creek

24   P

73

Oxford Trenton Road

Retreat Lane

2.5 Reach quiet Bonham Road. Cross the road, southbound, and soon come back along Harkers Run. A sheer bluff rises across the stream. You will be there later. Shoals and pools alternate on the stream. Ahead, bridge a tributary.

2.9 Stay left, still down Harkers Run, as a trail—part of the Bachelor Preserve Pine Loop—leaves right.

3.0 Come to the swinging bridge over Harkers Run. Cross the bridge and join the Bachelor Preserve East Loop. Curve back north into cedars.

3.3 Stay left at Bachelor Pond, now joining the Reinhart Preserve Loop. You might want to glimpse the pond before turning away from it.

3.7 Come to a sheer bluff overlooking Harkers Run. Look for the path running along Harkers Run, where you were earlier. Turn away from the high bluff; watch for huge hardwoods.

3.9 A spur trail leads left to Bonham Road. Stay right, heading easterly. Rise into cedar/grass complex. Watch for a spur trail leading left to Oxford Milford Road.

4.6 Reach Bachelor Pond. Stay left, walking along the banks of the small impoundment. Pass a spur leading to Oxford-Milford Road. Step over the pond outlet, then stay left with the southbound portion of the Bachelor Preserve East Loop.

5.1 Stay straight as a spur trail leads left to Bosel Pond and a loop near Oxford-Milford Road.

5.6 Cross Harkers Run on elevated concrete steps. You have completed the loop portion of the hike. Turn left downstream, backtracking in bottomland.

6.1 Arrive back at the trailhead, finishing the hike.

GREEN TIP

Please don't pick wildflowers or try to transplant other plant or animal life from wildlands. State natural preserves do just that, preserving the life within it and providing a place for the natural beauty of the region.

25 College Woods Loop at Miami University

This hike takes you through the southern part of Miami University Natural Areas. Head along big Four Mile Creek, a wide stream. Cruise deep in bottomland bordered by steep hills. Cross Collins Run to reach College Woods, a tract of mature hardwoods. Make a loop under impressive beeches, maples, and oaks. Your return route takes you back across Collins Run through the hills of Beck Preserve, where more tall trees stand guard over the path.

Start: OH 73 trailhead
Distance: 3.6-mile loop
Hiking time: About 2 to 3 hours
Difficulty: Moderate, has hills
Trail surface: Natural surface path
Best season: Year-round
Other trail users: None
Canine compatibility: Pets must be leashed at all times
Land status: Miami University property

Fees and permits: No fees or permits required to hike
Schedule: Open dawn to dusk year-round
Maps: Miami University Natural Area; USGS Oxford
Trail contacts: Miami University, 501 E. High St., Oxford, Ohio 45056; (513) 524-2197; http://miamioh.edu/student-life/natural-areas/

Finding the trailhead: From the intersection of OH 73 and OH 177 northwest of Hamilton, northwest of downtown Cincinnati, take OH 73 west for 2.7 miles to the University Natural Areas parking on the right, just before OH 73 bridges Four Mile Creek. Look for a sign indicating the Dewitt Homestead. This natural area is east of the main Miami University campus. Trailhead GPS: N39 30.500' / W84 42.968'

The Hike

Miami University Natural Areas is an agglomeration of acquired tracts of land located east of the main campus. The largest holding in the 1,000 acres is north of OH 73. What the south section may lack in size it delivers in scenery. Here, you will walk along a swift watercourse, over rich wooded hills, in wildflower-laden hollows. And while we may appreciate the scenery, the university also sees the scenic tracts as giant outdoor laboratories to conduct research on what lies within these lands. There is a bird-banding station here. Learning the migration patterns of birds helps students put together the interconnectedness of the environment within the natural area, beyond Ohio, and beyond the United States, for migratory birds know no government-created boundary lines. The streams of the natural areas provide accessible watercourses for those studying man's influence on the creeks of Southwest Ohio. And the area offers a great microcosm of this part of the state, with the agriculture and urbanity exuding influence on a tract of woodland and the waterways that flow through it. There's a prairie demonstration site here. This shows how you can change a simple

College Woods is a springtime wildflower haven.

regularly mown lawn to a prairie populated with native species that not only doesn't need mowing but also helps keep native grasses and other plants from being extirpated from the landscape. Along this hike you will see deer exclosures. Certain tracts have been fenced to keep deer out. Now, researchers can compare the changes in the vegetation inside the deer exclosure to changes outside the exclosure. The natural areas have many deer, and you will undoubtedly see them and their paths crisscrossing the maintained trails.

And the natural areas are also a teaching tool. For example, botany classes go out in the field and identify plants. Students can see the plants in their natural setting versus in a greenhouse or in a book. Identifying the plant in a natural setting also identifies competition, threats from nonnative plants and other habitat associations, where they can learn to put plant communities together. Other introductory classes use the natural areas to expose students to the outdoors, showing them what is literally in their own backyard. This way they get tuned into the environment. The natural areas are not only used by Miami University students but also school kids of all ages. Field trips to the natural areas are undertaken by thousands from the adjacent area. They may study stream life or fossils or the natural order of plants and animals. It's a great way for them to get in touch with the world beyond the smartphone, computer, and television screen.

A quick road bridge crossing of Four Mile Creek gets you started. Then you begin a pleasurable cruise along Four Mile Creek. At times, the trail travels directly alongside the streambanks. Trillium, toothwort, bloodroot, and Dutchman's breeches carpet the forest floor. You are now in the Beck Preserve, a 41-acre tract added to the natural areas in 1997.

The trail comes to the confluence of Collins Run and Four Mile Creek. An observation bench overlooks the confluence. This is also where you make the break for College Woods. The trail itself follows an auto ford used to maintain underground water lines. It requires a crossing of Collins Run, which can be tricky at high water. Other times Collins Run can be bone dry. If the crossing looks deeper than you prefer, walk upstream along Collins Run, seeking a wide part of the creek where rocky shoals make for an easier, safer passage.

Once across the creek, make sure to follow the hiker trail rather than the water line maintenance road. You will shortly find yourself at McKee Drive. A right-of-way granted by the city of Oxford allows trail passage between Beck Preserve and College Woods, which was once cut off from the rest of the natural areas. Big trees tower over this 15-acre tract.

After leaving College Woods, the hike returns to Beck Preserve, rambling through hills among more big trees. Join a high ridge and head north before dropping back to flatlands near the Miami University Police Station, bordered by a large student parking area. Ramble easterly along a grassy strip, coming back to Four Mile Creek. A backtrack up Four Mile Creek delivers you back to the trailhead.

Miles and Directions

0.0 Start at the trailhead off OH 73. Follow OH 73 west toward the university. Cross Four Mile Creek on the road bridge. Descend left off the road bridge before reaching the Oxford Water Works and pick up a single-track dirt path heading south along the west bank of Four Mile Creek. It first travels through a field then enters woods near a creekside building that is part of the water works.

0.3 Come to a trail intersection. Here, your return route comes in from the right, passing through a grassy clearing. For now, keep straight, continuing downstream along Four Mile Creek. Cottonwoods, maple ash, and sycamores tower overhead.

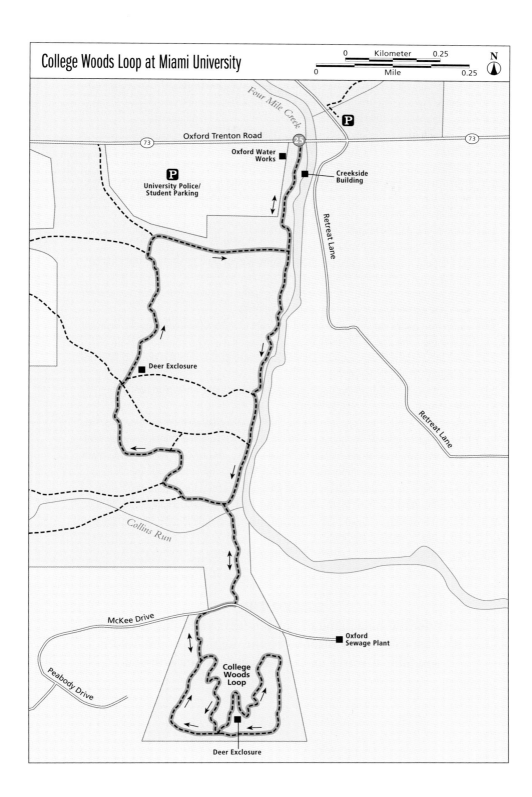

College Woods Loop at Miami University

Kilometer
0   0.25
Mile
0   0.25

N

Four Mile Creek

Oxford Trenton Road
73

25

Oxford Water
Works

Creekside
Building

Retreat Lane

P
University Police/
Student Parking

Retreat Lane

Deer Exclosure

Collins Run

McKee Drive

Oxford
Sewage Plant

College
Woods
Loop

Peabody Drive

Deer Exclosure

0.5 Bridge a normally dry tributary of Four Mile Creek. Keep downriver as the bottomland narrows.

0.6 Keep straight as a connector trail leaves right, westerly, shortcutting the loop. The path widens.

0.7 Stay straight as another connector trail heads west to shortcut the loop.

0.8 Reach an important intersection. Here, this hike keeps straight to cross Collins Run. You will return here later. For now cross Collins Run. After the stream a maintenance road leaves left but the hiker trail goes right. Stay right, traveling through rich forest.

0.9 Reach McKee Drive. The Oxford sewage plant is to your left. Turn right and walk along McKee Drive, soon reaching a house. Turn left at the first house, reentering foot trail after passing a trailhead kiosk. Dip to cross a tributary.

1.1 Come to the double loop of College Woods. Head left, curving along the perimeter of drainages dropping off to your left.

1.3 Stay left at the connector point of the two College Woods loops. Circle near the Oxford sewage plant in impressive hardwoods. Pass a deer exclosure.

1.8 Keep straight at the connector point of the two loops of College Woods. You are walking along the property boundary near some apartments.

2.0 Finish the College Woods double loop. Backtrack to McKee Drive and onward, crossing over to the north side of Collins Run.

2.4 Head left at the trail intersection on the north side of Collins Run. You are now following the water line maintenance road.

2.5 Turn right onto a raised hiking track as the waterline maintenance road keeps straight. Walk through potentially marshy woods.

2.6 Stay right at another intersection. You are turning back easterly then climbing hills. The other trail goes left and continues up Collins Run. Ahead, pass a shortcut leading right.

2.8 Reach the high point of the hike and a five-way trail junction. Keep straight on a single-track path, passing a deer exclosure on your right. Begin descending off the hill.

3.0 Keep straight as the university police and parking area comes into view. Walk to the fence along the large parking area and stay right, now heading easterly along the fence line.

3.3 Come to Four Mile Creek and a trail junction. You have completed the loop portion of the hike. Turn left, heading north.

3.6 Arrive back at the trailhead on OH 73, completing the hike.

GREEN TIP:
Consider the packaging of any products you bring with you. It's best to properly dispose of packaging at home before you hike. If you're on the trail, pack it out with you.

26 Cedar Creek Falls at Hueston Woods State Park

This short hike has plenty of highlights and is pretty much doable by anyone with time and a little stamina. The trek explores the highs and lows along Cedar Creek and beyond to the shores of Acton Lake. Start off at pretty Sycamore Grove Picnic Area then climb a bluff above Cedar Creek where views await. Drop to the limestone-bottomed stream, passing several cascades that comprise Cedar Falls. The hike then joins the Sycamore Trail, passing tall old-growth trees in a wide bottomland before nearing Acton Lake. Grab a lake view. Finally, backtrack to Sycamore Grove.

Start: Sycamore Grove Picnic Area
Distance: 1.9-mile double loop
Hiking time: About 1 hour
Difficulty: Easy, but does have a hill climb
Trail surface: Natural surface paths
Best season: Year-round, winter and spring for best water flow
Other trail users: None
Canine compatibility: Leashed dogs permitted
Land status: State park

Fees and permits: No fees or permits required
Schedule: Open daily year-round 6 a.m. to 11 p.m.
Maps: Hueston Woods Trail Map, available online; USGS College Corner
Trail contacts: Hueston Woods State Park, 6301 Park Office Rd., College Corner, OH 45003; (513) 523-6347; http://parks.ohio dnr.gov/huestonwoods

Finding the trailhead: From Oxford, Ohio, north of Cincinnati via US 27, take OH 732 north to the main park entrance of Hueston Woods State Park. Join Loop Road and follow it 0.5 mile before it splits. Turn right at the split and drive for 2.8 miles to Sycamore Grove Picnic Area, on your right. The trail starts at the back of the picnic area, near the gate that divides the upper and lower picnic areas. Trailhead GPS: N39 35.525' / W84 45.166'

The Hike

It's a shame this hike isn't longer. It certainly travels scenic terrain. The first part of the hike is a bit of a mess as a network of user-created trails climbs a big bluff above Cedar Creek. Some hikers want to travel the bluff's edge, while others prefer to stay back from the drop-off. Still others want to walk on the bluff slope itself, creating erosion problems and damaging the bluff. Don't follow this bad example. The views from atop the bluff are good enough without having to walk on the sloped part of the bluff. Cedars grow atop the hill. The cedar, often growing in poor soils, is important for wildlife. The thin stringy bark of cedar is used by birds for nests. Songbirds eat its berry-like fruit. Deer feed on the green foliage.

From the hilltop the Cedar Falls Trail dives toward its namesake creek. The path then curves downstream, below the bluff where you were earlier. Gaze at the

Cedar Creek cuts an impressive gorge.

sun–parched, west-facing rock as you walk along the stony watercourse. The slope and the sun create a microhabitat that adds biodiversity to the gorge. A bluff rises across the stream as well, revealing layers of limestone strata. Cedar Creek gurgles over the streambed, dropping farther and faster over a series of wide limestone ledges, below which lie pools, where the water briefly slows before pushing farther and faster toward Acton Lake. It's hard to declare one ledge as the Cedar Falls; rather, it is a series of several drops that occur in a short distance. Together they comprise the falls. Pick out the ledge you think is the highest.

The more exciting the falls, the more exciting the next part of the hike—your unbridged crossing of Cedar Creek. If the water is up, you will have to ford the stream, wetting your hiking boots. If the water is low it will be a dry-footed rock hop. If the water is excessively high, you may have to abandon a short section of the hike. In this case, simply backtrack up the bluff back to the picnic area/trailhead and pick up the Sycamore Trail down on Loop Road. Otherwise, after safely crossing Cedar Creek, you will travel amid thick woods, passing a humongous sycamore before emerging onto Loop Road. The Sycamore Trail continues downstream along Cedar Creek until it nears Acton Lake, amid sycamores, red bud, pawpaw, and oak.

Pawpaw trees are an interesting element of the floodplain forest along Cedar Creek. They are often found together in groups since they reproduce by root sprouts. Pawpaws have large leaves, 6 to 12 inches in length, which droop like their tropical cousins farther south. Their yellow banana-like fruit are favored by wildlife, especially raccoons and possums. Settlers made bread and puddings from pawpaw fruits. Attempts have been made to cultivate pawpaw as a fruit tree. Pawpaws range throughout Ohio and up the eastern seaboard to New England and down to North Florida.

The creek divides into channels as it works toward the lake. Culminate in a watery view of Acton Lake before turning away, traveling beneath more big sycamores. The rest of the trek rambles back to Sycamore Grove Picnic Area. Watch out for

REMEMBER SICK-A-MORE

Along Cedar Creek you will see many large sycamores, a few certainly hundreds of years old. Sycamores thrive in Ohio's bottomlands and prefer deep, rich, moist soils such as found along Cedar Creek. There's even a Sycamore State Park in the Buckeye State. It is in the Wolf Creek Valley of western Ohio and has trails aplenty. But you don't have to go to Sycamore State Park to find this tree. It is found throughout the state, and is generally accorded kudos for being the most massive tree in the state—not necessarily the tallest—but literally having more mass on an old-growth giant than any other tree in Ohio. You will see such a behemoth along this hike.

Even the most novice student of trees can identify the sycamore. Its bark is unlike any other tree. On older specimens the bark will be plated like other trees, but higher up the mottled white bark is a dead giveaway, no pun intended. See, sometimes the bark looks like it is peeling, hence the saying to help you remember the name, "sycamores look sick-a-more," pun intended. The leaves of the tree are large and have three to five points. In fall they turn a golden brown.

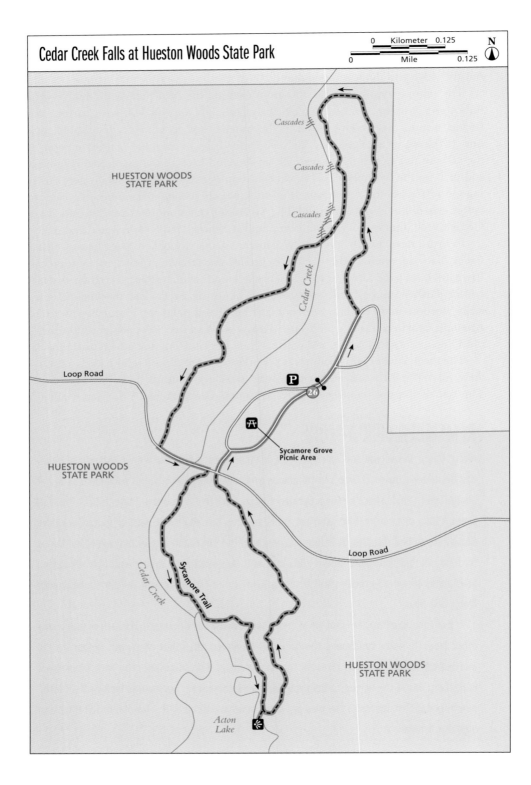

Cedar Creek Falls at Hueston Woods State Park

0   Kilometer   0.125

0   Mile   0.125

N

Cascades

Cascades

Cascades

HUESTON WOODS
STATE PARK

Cedar Creek

Loop Road

P

26

Sycamore Grove
Picnic Area

HUESTON WOODS
STATE PARK

Loop Road

Cedar Creek

Sycamore Trail

HUESTON WOODS
STATE PARK

*Acton
Lake*

abandoned trails that once connected to the park cabin area. They spur off the main track but then peter out, whereas the correct route remains well trod.

If this hike is too short for you, fortunately Hueston Woods State Park has many other trails, mostly short as well, that you can walk to lengthen your hike, including the Indian Mound Trail. It travels along Little Four Mile Creek before reaching the prehistoric Adena Mound. Gallion Run and the Equisetum Loop are nearby. They offer more biodiversity for the hiker. You can make a 1.4-mile trek on the Mudlick Loop on the north side of Acton Lake. It travels under a mature maple-beech forest and along an old country road, now abandoned after the flooding of Acton Lake. The showcase trails are located within the Hueston Woods Nature Preserve, along the south shore. Check the park map for a complete trail listing.

Miles and Directions

0.0   Start from the top of the lower loop at Sycamore Grove Picnic Area. The upper loop of the picnic area is gated. Walk around the gate and through the closed upper picnic area to join a natural surface footpath.

0.1   Cruise through cedars near Cedar Creek on a heavily used rooty and rocky track. Note the small sycamore-covered islands in Cedar Creek. Trails split and come together; follow the main track uphill.

0.2   Pass a massive old-growth white oak to the right of the trail. Shortly come alongside a high, white gravelly bluff above Cedar Creek.

0.3   Enjoy an upstream view of Cedar Creek through the trees. Stay straight as the loop descends toward Cedar Creek.

0.4   Reach the first of several limestone ledge cascades together comprising Cedar Falls. Low-slung bluffs rise across the water. The trail curves with the curves of Cedar Creek, passing more cascades, the final series of which drop about 6 feet over a 20-foot length of the creek.

0.5   Cross Cedar Creek. There is no bridge. After crossing, look up at the bluff where you were earlier. Ramble through wooded flats.

0.8   A user-created trail leads left back to the picnic area. Shortly pass a monstrous sycamore tree that would take several people with linked arms to circle.

0.9   Emerge on Loop Road. Turn left onto the road, bridging Cedar Creek. The Sycamore Trail starts across from the entrance to Sycamore Grove Picnic Area. The Sycamore Trail immediately splits; stay right, once again walking along Cedar Creek.

1.3   Reach a vista at the lake's edge. Your views are mainly of the Cedar Creek embayment. Turn away from the water.

1.9   Reach Loop Road. Walk through the picnic area to the trailhead parking.

GREEN TIP
**Keep to established trails as much as possible.
If there aren't any, stay on surfaces that will be least
affected, like rock, gravel, dry grasses, or snow.**

27 Big Woods Hike at Hueston Woods State Park

This hike travels through what is considered to be the largest stand of old-growth forest in Ohio. Hikers wander the Big Woods through Hueston Woods State Nature Preserve, enjoying large sugar maples, red oaks, and beech trees. Reach Sugar Camp, an old-time maple syrup tapping house on the shores of Acton Lake. Pick up the West Shore Trail where an undulating path offers multiple views and solitude. After backtracking, you will take new trails with yet more big trees before returning to the trailhead.

Start: Hueston Woods State Nature Preserve parking area
Distance: 5.2-mile double loop with out-and-back
Hiking time: About 2.5 to 3.5 hours
Difficulty: Moderate
Trail surface: Natural surface paths
Best season: Year-round
Other trail users: None
Canine compatibility: Dogs not permitted

Land status: State park
Fees and permits: No fees or permits required
Schedule: Open daily year-round 6 a.m. to 11 p.m.
Maps: Hueston Woods Trail Map; USGS College Corner, Oxford
Trail contacts: Hueston Woods State Park, 6301 Park Office Rd., College Corner, OH 45003; (513) 523-6347; http://parks.ohio dnr.gov/huestonwoods

Finding the trailhead: From Oxford, Ohio, north of Cincinnati via US 27, take OH 732 north to the main park entrance of Hueston Woods State Park. Join Loop Road and follow it 0.5 mile before it splits. Turn right at the split; stay on Loop Road and drive for 5.1 miles to Hueston Woods State Nature Preserve, on your left. Pick up the southbound trail, on the right-hand side of the parking area as you drive in. Trailhead GPS: N39 34.465' / W84 45.682'

The Hike

At one time, most of Ohio was wooded with tall, ancient trees, save for naturally occurring prairies. But as early Americans spread westward through the land, more and more timber was cut in order to till the rich land the forests once covered. Still other land was cut for lumber, much of which was used to build fast-expanding cities such as Cincinnati. A series of events kept this particular tract from being cut down. When Mad Anthony Wayne passed through this area during the Ohio Indian campaigns, one Matthew Hueston was with him. Later, Hueston was awarded a land grant for his military service. He then returned to Virginia, got his family, including his brother, and belongings, and they settled along what was then Four Mile Creek in 1797. Together they owned around 3,000 acres. They cleared the fertile, level land and went to work farming. What is now the Big Woods was too sloped to plow. The

Even beavers like the trails at Hueston Woods State Park.

forest was allowed to remain in its original state simply because there were better and easier farm and timber tracts to work. Later, the Huestons recognized the value of the sugar maples as a maple syrup resource. The family began a sugar maple tapping operation, converting the raw sap to maple syrup, which could then be sold. So the trees remained.

MAPLE SYRUP: THE PIONEER SWEETENER

American pioneers used whatever resources they could find in the great forests of the 18th and 19th centuries. They couldn't go to the grocery and get raw sugar or the myriad forms of artificial sweeteners we take for granted today. If they couldn't grow it or create it, they likely wouldn't have it. Today when looking at a sugar maple, we see a pretty tree producing golden leaves in autumn. The pioneers saw sugar and a trade product.

Even today maple syrup is made in Ohio, primarily in the northeast part of the state. Over 100,000 gallons are produced each year. First the sap must be tapped from the maple trees. This is known as the "sugar season." In the Buckeye State, this ranges from February through the middle of March. In our neck of the woods, the season starts at the early end of the spectrum. This is when the sap begins to move through the tree; it is collected in buckets (though hoses are used in the modern process) then boiled, removing the excess water, at the "sugar house" such as the one you pass on this hike. The liquid is then lowered to a precise temperature before being put in containers. Then you have not only good stuff for pancakes but also to flavor sweet treats, to make candy, and to make granulated maple sugar. Next time you are in the market, look on the label to buy Ohio-made maple sugar products.

Members of the Hueston clan lived on the original tract until the 1930s, when the final descendant passed away. The land was to be sold, and a resident of nearby Hamilton, Morris Taylor, stepped in to buy the tract and put it in trust. Taylor realized that by this time there were simply very few stands of old-growth forest left in the Buckeye State. In 1941 local legislator Cloyd Acton asked the state to buy the tract, and it became a state forest. Ironically, what is now the state park was originally used to house Ohio state inmates at an honor farm. Later, Four Mile Creek was dammed and the lake came to be, flooding the old Hueston homesite. The facilities we see today were added over time. Today you can still visit the Sugar Camp, a wooden building built in the 1930s used to process the sap to sugar. It sits on the foundation of the original sugar camp. Every March the state park holds a maple syrup festival and uses the sugar shack as a maple syrup-making demonstration area.

▶ Be careful around historic structures. They are often fragile and unfortunately subject to defacing. Respect closures of buildings that are opened only when park personnel are present.

The designated national natural landmark is composed of a climax beech-maple forest, along with stately red and white oaks. Wildflowers carpet the forest floor each spring. It won't take long during your hike to realize you are in truly "big woods." Tall trees tower overhead from your first step. Today's state natural area comprises a core tract of 200 special acres. Beyond the natural area, the hike travels the shore of Acton Lake. Spring high water will nearly

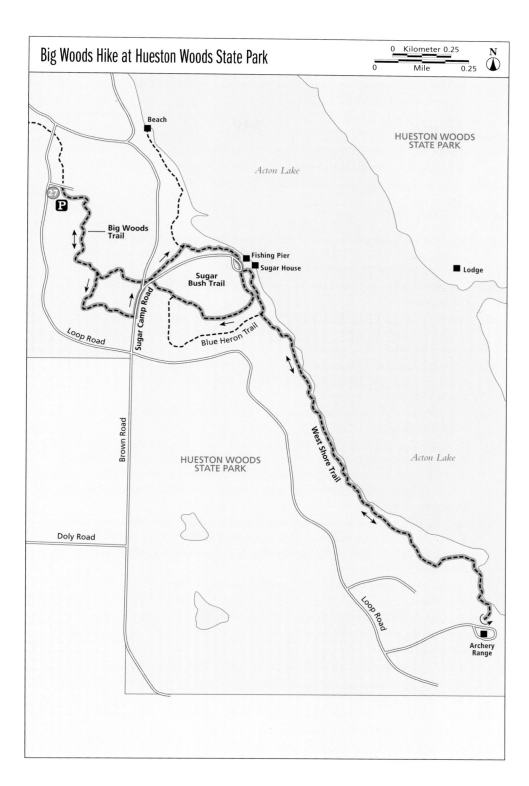

Big Woods Hike at Hueston Woods State Park

0   Kilometer 0.25

0   Mile   0.25

N

Beach

HUESTON WOODS
STATE PARK

Acton Lake

27 P

Big Woods
Trail

Fishing Pier
Sugar House

Lodge

Sugar
Bush Trail

Sugar Camp Road

Loop Road

Blue Heron Trail

Brown Road

HUESTON WOODS
STATE PARK

West Shore Trail

Acton Lake

Doly Road

Loop Road

Archery
Range

lap over the path while fall low water will expose small beaches. Expansive views give insight to the size of the impoundment. The park lodge stands boldly on a hilltop across the water. You will also note the plentiful fallen trees, a consequence of beavers' handiwork. The water dwellers call Acton Lake home.

You have to backtrack from the end of the West Shore Trail before rejoining the Sugar Bush Trail. A mini-network of trails near the Sugar Camp may briefly prove confusing. Many of the big beech trees have been carved on, and after a while you wonder about the aggregate hours spent carving on the trees by thoughtless hikers. However, it is better to have big carved-upon trees than no big trees at all.

Miles and Directions

0.0   Start from the Hueston Woods State Nature Preserve Area parking lot. Head south to join a natural surface footpath. Big trees are immediately evident—maple, beech, and oaks. Cross streamlets on little wooden bridges between hills.

0.4   Rock-hop a stream, as another trail, your return route, leaves left. Most hikers miss this trail leaving left.

0.6   Emerge onto Sugar Camp Road. Turn left and follow the road, passing a parking area on your left with your return route leaving from a kiosk beside the parking area. Stay right with Sugar Camp Road.

0.7   The Sugar Bush Trail crosses Sugar Camp Road. Go left from Sugar Camp Road. The other end of the Sugar Bush Trail leaving right is also your return route. Travel under a tall canopy toward Acton Lake.

0.9   A spur trail leaves left to the park beach. Stay right on the Sugar Bush Trail. Acton Lake is visible through the trees.

1.1   Come to the parking area near the old Sugar Camp. A fishing pier is nearby as is the sugar-making building. Check out the camp then pick up the West Shore Trail. The Sugar Bush Trail leaves from the parking area. Ahead, soon pass the intersection with the Blue Heron Trail. Travel in big trees with a light understory along the shore of Acton Lake, leaving any crowds behind.

1.5   Leave the designated state nature preserve. The path sometimes is pushed directly to the shore by steep hills. Gain numerous views as you alternate between bisecting drainages feeding the lake and hills dividing the drainages. A few pines add an evergreen touch to the woods.

2.6   Emerge onto a grassy area near Acton Lake Dam and the archery range. Backtrack to the Sugar Camp.

4.1   After passing the Blue Heron Trail, rejoin the Sugar Bush Trail. It leaves from the Sugar Camp parking area, passing a capped water cistern. Turn away from the water, ascending through big trees.

4.5   Meet the other end of the Blue Heron Trail. Keep straight, still in large oaks and other giants.

4.6   Come to Sugar Camp Road. Turn left onto the road, then pick up new trail from the parking area and kiosk nearby.

4.8   Meet the Big Woods Trail near a stream. Begin backtracking for the trailhead, enjoying a second look at some of Ohio's largest trees.

5.2   Arrive back at the trailhead, completing the hike.

Southeast Indiana

S ome fantastic hikes await across Ohio's western border in the Hoosier State. Explore wild and hilly terrain bordering Brookville Lake, where a trail system literally encircles the huge impoundment. The Adena Trace will challenge your assumptions about trails in greater Cincinnati. See mounds made by lost cultures on the Glidewell Mound Loop. Grab some views at Whitewater Memorial State Park. Observe wildlife at Mary Gray Bird Sanctuary, privately held by the Audubon Society. Hike along an abandoned waterway at Whitewater Canal Historic Trail.

Lakes and views are two attractions of Southeast Indiana trails.

28 Whitewater Memorial State Park

This adventure uses three trails to achieve a hiker's overview of Whitewater Memorial State Park. First, the Lakeshore Trail makes an undulating jaunt along Whitewater Lake through the Hornbeam Nature Preserve to a waterfowl observation deck. Backtrack to the trailhead, then pick up the Red Springs Trail. It also wanders along the lakeshore before dropping to a hillside where mineral-rich seep springs emanate. After looping back to the trailhead, make a short drive to the Veterans Trail. The Veterans Trail makes a circuit of its own beyond Brookville Lake and into hills, finally passing a homesite and limited vista.

Start: Hornbeam Nature Preserve trailhead
Distance: 5.5 miles in 2 loops and 1 out-and-back, with shorter options
Hiking time: About 3 to 4 hours
Difficulty: Moderate, some hills
Trail surface: Natural surface path in forested woods
Best season: Sept through May
Other trail users: None

Canine compatibility: Leashed dogs permitted
Land status: State park
Fees and permits: Entrance fee required
Schedule: Open daily year-round
Maps: Whitewater Memorial State Park, available at park office; USGS New Fairfield
Trail contacts: Whitewater Memorial State Park, 1418 State Rd. 101, Liberty, IN 47353; (765) 458-5565; www.in.gov/dnr

Finding the trailhead: From exit 169 on I-74 in Indiana, west of downtown Cincinnati, take US 52 to Brookville and IN 101. Take IN 101 north for 11 miles to the Whitewater Memorial State Park on your left. Enter the state park and follow the main road toward the park cabins, bridging Whitewater Lake Dam, driving 2.6 miles from the park entrance to the trailhead, on your right. Trailhead GPS: N39 36.426' / W84 58.653'

The Hike

If you are going to make the drive to Whitewater Memorial State Park, you may as well bag three hikes. Each trail has its own desirable characteristics. The park offers even broader appeal, so consider combining park activities with your walk. I have camped here and found it a good base camp to enjoy not only the trails but also 200-acre Whitewater Lake. Anglers can vie for warm-water species such as bass and bluegill that swim the waters. You can also bring your own canoe, kayak, or other watercraft on the quiet trolling-motors-only lake. Or you can swim at the park beach. If you want to explore the land other than hiking, consider a guided horse ride during the warm season. Furthermore, you can walk each of the three hikes separately or as one. The important thing is getting out there and having some healthy fun!

Your first hike is on the Lakeshore Trail. True to its name, it skirts the shoreline of Whitewater Lake on steep terrain, continually bisecting wooded ravines in

Asters brighten the trails at Whitewater Memorial State Park.

pawpaw-filled hollows that reach to the water. The path dead-ends at an observation deck. Start the Red Springs Trail after returning to the trailhead. Your return to the trailhead is an opportunity to make a "Hudson Bay start." Centuries back, trappers of northern Canada would get their supplies from Hudson Bay Company then go but a short day's journey, camp out, and subsequently figure out what they forgot to bring. Since they were close to civilization, they returned to the outpost and obtained the forgotten supplies, then moved on to far reaches for a winter or more of trapping.

Beyond the trailhead, the Red Springs Trail meanders through big woods between Whitewater Lake and the main park road. Pass under a canopy of beech and maple,

INDIANA'S NATURE PRESERVES

Hop Hornbeam Nature Preserve is but one of over 280 preserves located throughout the Hoosier State. The preserve program was established in 1967, with the first preserve being established in 1969. The preserves maintain or restore unique natural communities in the state. The powers that be try to keep them open to the public, the exception being if flora or fauna is especially imperiled. Even at that, all preserves are open for scientific research. Over 53,000 acres of land harboring the rarest plant and animal species are protected under the program. Most of the preserves are managed by various units of Indiana's Department of Natural Resources. The state is also on the lookout—with the help of citizens and scientific groups—to locate other special areas in the state to include in the program.

The Hornbeam Preserve covers 83 acres. Its name comes from the large proliferation of hornbeam trees, but the preserve primarily protects the red springs that you see along the hike. Given the thousands of acres within the Indian preserve system, there must be many other special places within the Hoosier State.

ultimately crossing the park road. From there, the path slips onto a hornbeam slope from which emit "red springs." Iron and other minerals in the water give the emergent aqua an odd but naturally occurring shimmer. Stop at the observation deck to see the wide, shallow springs slowly flowing toward Silver Creek. The springs also provide wetland habitat. Climb back to the trailhead, still on a slope.

Your next hike requires a short 0.7-mile drive to reach the Veterans Trail trailhead at the Silver Creek Boat Ramp. You can make a second Hudson Bay start here. It snakes through a lakeside bottom before turning toward park cabins. From the cabins the trail climbs to find an old homesite, now part of the park. Cross the park road then hike through a mix of field and forest, to reach Veteran's Vista, a limited overlook with a picnic shelter. While here, contemplate the sacrifices of our United States military veterans, for whom this park was dedicated in 1949.

Miles and Directions

0.0 Start from the Hornbeam Nature Preserve parking area on the Lakeshore Trail. The Red Springs Trail also leaves from this same trailhead. Join a wide grassy track.

0.1 The Lakeshore Trail splits. Go right, now on a single-track path skirting a steep ravine in mature hardwoods of maple, oak, and beech. Come alongside the lake.

0.3 Reach the other end of the Short Loop. Stay right on the Lakeshore Trail.

0.4 A spur trail leads right to a point overlooking Whitewater Lake. Continue northeast on hills above the shoreline.

0.6 Cut through a lakeside cedar thicket. You are now along the lake.

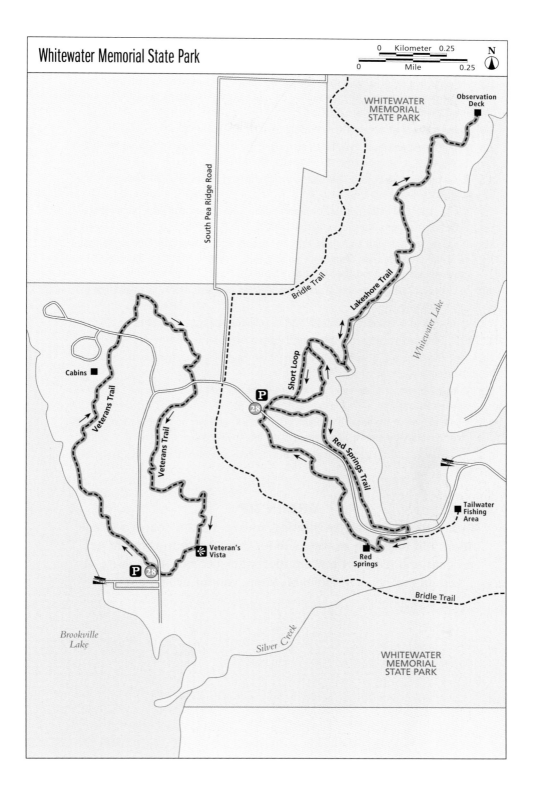

Whitewater Memorial State Park

0   Kilometer   0.25

0   Mile   0.25

N

WHITEWATER
MEMORIAL
STATE PARK

Observation
Deck

South Pea Ridge Road

Bridle Trail

Lakeshore Trail

Whitewater Lake

Short Loop

Cabins

Veterans Trail

Veterans Trail

P
28

Red Springs Trail

P
28

Veteran's
Vista

Red
Springs

Tailwater
Fishing
Area

Bridle Trail

Brookville
Lake

Silver Creek

WHITEWATER
MEMORIAL
STATE PARK

0.9 Leave the lakeshore and climb into piney woods. Soon return to the lake. Continue in and out of ravines.

1.3 Reach a long set of wooden steps. Descend to reach a wooden observation deck. The locale overlooks a cove where waterfowl may be observed in season. Backtrack toward the main trailhead.

2.3 Come to the Short Loop. Stay right this time, picking up new trail.

2.5 Return to the trailhead. If you forgot something, get it now; otherwise, pick up the Red Springs Trail. It leads directly into woods on a level track.

3.1 Cross the paved park road. Just after crossing the road an angler's trail leads left to the Whitewater Lake Dam tailwater.

3.2 Come to the first of the red springs before reaching an observation deck overlooking a large mineral spring. Continue cruising a slope.

3.5 Return to the trailhead. From here, drive 0.7 mile down the main park road to the boat ramp on Brookville Lake. Once in the parking area, pick up the Veterans Trail leaving from the west side of the road, toward Brookville Lake.

3.9 Walk through wooded flats on a grassy track. Come very near Brookville Lake. Enjoy your second lake.

4.1 Pass near park cabins, then cross a branch. Look for a big sycamore here.

4.2 Bisect the cabin access road, traveling the nexus of field and forest.

4.6 Pass the stone wall of an old homesite after climbing a hill. Shortly cross the main park road, entering a mixed hardwood cedar forest.

5.1 Bridge a streamlet at the head of a hollow. Shortly bridge a second streamlet after entering another hollow.

5.3 Come to a picnic shelter and Veteran's Vista. Trees have grown up partially obscuring the view. Hopefully the view will be cleared in the future. Descend.

5.5 Arrive back at the trailhead, completing the last hike at Whitewater Memorial State Park.

GREEN TIP

If you see someone else littering, muster up the courage to ask them not to. The best way is to let them know they might get a ticket and lecture from a park ranger, not raising their ire at you. In fact, they might even thank you for avoiding a fine.

29 Adena Trace Sampler

This out-and-back ramble travels a portion of the Adena Trace, a trail circling Brookville Lake. This particular segment offers a quality footpath, first exploring the valley of Salt Well Creek then heading south for the Wolf Creek embayment. This hike's end is on a bluff high above Wolf Creek that presents winter views. Should you feel extra energetic, continue on to the crossing of Wolf Creek, then backtrack.

Start: Fairfield Causeway
Distance: 6.0 miles out-and-back
Hiking time: About 3 to 3.5 hours
Difficulty: Moderate, but does have hills aplenty
Trail surface: Natural surface path in forested woods
Best season: Sept through May
Other trail users: None
Canine compatibility: Leashed dogs permitted

Land status: US Army Corps of Engineers land managed by state of Indiana
Fees and permits: No fees or permits required
Schedule: Open daily year-round
Maps: Adena Trace Hiking Trail at Brookville Lake available online; USGS Whitcomb, Brookville
Trail contacts: Brookville Lake, P.O. Box 100, Brookville, IN 47012; (765) 647-2657; www .in.gov/dnr

Finding the trailhead: From exit 169 on I-74 in Indiana, west of downtown Cincinnati, take US 52 to Brookville and the intersection of IN 1 and IN 101 on the north side of Brookville. Take IN 101 north for 8 miles to Fairfield Causeway. Turn left onto Fairfield Causeway and follow it for 2.8 miles just past the bridge over Brookville Lake. The parking area is on the right, just after the bridge. The trailhead is just after the bridge on the southwest side of the causeway. Trailhead GPS: N39 30.357' / W85 0.041'

The Hike

This hike travels the Wolf Creek Trail, part of the greater Adena Trace. The Adena Trace makes a 25-mile circuit around Brookville Lake. It uses already established trails on the east side of Brookville Lake, along with some new sections. The west side of Brookville Lake is rugged and remote, without the developed park features that dot the impoundment's eastern shore. This section of trail follows a formerly trackless shore, creating as wild a setting as you can find in this part of the country. The easy-to-follow trail contrasts with the Wolf Creek Trail near Brookville Dam, where it is lesser-used and harder to follow. So if you want a wilder trek yet desire good trail on which to do it, this hike is for you. Winter is a good time for this hike. The leaves in the lush forest will be down, maximizing lake views. Also, boats will be absent on Brookville Lake, cutting down on motor noise,

▶ Plan ahead. Know your equipment, your ability, and the area where you are hiking—then prepare accordingly.

This hike leads you past wooded hills along Brookville Lake.

leaving the sounds of nature and the wilderness atmosphere to enjoy while you walk the preserve.

A steeply sloped wooded hillside characterizes the west shore of Brookville Lake. Rocky drainages flow toward the water. You cross them repeatedly. Depending upon the season, they may or may not be flowing. Expect stream flows in winter and spring.

THE HOOSIER HIKERS COUNCIL: INDIANA'S TRAIL BUILDERS AND MAINTAINERS

The Adena Trace was scouted and built between the years 1996 and 2001 by volunteers from the Hoosier Hikers Council. It was a lot of work just scouting a potential trail on the mean slopes, much less building it. This accomplishment, building the Adena Trace, cemented the Hoosier Hikers Council's reputation as *the* trail building group in Indiana.

When you want something done, do it yourself, the old adage goes. Avid hikers in Indiana saw trails in their state becoming grown over, losing signage, and becoming hard to follow. Rather than complaining to a government entity, a hard-core group of trail trekkers formed the Hoosier Hikers Council (HHC) back in 1994. It was later incorporated as a nonprofit group.

The HHC went into action, using volunteer labor to restore and improve existing trails throughout the state, also scouting and building trails such as the Adena Trace. The Knob-stone Trail, ultimately to reach 140 miles in length, is the biggest project to date. The HHC are not hiking snobs; rather than eschewing other trail users, namely mountain bikers and equestrians, they instead work with these groups to create trails that each group can use. This policy, creating single-use trails for each group, keeps hikers using trails for hikers only, mountain biking trails for bikers only, and equestrian trails for horseback enthusiasts only. The Adena Trace is a great example of a hiker-only trail. This "single-user" trail policy is also advocated by the American Hiking Society.

Finally, the Hoosier Hikers Council works to secure funding for trails and works to involve other hikers and hiking groups in issues involving hiking and trails. They also recruit other groups to get "down and dirty," doing actual trail work, the hard stuff that makes life easier for users who get to a trailhead and expect pathways to be groomed and ready to go.

If you think that you are incapable of the physical work involved with trail building and maintenance, think again. Most of the active members of the HHC are trail enthusiasts who have recently retired from their previous careers, so they aren't exactly spring chickens. The trail work not only keeps them in good physical shape but the intangible rewards of making Indiana's beauty accessible for hikers, being part of a project seen through from beginning to end, the camaraderie while working with other trail enthusiasts, and simply being "out there" make it all worthwhile. It's also an opportunity to express your love of hiking by giving your time, talent, and treasure. They generally meet the third Saturday of every month to do this worthwhile trail work. If you are interested in supporting the Hoosier Hikers Council, please visit hoosierhikerscouncil.org.

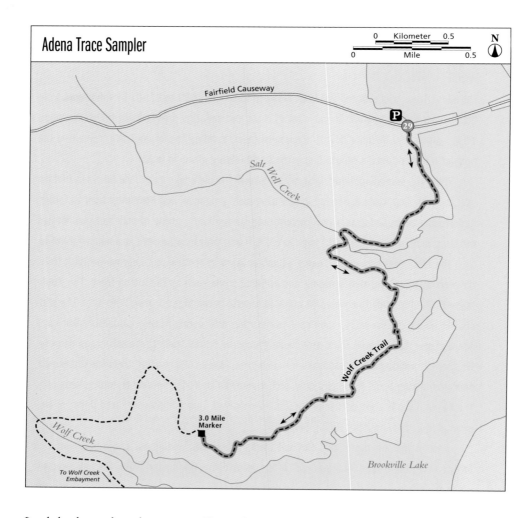

0   Kilometer   0.5

0   Mile   0.5

N

Fairfield Causeway

P
29

Salt Well Creek

Wolf Creek Trail

3.0 Mile
Marker

Wolf Creek

Brookville Lake

To Wolf Creek
Embayment

Look back north and you can still see the Fairfield Causeway. This road spans long and relatively narrow Brookville Lake near the center of the impoundment. The trail enters younger woods. This was likely pastureland before the dam project claimed the territory by eminent domain.

Beyond the young woods, the singletrack path—marked with white blazes and occasional metal mile markers—turns west. The serpentine still lake is visible through the trees below. Continue deeper into a hollow, leaving the lake behind, to reach and cross Salt Well Creek. Take your time and take in this scenic little vale, where the stony stream flows under regal trees bordered by forested hills that lend an intimate feel to the woodsy setting.

Lose Salt Well Creek and you meander through cedar forest on hills alternating with beech and pawpaw woods in the hollows. The Wolf Creek Trail is aiming for the Wolf Creek embayment. The path surprisingly and suddenly opens onto a power line, then climbs. You are coming nearer to the drop-off into Wolf Creek. Obscured views open of the water below and land beyond. Look for the 3.0-mile marker posted to a tree. This is a good turnaround point. Should you desire to travel on, it is about a mile to the Wolf Creek crossing. This added mile down to Wolf Creek will make your round-trip hike 8 miles.

Miles and Directions

0.0   Start beside the west end of the Fairfield Causeway, very near the end of the bridge on the southwest side. Look for a sign indicating the Adena Trace. Immediately join a single-track path traveling south. Brookville Lake lies to your left. The forest can be rocky in places.

0.1   Look for a big multi-trunked oak tree to the left of the trail.

0.4   Enter younger woods, perhaps a former field regenerating. Begin turning west into the Salt Well Creek embayment.

1.0   Cross Salt Well Creek. Depending on water levels, it could be a rock hop, a ford, or a completely dry endeavor. A hill-encircled flat stretches toward Brookville Lake and makes for an alluring relaxation spot. Turn into a side hollow then climb out by short switchbacks.

1.2   Level out in tall maple-beech flatwoods. The hiking is easy. Soon saddle alongside a bluff overlooking the lake.

1.5   The trail turns south and curves past the head of another embayment.

1.8   Turn southwesterly into the greater Wolf Creek embayment, though you won't know it, since the lake is out of sight.

2.5   Pass through a stand of straight-trunked tulip trees regenerating an old field.

2.6   Open onto a power line, then reenter woods.

2.9   The trail levels off, but the land drops left toward Wolf Creek below. Continue on the wooded rim of the gorge. You can see the far side of the embayment and the water below.

3.0   Come to a tree with a 3.0 mile marker nailed to it, on the left side of the trail. This is a good turnaround point. Otherwise you can continue a mile to Wolf Creek crossing.

3.4   Pass back under the power line.

5.0   Cross Salt Well Creek. Continue backtracking toward the trailhead.

6.0   Arrive back at the trailhead and Fairfield Causeway.

30 Garr Hill Wildlife Wander

This hike takes you through many environments of Mounds State Recreation Area, on a lesser-used trail. Start off by big Brookville Lake, then turn up a large but unnamed tributary, traveling moist bottomland. The hike then wanders a dry cedar hill presenting elevated lake vistas. Turn up the nose of Garr Hill and climb. The hike finds mature woods full of shagbark hickories, among other trees. Make a little loop through the big forest, then backtrack to the hike's beginning.

Start: Garr Hill Boat Ramp
Distance: 5.8-mile out-and-back with short loop at far end
Hiking time: About 2.5 to 3 hours
Difficulty: Moderate
Trail surface: Natural surface path, pea gravel on short loop
Best season: Sept through May
Other trail users: None
Canine compatibility: Leashed dogs permitted

Land status: State recreation area
Fees and permits: No fees or permits required
Schedule: Open daily year-round
Maps: Brookville Lake and Whitewater Memorial State Park, online and available at Mounds SRA office; USGS Whitcomb
Trail contacts: Mounds State Recreation Area, 4306 Mounds Rd., Anderson, IN 46017; (765) 647-2657; www.in.gov/dnr/

Finding the trailhead: From exit 169 on I-74 in Indiana, west of downtown Cincinnati, take US 52 to Brookville and the intersection of IN 1 and IN 101 on the north side of Brookville. Take IN 101 north for 4.8 miles to Garr Hill Road. Turn left onto Garr Hill Road and follow it 1.0 mile to dead-end at the Garr Hill Boat Ramp. Park on the left before reaching the boat ramp. The Garr Hill Trail starts on the right just before reaching the parking area. Trailhead GPS: N39 28.795' / W84 57.666'

The Hike

Most people starting at this trailhead hike the Scenic Trail. It is a fine path but it is paved, thus losing some of its luster. By the way, the natural surface trails are best for the long-term health of your feet and legs, as opposed to concrete or asphalt paths. Natural surface trails absorb the pounding of your feet while walking as opposed to hard surface trails, where the shock of walking is sent back up to your feet, ankles, and knees. However, a hard surface trail is better than none at all. Consider bicycling the 3-mile one-way Scenic Trail if you want to try that trek.

Begin your hike on the solitude-filled Garr Hill Trail, walking through bottomland of an unnamed creek, a tributary of Templeton Creek. The tributary and Templeton Creek now meet under the waters of Brookville Lake. Garr Hill rises on the far side of the tributary.

After walking upstream shaded by sycamores, the trail crosses the creek via concrete ford. Like most streams flowing into Brookville Lake, this one can be bold in

An afternoon autumn sun warms the woods along the Wildlife Wander.

winter and spring and just a collection of still pools come fall. The forest changes after you cross the creek. Cedars, oaks, and hickories populate the south-facing slope. Brookville Lake comes into view before making your way up Garr Hill. The walking becomes easy and pleasant, though it does undulate a bit before you cross the upper end of a different unnamed drainage.

A SHAGGY TREE GOOD FOR EATING

There are some big shaggy trees along this hike at Mounds State Recreation Area. And you will be able to pick them out without problem. Shagbark hickories look like what their name implies, a tree with loose plated bark sloughing off the main trunk, looking like they could use a trim, much as shaggy-haired humans may. The loose bark plates run vertically up the trunk of the tree.

Found all over the Buckeye State, shagbark hickories once were an important food source for aboriginal Ohioans, who sought out their surprisingly sweet nuts. The nuts were used by American pioneers much as you would use a pecan. However, attempts at commercial propagation of the shagbark hickory have been unsuccessful. In the wild, nut production varies wildly year to year. The thinner shell and greater nutmeat make shagbark hickory nuts an attractive choice. Indians even made hickory nut soup. They also broke open the nuts, collected the meat, and pounded them down, releasing oils in the nut. They would then form the meat into balls, with the oil of the nut keeping the pulverized acorn pieces together. These "nutballs" were an ideal way to store the food for later use, since they could be quickly and easily eaten, as opposed to breaking the shells and removing the meat. The best time to collect the treat was soon after the acorns fell and before the first frost of autumn. Birds and mammals competed with the Indians in getting to the sought-after nuts, especially in times when the shagbark's nut production was down.

Shagbark hickories also aided the Indians in obtaining food another way. The strong wood was fashioned into bows, with which they could hunt game. Ohio pioneers used the tough yet resilient wood for everything from axe handles to wagon axles. The big shagbark hickories you see on the Garr Hill Wildlife Wander may seem like mere shade trees, but at second glance they have been providing the peoples—and the beasts—of Ohio with a good food source. Nutty, isn't it?

Ahead lays an old farm pond. These ponds are important for wildlife because they provide a year-round water source, since most streams dry up in summer and fall. They also provide habitat for aquatic creatures such as frogs. So even though they aren't part of the native landscape, they do enhance circumstances for the wild creatures of Mounds State Recreation Area. Look for animal tracks near the water's edge. On your return trip it may pay to set up and be still near the pond, to see what wildlife the pond may attract, especially during drier times.

Enter mature woods beyond the pond. Look how much higher the canopy rises. Hickories and maples thrive here. Soon reach civilization and the access road for the

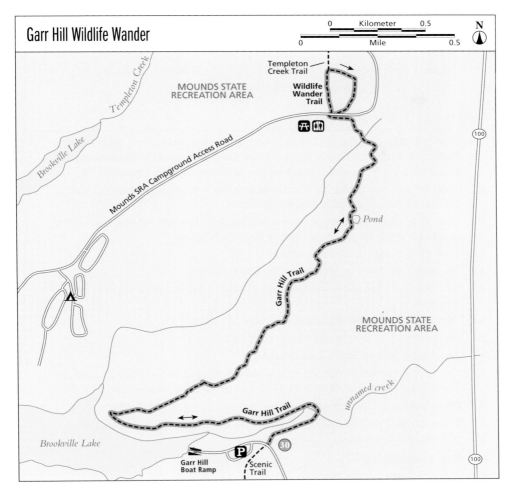

Garr Hill Wildlife Wander

0 ——— Kilometer ——— 0.5

0 ——— Mile ——— 0.5

N

Templeton Creek

MOUNDS STATE RECREATION AREA

Templeton Creek Trail

Wildlife Wander Trail

Brookville Lake

Mounds SRA Campground Access Road

Pond

Garr Hill Trail

MOUNDS STATE RECREATION AREA

unnamed creek

Garr Hill Trail

Brookville Lake

Garr Hill Boat Ramp

P

Scenic Trail

100

100

30

park's campground. A shady picnic shelter and restrooms are within sight should you desire a break. The Wildlife Wander is an interpretive nature trail; hopefully, the box will have handouts for you to absorb information at the numbered stations. An easy walk takes you past some big trees, including shagbark hickories and oaks.

Look for a massive white oak, too. It's no surprise this big tree is here—white oaks are known for their longevity. Interestingly, oaks are technically part of the beech family. White oaks grow throughout the state of Ohio, with the greater Ohio River valley offering near ideal conditions. The range of white oak covers most of the eastern United States, from Texas north to Minnesota, then east to Maine and south to Florida.

The high-quality wood has been prized by Americans for generations. Among other uses it once was made into barrel staves, bringing about the all but forgotten nickname barrel oak. Wildlife may love white oaks more than people do. Woodpeckers and turkeys are among the birds that enjoy the nuts. Raccoons and chipmunks savor the nutrient-packed treat, too. Deer eat the acorns and browse on tender white oak twigs.

The short loop is over quickly, especially if you don't have a handout. Enjoy your return ramble, traveling through a variety of environments.

Miles and Directions

0.0   Start from the northeast side of Garr Hill Road, across from the beginning of the paved Scenic Trail. Pass around a pole gate and follow a double track through sycamore-laden bottomland. A large, unnamed creek flows to your left and divides you from Garr Hill.

0.2   Cross the unnamed creek at an old concrete auto ford. Turn back downstream, climbing a bit. The lake embayment reflects the sunlight below.

0.9   Enter young brushy woods. Enjoy one last view, then turn away from the lake. Make a hard switchback to the right and begin climbing the nose of Garr Hill.

1.4   Level off amid ridgetop maples and oaks.

1.5   The trail turns left from an old roadbed. This turn is signed.

1.7   Pass through a small grassy meadow. Come alongside a field across an old fence line to your right.

2.1   Step across a normally dry drainage. Make one more climb.

2.2   Come along an old farm pond. Cross the pond dam.

2.5   Bridge a last drainage. Bisect a grassy road.

2.6   Emerge on the paved campground access road of Mounds State Recreation Area. Turn left and walk the road a short distance then look right for the Wildlife Wander Trail.

2.7   Bridge a grassy roadside drainage ditch and begin the all-access Wildlife Wander.

2.8   The Templeton Creek Trail leaves left. You stay right, making the Wildlife Wander circuit.

3.1   Complete the Wildlife Wander. Begin backtracking.

4.4   Start descending Garr Hill.

4.9   Return to Brookville Lake. Make a sharp left.

5.6   Cross the unnamed stream on the concrete ford.

5.8   Arrive back at the trailhead, completing the hike.

GREEN TIP
**Go out of your way to avoid birds and animals that
are mating or taking care of their young.**

31 Glidewell Mound Loop

Hike to an ancient mound built by prehistoric residents of the East Fork Whitewater Valley. The Adena Mounds, built around the time of Jesus, have weathered down and aren't impressive themselves, but their mere presence impresses. Beyond the mounds, pass a pond to reach a decision point—the long loop or the short loop? Of course, we'll take the long loop. The hike commences dropping 200 feet to Brookville Lake. Here, you will soak in near and far views of the impoundment. What goes down must come up, and you leave the lake, climbing back to the trailhead.

Start: Adena Mounds trailhead
Distance: 3.3-mile loop
Hiking time: About 1.5 to 2 hours
Difficulty: Moderate
Trail surface: Natural surface path in forested woods
Best season: Sept through May
Other trail users: None
Canine compatibility: Leashed dogs permitted

Land status: State recreation area
Fees and permits: Entrance fee required
Schedule: Open daily year-round
Maps: Brookville Lake and Whitewater Memorial State Park, available online and at Mounds SRA office; USGS Whitcomb
Trail contacts: Mounds State Recreation Area, 4306 Mounds Rd., Anderson, IN 46017; (765) 647-2657; www.in.gov/dnr/

Finding the trailhead: From exit 169 on I-74 in Indiana, west of downtown Cincinnati, take US 52 to Brookville and the intersection of IN 1 and IN 101 on the north side of Brookville. Take IN 101 north for 6.0 miles to the entrance to Mounds State Recreation Area. Turn left here into the recreation area, then follow the main road past the campground and to the trailhead at 2 miles, on your left just after you top over a hill. The trailhead is at the hilltop. Trailhead GPS: N39 29.594' / W84 58.929'

The Hike

The Glidewell Mound is one of ten Indian mounds located within the bounds of Mounds State Recreation Area. Over time, the mound has been partially excavated by archaeologists and probably others before the area was protected. While all you will see is an elevated piece of land topped with trees, it serves as a reminder that civilizations existed long before we ever came to the greater Ohio River valley. And as you hike, imagine what the mound builders would think of how we have altered the landscape with the damming of East Fork Whitewater River, creating massive Brookville Lake. I am sure our ability to create such a body of water would impress them at least as much as we are impressed by a 2,000-year-old mound!

The hike starts atop a ridge now encircled on three sides by Brookville Lake. Chestnut oaks, maple, and red bud shade the wide track. It isn't long before you reach Glidewell Mound. Signs mark the spot. As you will see, it's no Egyptian pyramid when it comes to awe-striking ancient history, but the mound is significant nonetheless.

These sugar maples display hues of orange and red.

Beyond the mound, the trail curves along a southwest-facing slope. Hickories and oaks increase in the drier conditions. Reach a farm pond, where hikers can go short or long. Even the Long Loop isn't really long, 3.3 miles, so take the Long Loop and drop to Brookville Lake. Wolf Creek embayment stretches west, while Brookville Dam rises to the south.

The shoreline is scenic, but the trail itself may be brushy in summer. Anglers will be fishing the lake during warmer times, boats along the shoreline distant and near. Watch for driftwood piling on the land. Shortly turn away from the lakeshore and climb into deep woods. The walking is easy and before you know it, the walk is completed.

MORE MOUNDS ANYONE?

The mounds here are significant, but the greatest preserved concentration of mounds, also built by the Adena Indians, stands at Mounds State Park, north of here, near the town of Anderson (Mounds State Recreation Area, where the above hike takes place, is under the greater Brookville Lake state parks umbrella). Mounds State Park protects and preserves ten mounds. Set above the White River, the Adena did the earthwork around the same time as the mounds you see on this hike. Of course, there is no way to prove exactly why the Adena worked to build these mounds, but most theories center around them being used to track the changing seasons here on earth and of the brightest constellations in the skies above. This tracking of the seasons perhaps helped them plan their agriculture, enabling the most bountiful harvests. And the mounds likely had a religious significance lost to time. Also, it is theorized that the Hopewell Indians came later and added to the mounds.

Among the ten mounds is the so-called Great Mound, the largest of its kind in the Hoosier State. The Great Mound is more of an earthwork, with walls that make a circle almost 0.25 mile in length. It has a flat mound in its center, sort of a "stage." Now that's a lot of dirt moving using the tools available 2,000 year ago! Trees grow among the mounds today, but back then, the Adena cleared the land to allow for the best views of the night sky possible.

For hikers like us, Mounds State Park has a great trail system to explore records left behind. Here, you will find not only the ancient history but also the Bronnenberg house, built in the 1840s. Paths wander among the earthworks and by the Bronnenberg house and also down to the White River. The trails connecting the upland to the White River and its limestone bluffs can be steep. The riverside is a rich wildflower habitat. The state park claims 6 miles of hiking trails. Perhaps you could add this to your hiking wish list. Make a weekend of it, visiting the mounds and staying in the campground. Of course, Mounds State Recreation Area also has its own campground with electrical hookups. It also has a swim beach and boat ramp for enjoying Brookville Lake. So whether you go to Mounds State Park, up Anderson way, or Mounds State Recreation Area, near Cincinnati, you can explore ancient history and have a good time in Indiana's state parks.

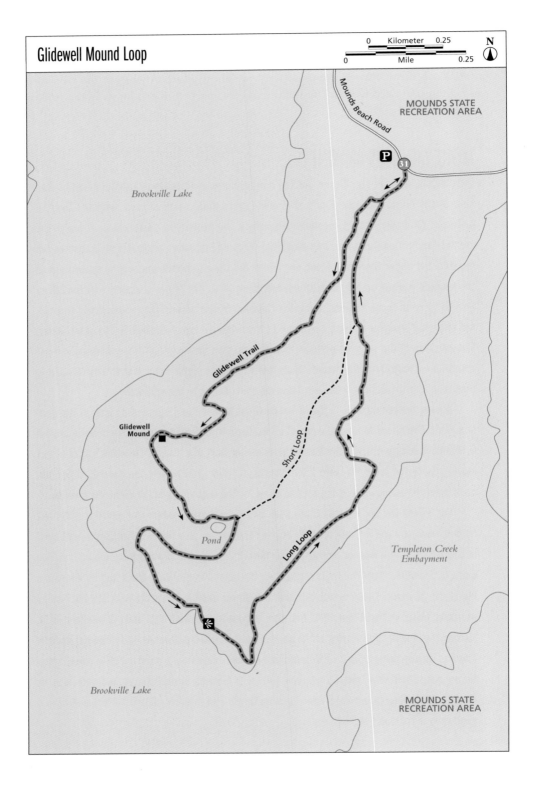

Glidewell Mound Loop

0 Kilometer 0.25
0 Mile 0.25

N

MOUNDS STATE
RECREATION AREA

Mounds Beach Road

P 31

Brookville Lake

Glidewell Trail

Short Loop

Glidewell
Mound

Pond

Long Loop

Templeton Creek
Embayment

Brookville Lake

MOUNDS STATE
RECREATION AREA

Miles and Directions

0.0 Start from the hilltop before the main park road descends to Mounds Beach. A large informational sign marks the trailhead on the left. A shaded picnic table stands at the trail's beginning. The trailhead is easy to miss while driving in. Pass around a gate and join a double-track path heading south atop the ridge.

0.1 Reach the loop portion of the hike. Turn right and join a single-track semi-rocky path in tall forest. Drop over to the north slope of the ridge. Brookville Lake is visible nearly 130 feet below.

0.8 The trail turns left and climbs toward the crest of the ridge. Level off.

1.0 Reach Glidewell Mound. In truth, you might not know it was there, save for the sign. Trees grow atop the irregular elevated soil. The trail circles partly around the mound before turning away.

1.2 Come to a ridgetop pond. Fields are nearby. Continue left to reach a trail junction just ahead. Here, the Long Loop leaves right and the Short Loop keeps straight, running along a field. Turn right onto a double-track path, descending south into woods. Angle down the slope of a hill.

1.7 Come along the wooded shoreline. Unobstructed views open ahead, as you come very near the water.

2.0 Turn into the Templeton Creek embayment, which delineates the southeast side of the ridge atop which the mound stands. Drop back from the water and climb into thick oak woods and soon level off.

2.6 The climb resumes. Make a short uptick then reach the ridgetop.

3.0 Join a woods road and the Short Loop. Stay right, now on double-track path.

3.2 Complete the loop portion of the hike. Backtrack.

3.3 Emerge from the woods, finishing the hike.

▶ Be courteous of others. Many people visit natural areas for quiet, peace, and solitude, so avoid making loud noises and intruding on others' privacy.

GREEN TIP

Pass it down—the best way to instill ecologically sound habits in your children is to set a good example.

32 Wolf Creek Trail from Brookville Dam

This rugged wilderness walk starts atop high Brookville Dam. Cross the dam on foot, taking in the far-reaching views up Brookville Lake and also down to Brookville below. Join the slender Wolf Creek Trail as it wanders wooded and rocky slopes above Brookville Lake. The path nears the lake then climbs to Battle Point, a steep wooded bluff 200 feet above Brookville Lake. Enjoy partial views of the lake and beyond. You will be able to follow the trail much more easily on your return trip. Allow plenty of time when hiking this lesser-used track.

Start: Brookville Dam
Distance: 6.8 miles out-and-back
Hiking time: 3.5 to 4.5 hours
Difficulty: Difficult due to rugged terrain and potentially faint trail
Trail surface: Asphalt over Brookville Dam, natural surface path in forested woods
Best season: Sept through May
Other trail users: None
Canine compatibility: Leashed dogs permitted

Land status: US Army Corps of Engineers land
Fees and permits: No fees or permits required
Schedule: Open daily year-round
Maps: Adena Trace Hiking Trail at Brookville Lake available online; USGS Whitcomb, Brookville
Trail contacts: Brookville Lake, P.O. Box 100, Brookville, IN 47012; (765) 647-2657; www .in.gov/dnr/

Finding the trailhead: From exit 169 on I-74 in Indiana, west of downtown Cincinnati, take US 52 to Brookville and the intersection of IN 1 and IN 101 on the north side of Brookville. Take IN 101 north for 0.9 mile to the Brookville Dam and Spillway. Turn left here, climbing a hill to dead-end at the trailhead on the dam. Trailhead GPS: N39 26.322' / W84 59.697'

The Hike

This hike starts off in unique fashion with a 0.5-mile walk across Brookville Dam, on an asphalt track closed to all but foot travelers. From here you can look north at Brookville Lake but also south at the town of Brookville, where church steeples and other buildings rise above the trees. Below, you see the dam outflow, as seemingly tiny East Fork Whitewater River flows south toward Brookville to meet West Fork White-water River just south of Brookville, forming the Whitewater River. From there the Whitewater River flows southeast into Ohio, meeting the Great Miami River just before its confluence with the mighty Ohio River. Just a simple map perusal shows the possibility of flooding at Brookville.

Brookville Lake, 5,260 acres, not only prevents flooding but also stores water for public use as well as provides aquatic recreation. Be apprised the road to the dam could be closed during times of heightened national security. The land around the impoundment and the water itself create habitat for wildlife and also a place to lay

A lone boater banks up against Brookville Dam.

out hiking trails, as was done here. The Wolf Creek Trail is also part of the greater Adena Trace Hiking Trail. The Adena Trace cobbles together several hiking paths to create a 24-mile circuit around Brookville Lake. The 12-mile Wolf Creek Trail forms the longest link in this network. It is also the most remote, rough, and rugged. You will find this out beyond your 0.5-mile jaunt across Brookville Dam. Finally, consider wearing long pants as the lightly maintained trail may be brushy.

After crossing the dam, the hike bisects the wide overflow spillway before entering woods and more—or less—of a standard foot trail. This tread is a slender, single-track path marked with white paint blazes on trees spaced at intervals. You will undoubtedly lose the trail a time or two on your hike. Fear not: just backtrack to your last known blaze. This warning isn't to scare you from doing the hike. On the contrary, the Wolf Creek Trail is in the "best of the best" greater Cincinnati hikes category. I just want you to know this isn't a well-beaten nature trail you might find at a busy state park.

The Wolf Creek Trail heads north along the west shore of Brookville Lake. It is almost always on a rocky slope, which adds to the challenge of the trail. Always be

MAKING THE CIRCUIT

The Adena Trace makes a 24-mile loop, completely encircling Brookville Lake State Park. The circuit was finished using some existing trail but mostly new path. The trail was scouted and built between the years 1998 and 2001 by volunteers from the Hoosier Hikers Council. It was a lot of work just scouting a potential trail on the mean slopes.

Some argue the Adena Trace as being the Hoosier State's most celebrated path, though the Knobstone Trail, with which the Hoosier Hikers Council is also involved, is longer. What is so great about the Adena Trace, about making the loop in its entirety? Geologically speaking, it wanders among the oldest rocks in Indiana, and their age is but one feature of this stone—it is also fossilized, revealing a record of underwater sea life eons ago. When crossing the many streams flowing toward Brookville Lake, stop and look at the streamside stones. You will find a record of the past, of Ordovician fossils imprinting life as it was when this land was submerged.

Beyond the streams, the woods are also rocky and steep. Along the way the Adena will take you from the lake's edge to bluffs where panoramas open of Brookville Lake below. As night falls on your campsite and the skies are clear, a mural of constellations will paint the night sky, a just reward for a day of hiking the Adena.

You will also feel a sense of completion—on a much smaller scale—of what thru-hikers feel when they complete the Appalachian Trail. But before you tackle the Appalachian Trail, you might want to take on Indiana's longest path, the Knobstone Trail, then decide for yourself which is the Hoosier State's kingpin hiker highway—the Adena Trace or the Knobstone.

watching for the white blazes as the trail sometimes goes where you think it won't. Chestnut oaks, sugar maple, and shagbark hickory shade the path. You will repeatedly bisect wet-weather limestone drainages cutting steeply toward the lake. Up and down, up and down, you go.

Climb way above the lake on a very sloped trail. You will work into the steep-sided valley of a significant stream, dipping to cross the rocky watercourse before venturing farther up the west shore. At one point you descend and come to a lake access and campsite, which makes for a great shoreline breaking point. From there it's all uphill to Battle Point. Your best views will come in winter, when the leaves are gone. Look across the water to Templeton Creek embayment and facilities of Mounds State Recreation Area. Battle Point is a good ending for a great journey. Save a little energy for the backtrack.

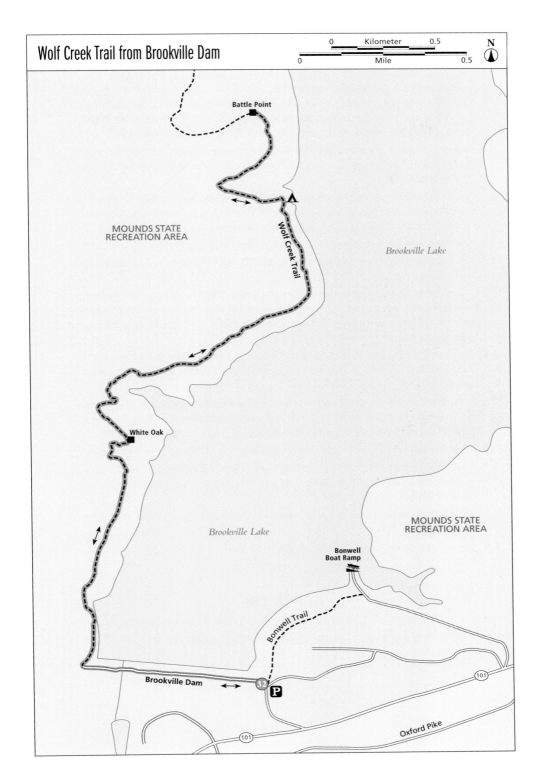

Wolf Creek Trail from Brookville Dam

Battle Point

Wolf Creek Trail

MOUNDS STATE
RECREATION AREA

Brookville Lake

White Oak

Brookville Lake

Bonwell
Boat Ramp

MOUNDS STATE
RECREATION AREA

Bonwell Trail

Brookville Dam

32

P

101

Oxford Pike

101

0   Kilometer   0.5

0   Mile   0.5

N

Miles and Directions

0.0 Start from parking area on the east side of Brookville Lake Dam. The Wolf Creek Trail passes around a gate and begins tracing an asphalt track atop the dam. The busy Bonwell Trail leaves right as a natural surface path. Absorb spectacular views as you cross the dam, as well as interpretive information placed by the Army Corps of Engineers. Look for the farthest point you can see on the west lake shore. You will be hiking beyond that.

0.6 Reach the far end of the dam. Turn right off the dam and cross the dam spillway on a gravel track. Look for buzzards riding the thermals on the artificial bluff created by digging the spillway.

0.7 Reach the signed woodland entrance of the Wolf Creek Trail. Begin looking for white blazes as the trail ascends through trees and grass before entering full-blown woods. Be careful not to follow an angler's path heading down to the water.

1.3 The Wolf Creek Trail turns into a steep drainage then climbs out.

1.5 On a hilltop, pass an eye-catching, multi-trunked old-growth white oak. Turn into a bigger drainage, descending.

1.7 Switchbacks lead downhill to the crossing of a stream that has cut its own valley. Look for fossils in the limestone rock of the streams, especially when they run dry in late summer and fall. Continue on a rocky mid-slope running parallel to the shoreline. Lake views open through the trees.

2.6 Turn northwesterly, after curving out toward a point but never getting too close to the lakeshore. Pass through an area with many piled rocks, indicating former pasturage or cropland.

2.8 Drop to a drainage and come very near the lake. Look for a campsite with a large rock fire ring and rock sitting stones by the water. A small gravelly beach avails water access. Beyond the campsite, turn away from the lake, climbing up a hollow.

3.1 Cross the head of the hollow, and continue climbing toward a steep bluff, Battle Point.

3.4 Reach Battle Point. The bluff drops severely but it is wooded; therefore, it offers a wide but partly obscured view of Brookville Lake and Mounds State Recreation Area across the water. Backtrack.

6.1 Emerge from the woods, Cross the dam spillway then join the dam itself for more spectacular views.

6.8 Come to the parking area after crossing Brookville Dam.

GREEN TIP
Observe wildlife from a distance. Don't interfere in their lives—both of you will be better for it.

33 Mary Gray Bird Sanctuary Loop

Thank the Indiana Audubon Society for this hike. It takes place on property owned and operated by this nature-oriented philanthropic outfit. The sanctuary is located amid picturesque woodland, field, and pond. Trails have been developed, allowing you to visit all the streams, hills, and hollows at this great wildflower destination. As you may imagine, it is even better for birding.

Start: Markle Barn trailhead
Distance: 3.2-mile loop
Hiking time: About 1.5 to 2 hours
Difficulty: Moderate, some hills
Trail surface: Natural surface path in forested woods
Best season: Year-round
Other trail users: None
Canine compatibility: Leashed dogs permitted
Land status: Indiana Audubon Society property

Fees and permits: No fees or permits required, donations welcomed
Schedule: Open daily year-round
Maps: Mary Gray Bird Sanctuary Trail Map; USGS Alpine
Trail contacts: Mary Gray Bird Sanctuary, 3499 S. Bird Sanctuary Rd., Connersville, Indiana 47331; (765) 827-5109, www.indiana audubon.org

Finding the trailhead: From exit 169 on I-74 in Indiana, west of downtown Cincinnati, take US 52 west for 25 miles to IN 121. Turn right onto IN 121 and follow it 11.5 miles to CR 350S. Turn left on CR 350S and follow it for 3.1 miles to a sharp right turn. Keep straight here, entering the signed sanctuary. Continue on the sanctuary road to the trailhead, near the caretaker's house. The picnic shelter and the red Markle Barn will be to your left. Trailhead GPS: N39 35.380' / W85 13.511'

The Hike

Mary Gray Bird Sanctuary is a privately owned nature preserve open to the public. It all started back in 1943 when Mary Alice Gray donated a tract of land to the Indiana Audubon Society (IAS). Adjoining property was willed to the IAS in 1947. Since then additional contiguous property has been purchased, and the preserve stands at an impressive 700-plus acres. Singletrack nature trails have been overlain upon the property, allowing hikers and nature enthusiasts to explore this swath of Fayette County, Indiana. And this is no static property, frozen in time as a museum. On the contrary, the property continues to be managed as a wildlife preserve and supports ongoing research on its grounds.

The hike makes a big loop through the eastern section of the property, where the trails are concentrated. The trail system is excellent. The paths head for all the highlights of the terrain in the hilly watershed of North Branch Garrison Creek. The paths are almost all singletrack, well managed but not beaten down, nor too faint. Footbridges and trail signage are effective but not obtrusive. Simply put, the trail system

Rue anemone is fascinating up close.

is suitably integrated into the landscape. Be apprised the paths are numbered, with a corresponding name, and numbered trails can run in conjunction with one another.

The trailhead parking area has an information kiosk, a simple restroom, a shaded picnic pavilion, and a donation box for the privately run preserve. Please carry out your own trash to minimize the burden on the sanctuary. Your hike starts by visiting the ponds below the trailhead. These small impoundments attract more songbirds and other wildlife than would be here otherwise. You will then climb away from this valley on the first of many ups and downs. Big trees shade the path as you then come near the property boundary, looking on much of what is the Midwest—agricultural fields. Properties such as the Mary Gray Bird Sanctuary balance the need for agriculture with the need to preserve natural areas. Note how the level uplands are often used for agriculture while the sloped lands are kept forested. This is the best setup for erosion control, preserving the rich soils for cultivation, yet allowing the woodlands to thrive on the less productive slopes.

After crossing the entrance road, the hike picks up the appropriately named Wildflower Trail. In April, hikers will be rewarded with a carpet of spring beauties, trillium, mayapple, toothwort, and trout lilies. Watch for big tulip trees, too. The loop climbs to a high point and turns westerly. More intersections lie ahead, but this loop takes the longest, outside track, in order to maximize the trail mileage. A highlight along this section is a trip through a meadow, where a mix of field and forest improves wildlife habitat.

The next highlight is a side trip to a pair of small ponds and wetland. This area was improved for wildlife, adding another habitat to the landscape. A viewing blind that overlooks the wetland adds to the possibilities. Of course, a little patience is in order. The final part of the hike rambles through more wildflower-covered hollows before returning to the ponds near the trailhead.

Miles and Directions

0.0 Start at the trailhead parking area below the caretaker's house. Walk downhill on a grassy track toward the red Markle Barn and the sanctuary ponds. A service road continues beyond the parking area. Split two ponds, getting to the far side of the ponds. Turn right beyond the ponds.

0.1 Reach a footbridge. Turn left here and cross the footbridge. Stay right with Trail #3/#5, continuing downstream. Trail #4/#5 head left.

0.2 Come to another intersection. Here, Trail #3, your return route, comes in. You turn left and uphill on Trail #5. Pines, tulip trees, sycamore, and beech tower overhead.

INDIANA AUDUBON SOCIETY

The Indiana Audubon Society is about more than just birds. It strives "to engage in educational, scientific, investigative, literary, historical, philanthropic, and charitable pursuits which protect and conserve our natural resources including water, air, soil, plants, and wildlife, stimulating public appreciation of the values of such natural resources and the need for their conservation." Pretty comprehensive. You might say that bird-watching is the vehicle for improving the environment.

But they aren't just a bunch of nerdy do-gooders with binoculars around their necks and field guides in their hands. They like to have fun in the outdoors. The IAS goes on adventurous birding trips throughout the state and region, and gather for camping outings and nature classes led by experts.

The Indiana Audubon Society is no Johnny-come-lately in the outdoor conservation field. They were founded back in 1898. Then-governor of Indiana, James A. Mount, was a charter member. So if you are looking to become part of a conservation group that has stood the test of time, consider this bunch, whose main stomping ground is right here at Mary Gray Bird Sanctuary.

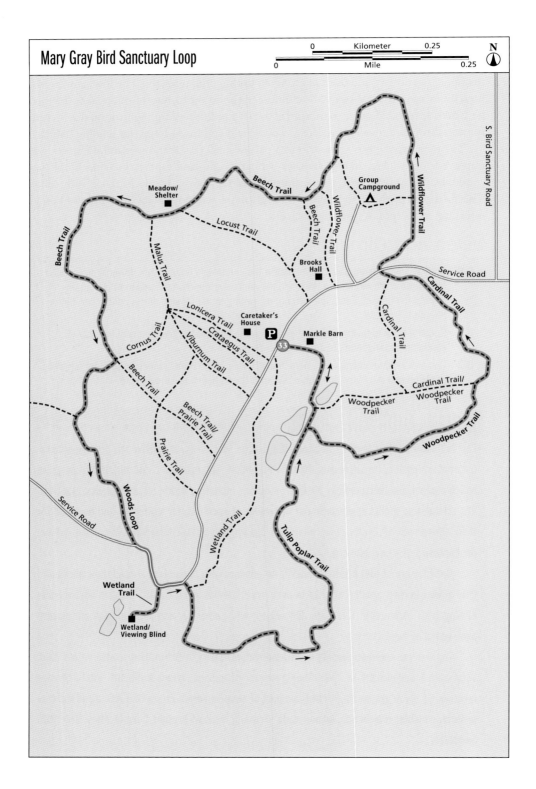

Mary Gray Bird Sanctuary Loop

Kilometer
0   0.25

Mile
0   0.25

N

Meadow/Shelter

Beech Trail

Locust Trail

Group Campground

Wildflower Trail

S. Bird Sanctuary Road

Beech Trail

Beech Trail

Malus Trail

Brooks Hall

Service Road

Cardinal Trail

Lonicera Trail

Caretaker's House

Crataegus Trail

Markle Barn

Cornus Trail

Cardinal Trail

Viburnum Trail

P

33

Cardinal Trail/Woodpecker Trail

Beech Trail

Woodpecker Trail

Woodpecker Trail

Beech Trail/Prairie Trail

Prairie Trail

Woods Loop

Service Road

Wetland Trail

Tulip Poplar Trail

Wetland Trail

Wetland/Viewing Blind

Dutchman's breeches are an early spring wildflower.

0.5 Make a high point and trail intersection. Keep straight, picking up Trail #4, the Cardinal Trail. Descend off the hill.

0.8 Reach the entrance road, just after passing Trail #4 leaving left and uphill. Join the road and walk left just a short distance, then pick up the Wildflower Trail, Trail #1, leaving right. Wander up a stream-bottomed hollow, crisscrossing the streambed on bridges.

0.9 Pass a spur trail leading left to the property campground. It is open only to members of the Indiana Audubon Society.

1.1 Pass a second spur trail leading to the campground.

1.2 Trail #1 ends. It leaves left toward the entrance road. Just ahead, after bridging a stream, meet Trail #2. It leaves left and right. Keep right, climbing from the stream and leaving the forest on Trail #2.

1.4 Reach a trail junction in a meadow. Here, Trail #10 leaves left. Just ahead, come to a trail shelter bordered by cedar trees and another intersection. Here, Trail #8A leaves left. Keep straight, continuing in the meadow on Trail #2. Wander into beech-dominated woods.

1.8 Come to a four-way trail intersection. Turn right, joining Trail #9. The path joins an old roadbed.

1.9 Trail #9 splits. Stay left. The valley widens. Watch for big white oaks.

2.1 Meet the property service road. Stay left and shortly turn right on a grassy track, Trail #6, heading for the property wetland.

2.3 Reach the covered blind and ponds. Look for amphibians, waterfowl, and other birds. Backtrack, then turn right onto Trail #3. Reach a bluff, then enter a wooded hollow with more wildflowers.

3.0 Complete the loop portion of the hike. Keep straight, then turn left at the ponds.

3.2 Arrive back at the trailhead.

34 Whitewater Canal Historic Trail

Follow an old towpath along the Whitewater Canal, once used to transport people and goods. You will start in quaint Metamora, Indiana, then curve along a huge flat of the West Fork Whitewater River. Views of fields and hillsides stretch before you. The trek parallels an old railroad grade that was built atop the towpath. The railroad tracks end and you follow the towpath through woods, coming to a great vista along the Whitewater River. Your trip ends at an old stone lock. You can explore the remnants of these structures used to raise and lower boats on their canal journeys.

Start: Metamora trailhead
Distance: 5.2-mile out-and-back
Hiking time: About 2.5 to 3.5 hours
Difficulty: Easy, level trail
Trail surface: Gravel
Best season: Sept through May
Other trail users: Bicycles
Canine compatibility: Pets must be leashed at all times

Land status: Indiana State park property
Fees and permits: No fees or permits required
Schedule: Open dawn to dusk year-round
Maps: Whitewater Canal; USGS Metamora, Brookville
Trail contacts: Whitewater Canal State Historic Site, 19083 Clayborn St., Metamora, IN 47030; (765) 647-6512; www.indiana museum.org

Finding the trailhead: From the intersection of US 52 and Indiana 101 in Brookville, Indiana, northwest of downtown Cincinnati, take US 52 west for 7.8 miles to Metamora. Turn left onto Columbia Street. Follow it for 0.1 mile to a T intersection. Turn left onto Pennington Street and follow it for 0.2 mile to the large gravel trailhead parking on the right, just past the covered Duck Creek Aqueduct. Trailhead GPS: N39 26.738' / W85 7.789'

The Hike

This is a fun learning experience. And you can exercise while doing it! You will start out this hike in the quaint and quirky town of Metamora, Indiana, a place that prides itself on being a throwback city, a town that time forgot. That historic theme is consistent with this hike, as you will be following a canal that was built in the 1830s and 1840s. Now the Whitewater Canal Historic Site, this 2.6-mile segment of the old canal towpath is also complemented with boat rides, and a train ride during the warm season, all making for a fun way to explore the past.

Start your trek on the east side of Metamora, an enjoyable berg to visit, especially in summer when all the tourist attractions are open. Before you hit the trail, check out the Duck Creek Aqueduct, registered as a National Historic Landmark in 2014. This is where the Whitewater Canal was carried over Duck Creek. The aqueduct resembles a covered bridge. It is strange to think of a canal flowing above a creek. The trail starts out below the historic towpath, heading easterly away from Metamora. At

The curve of the trail and old railroad bend with the Whitewater River

this juncture a small gauge railroad track covers the actual towpath. At one time a commercial train utilized the towpath for its bed after the canal was rendered obsolete.

This is a historic hike rather than a woods hike. Therefore civilization will be in view much of the time. However, the natural beauty of the West Fork Whitewater River Valley is in view at all times. Be apprised that much of the trail is open to the sky overhead. Bring a hat and sunscreen, especially during the summer season. After a while the railroad tracks running atop the towpath end and the trail itself follows the track where horses and mules once pulled cargo-laden barges up and down the canal.

On a warm day the now-wooded path can be a delight. In contrast, on a cold day the open sun will be more welcome. No matter the weather, you will come to an overlook with a sweeping view of the West Fork Whitewater River. A resting bench begs a seat here. Continuing on, you will pass a campground, then a few dwellings. A big highlight awaits at the end of the trek—Twin Locks. Here, you can see the structures firsthand that helped boats conquer the elevation changes of the canal. Interpretive information adds to the locks themselves. From here, you must backtrack to Metamora.

LOCKING DOWN

After the heyday of the horse and before the rise of the railroads, there was a time in American history when canals were looked upon as the transportation answer of the future. Canal building took off in the lower Ohio River Valley with the US government's passage of the Internal Improvements Act of 1836. Indiana literally got in on the act, with the development of the 76-mile-long Whitewater Canal. This canal ultimately connected Hagerstown, Indiana, with the Ohio River at Lawrenceburg. A 25-mile spur canal connected the Whitewater Canal to Cincinnati. Building the canal was slow work, especially when you consider that over the 76 miles canal engineers had to account for an elevation change of nearly 500 feet from one end of the canal to the other. Boats were either moved up or down on these fifty locks.

The locks you see along this hike were built of cut stone. There was no uniformity of lock construction because each contractor built using the availability of materials on hand and what they personally knew about constructing locks in the first place. They did have standard dimensions, with each lock being 100 feet long and 15 feet wide, to accommodate your typical transportation boat of that era. The depth of a lock depended upon how much elevation had to be gained or lost. Most locks changed the elevation of the canal by 6 to 11 feet. The twin locks at the end of this hike were typical of those that needed a greater elevation change than 11 feet, using two locks side-by-side rather than just one.

To get up or down the canal, boats were pulled into a watertight chamber with gates closed at either end. Next, water was let out of the lower gates through sieves, known as wickets. Shortly, the water level was equalized to that of the canal downstream. Then the downstream gate was open and the boat kept going. If the boat was going upstream it was pulled into the watertight chamber, then water was allowed to flow into the chamber from the upstream side until it rose enough to equal the water level of the upper canal. The upper gate was opened and on the boat went.

You may wonder about the sensibility of putting a canal right alongside a flowing river. The water levels on canals could be controlled and stabilized, whereas rivers rose up and down, often radically, limiting the reliability of using them. Also, draft animals or horses could pull boats along canals in both directions. Getting a boat upstream on a river in those days was very challenging. Canals had the advantage of two-way transportation. However, by the 1840s railroads proved to be a cheaper form of transportation, and canals became a thing of the past.

Whitewater Canal Historic Trail

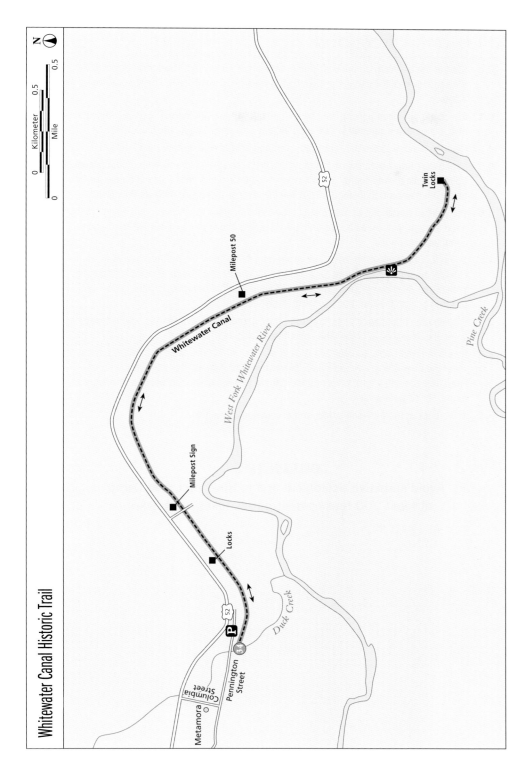

Metamora
Columbia Street
Pennington Street
Duck Creek
52
Locks
Milepost Sign
Whitewater Canal
West Fork Whitewater River
Milepost 50
52
Pine Creek
Twin Locks

N

Kilometer
0   0.5
Mile
0   0.5

Miles and Directions

0.0 Start at the trailhead on the east side of Metamora. Follow the gravel track below and on the south side of the canal. The West Fork Whitewater River is to your right, southerly, in the distance.

0.2 Reach the handicap parking area beyond a large red trailside barn. The gravel trail continues. A large valley spreads to your right. Horses may be grazing in the fields.

0.3 Come to a set of locks. They are to your left and are accessible from US 52 as well.

0.6 Reach Park Road, then railroad marker post 51. Cross the road and keep on the historic trail. A cornfield rises nearby and hills rise in the distance. A picnic area is on the far side of the Whitewater Canal along US 52. You can access this picnic area via Park Road.

1.6 The railroad tracks end at milepost 50. The trail then joins the towpath and enters woods. Keep easterly, now on a shaded trail. US 52 is well above you on a hill. The road and trail continue to separate.

2.2 Come to a bluff along the West Fork Whitewater River. Enjoy an elevated view of the curving stream as it continues for the East Fork Whitewater River in Brookville. The main Whitewater River meets the Great Miami River just before dumping into the Ohio. The trail turns away from the river but stays with the Whitewater Canal.

2.5 Emerge onto a road with a few houses nearby. It looks like the trail ends. Keep forward along the grassy edge of the canal past the houses.

2.6 Reach the Twin Locks. You can see the cut stone used to build the locks. Imagine the days when these were used to help boats gain or lose elevation as they traveled the canal. From here the canal towpath is not open to the public. Hopefully it will be extended in the future. For now, backtrack.

5.2 Arrive back at the trailhead in Metamora, completing the hike.

GREEN TIP:
Avoid sensitive ecological areas. Hike, rest, and camp
at least 200 feet from streams, lakes, and rivers.

35 Versailles State Park Hike

Explore the heart of historic Versailles State Park on this trek. First, travel up Fallen Timber Creek, crossing it a few times before climbing into hills to reach the architecturally attractive Oak Grove Shelter. From here, hike to a vista overlooking Laughery Creek. The excitement continues as you circle past interesting sinkholes and a small cascade before returning to Versailles Lake. The Civilian Conservation Corps developed this park and you will see their handiwork throughout, including the trails themselves. Expect some challenges with the numerous ups and downs.

Start: Trail #3 trailhead near the Nature Center
Distance: 4.7-mile double loop
Hiking time: About 2.5 to 3.5 hours
Difficulty: Moderate, but does have hills to climb and a plethora of trail junctions
Trail surface: Natural surface path in forested woods
Best season: Year-round
Other trail users: None

Canine compatibility: Leashed dogs permitted
Land status: State park
Fees and permits: Entrance fee required
Schedule: Open daily year-round
Maps: Versailles State Park; USGS Whitcomb, Brookville
Trail contacts: Versailles State Park, 1387 E. US 50, Versailles, IN 47042; (812) 689-6424; www.in.gov/dnr/

Finding the trailhead: From exit 16 on I-275 in Indiana, west of downtown Cincinnati, take Eads Parkway to US 50. Take US 50 west toward Versailles. Just before reaching the town of Versailles, come to the right turn to Versailles State Park. Enter the park and follow signs for the Nature Center and Camp Store. Bridge the Fallen Timber Creek embayment at 1.4 miles, then turn left to park in the large lot near the Nature Center. Trailhead GPS: N39 4.885' / W85 14.041'

The Hike

You will find this hike pleasing to the eye and easy to execute as well. Wooden posts are located at the major trail junctions, of which there are many. You won't get lost here, but may get turned around for a moment. We begin the double loop on Trail #3, Fallen Timber Trail. It travels up the valley of Fallen Timber Creek, crossing it three times without benefit of a footbridge. However, hikers have built elevated stones extending across the stream that may allow dry passage when it is flowing. Look for fossilized invertebrates in the stream rocks. In late summer and fall the stream can completely dry up. If the water is too high, simply execute the hike in reverse, and avoid the stretch along Fallen Timber Creek.

The climb comes near Versailles' campgrounds. Don't be surprised if a little campfire smoke wafts into your nose. I have stayed here and found it a fine experience. Work your way through the campground and come to Oak Grove Shelter. This structure is of special note. Versailles State Park was developed during the 1930s as

The historic Oak Grove Shelter stands proudly atop a wooded hill.

a Great Depression–era work project. The valley of Laughery Creek was chosen to turn less than ideal farmland into a recreation area all could enjoy. The young men, ranging from eighteen to twenty-eight years of age, were part of the Civilian Conservation Corps. They gathered on-site and first built their own housing, then went to work developing the park. They built the roads, trails, and quaint stone structures we see today. This initial infrastructure became Versailles State Park, when the land was deeded over to the state of Indiana in 1943. Versailles Lake was constructed a decade later. This time prison workers developed the 230-acre impoundment for water storage and recreation. The lake became operational in the late 1950s. Over time Versailles State Park has been further improved, but the core of the park developed by the CCC remains intact. As you make this hike, continue looking for their handiwork.

▶ **Regular hiking and walking combined with a good diet is a great way to stay in great health and save money on your health care!**

Trail #2, Orchard Trail, is actually several trails all in the vicinity of the park's two campgrounds—A and B. They didn't do much better naming their campgrounds than they did the trails. Once you get past the maze that is Trail #2, you will climb to a bluff way above Laughery Creek. Views open and include a designated overlook with resting bench. Look west across the creek valley, 175 feet below, toward the town of Versailles. The trek continues in tall beeches and oaks, which shade the path. Undulate in and out of small ravines draining the hilltop on which you walk, finally reaching the developed overlook of the Laughery Creek valley.

Your hike then enters an area pocked with sinkholes large and small. Look for streams that simply drain into a hole and disappear. After the hike turns back north, you are treated with a hidden waterfall in a ravine. The low–flow cascade spills over a limestone lip. Though the stream is perennial, the waterfall is more often a drip than a splash. Finally, work your way past the Oak Grove Shelter and down to the trailhead.

Miles and Directions

0.0   Start on the northeast side of the bridge over Fallen Timber Creek, picking up Trail #3, Fallen Timber Trail. Join a double-track path with Fallen Timber Creek to your right. The trail is pinched in by the stream on the right and a steep hill on the left. Sycamores and pawpaws rise from the stream banks, which contrast with the oak-studded hill.

0.4   Cross Fallen Timber Creek.

0.5   Cross Fallen Timber Creek again. You are back on the left-hand bank.

0.8   Cross Fallen Timber Creek a third and final time. Now curve right, climbing away from the creek on a very rocky path.

RESTORING INDIANA'S DEER

Deer weren't always as plentiful as you see them today, along the roads, fields, and forests of the Hoosier State. As America pushed west and settlers filtered into Indiana, unregulated hunting nearly decimated the four-legged critter's numbers. In the 1930s the Department of Natural Resources rounded up deer from several other states and let them loose on state and federal lands in the hilly southern part of the state. They began reproducing and expanding, following the river drainages up the state. Additionally deer migrated down from Michigan. Deer numbers began to rise. In counties that still didn't have deer, the Department of Natural Resources trapped and relocated deer into those counties, further expanding their range.

The first regulated hunting season opened in 1951. Licenses were purchased and deer harvested. The numbers continued to rise. Today, thanks to monies raised from hunting licenses, deer are found in all ninety-two counties in Indiana. The monies go into the Wildlife Restoration Fund, along with revenue from fishing licenses, all of which is used for game and non-game species. These monies are also used for buying new state lands for natural preservation to animal research to eradicating exotic plants and, of course, for improving deer habitat. The return of the deer in Indiana has become a good thing for the cornucopia of wildlife in the Hoosier State.

Trails like this keep us moving forward, excited to see what lies ahead.

1.0 Trail #3 ends at a junction. Here, Trail #2, Orchard Trail, goes right and straight. Stay straight, now on Trail #2, still ascending. Come near Campground B. Watch for user-created trails connecting to the campground.

1.3 An official spur trail leads left to Campground B. Other user-created trails before here may confuse. Stay right at the official intersection.

1.4 Reach another intersection. Go left this time to cross a streamlet near a big white oak. Come to another junction. Stay left. The trail going right, also Trail #2, will lead you back toward the nature center.

Versailles State Park Hike

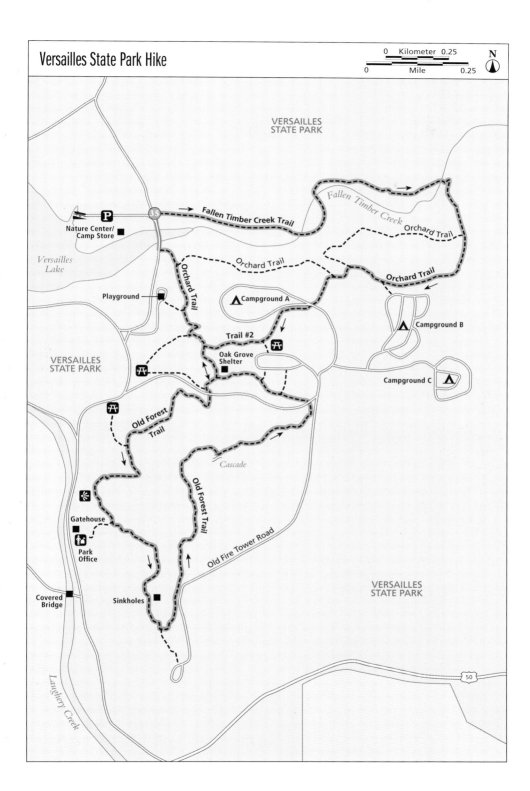

VERSAILLES STATE PARK

0   Kilometer 0.25
0   Mile   0.25

N

Fallen Timber Creek

Nature Center/
Camp Store

Fallen Timber Creek Trail

Orchard Trail

Orchard Trail

Orchard Trail

Versailles Lake

Playground

Orchard Trail

Campground A

Campground B

Trail #2

Oak Grove
Shelter

Campground C

VERSAILLES
STATE PARK

Old Forest
Trail

Cascade

Old Forest Trail

Old Fire Tower Road

Gatehouse

Park
Office

VERSAILLES
STATE PARK

Covered
Bridge

Sinkholes

Laughery Creek

50

1.5 Cross the access road to Campground A. Keep westerly, passing below the park picnic area.

1.7 A spur trail leads right to the picnic area. Keep straight.

1.8 Reach a T intersection near some cut stones. You will be here later. For now, turn left and circle around to reach the Oak Grove Shelter and a trail junction. The stone and wood structure is the CCC standout of the park. Turn right here at the shelter, beginning Trail #1, Old Forest Trail. Descend wood and earth steps to cross a paved road. Climb steeply to a bluff well above Laughery Creek valley. Views open to the north.

2.4 A spur trail leads right and downhill to another picnic area. Stay with Trail #1. The slope of the hill sharpens.

2.7 Come to a developed overlook. Westerly views open of Laughery Creek valley. Stones and a park bench mark the spot.

2.8 A spur trail leads right down toward the park office. Stay straight.

3.0 Enter an area with many sinkholes amid big trees.

3.1 A spur trail leads right to Old Fire Tower Road. Trail #1 turns back north, passing through more sinkholes.

3.2 Come within sight of Old Fire Tower Road. Keep north under oaks and maples.

3.7 Dip into a hollow to reach a stream and multitier limestone cascade. Continue north, watching for more sinkholes.

4.0 Cross a park road left, near the intersection with Old Fire Tower Road. Walk along an exposed limestone outcrop. Note the yucca plants in the woods.

4.1 A spur trail leads right to the picnic area. Keep straight.

4.2 Another spur trail leads right to the picnic area. Keep straight again.

4.3 Return to the Oak Grove Shelter. Backtrack to the T intersection you were at earlier. Keep straight this time, descending wood and earth steps back on Trail #2.

4.7 Reach your final trail junction near some wooden steps. Trail #2 leaves right. Stay left, joining the wooden steps to emerge near the bridge over Fallen Timber Creek embayment. Cross the bridge and shortly reach the parking area.

Northern Kentucky

Hikers venturing south across the Ohio River will be pleasantly surprised at the hikes included from the Bluegrass State. Kentucky offers huge old-growth trees at Middle Creek Park and rare natural communities at Boone Cliffs Nature Preserve. Combine hiking with other pursuits at quiet Kincaid State Park. Check out the buffalo at Big Bone Lick State Park. Make sure to visit the museum there, too, and learn about the prehistoric past of now–extinct creatures. Quiet Trails State Nature Preserve presents varied landscapes along and above the Licking River.

Preserves like this allow you to get back to nature on nature's terms.

36 Middle Creek Park Loop

This Boone County park trail system will surprise. Your hike traverses bottomlands where ancient and enormous sycamores curve skyward in incredible arcing beauty. Middle Creek is an alluring stream in its own right. Leave the bottomlands to roam among deeply wooded hills draining into Middle Creek. Along the way you will visit an old chimney from a forgotten cabin before dropping back to Middle Creek and completing the loop. The establishment of adjacent Camargo Hunt Park adds more acreage—and more trails.

Start: Middle Creek Park
Distance: 3-mile loop
Hiking time: About 2 to 2.5 hours
Difficulty: Moderate due to shorter distance but has significant elevation changes
Trail surface: Natural surface path in forested woods
Best season: Fall will have driest trails
Other trail users: Equestrians
Canine compatibility: Leashed dogs permitted

Land status: County park
Fees and permits: No fees or permits required
Schedule: Open daily year-round sunrise to sunset
Maps: Middle Creek with Camargo Trails; USGS Rising Sun
Trail contacts: Boone County Parks and Recreation, 5958 Garrard, Burlington, KY 41005; (859) 334-2117; www.boonecountyky.org/parks

Finding the trailhead: From exit 181 on I-75 south of downtown Cincinnati, take KY 18 west for 11.0 miles, passing the historic Dinsmore Homestead on your right just before making the left turn into the Middle Creek Park entrance road. The trailhead is a short piece down the entrance road. Trailhead GPS: N38 59.893' / W84 48.864'

The Hike

Middle Creek Park is a pure nature park overlain with trails. It was once part of the greater Dinsmore Homestead, a historic preserved farm located just across KY 18, the two-lane road leading from nearby Burlington to the park. Being a part of the homestead property allowed for the preservation of the massive sycamores located along Middle Creek. It remained an unused tract of the greater farm, was never sold or cut down, thus remaining in its natural state. One double-trunked sycamore may have more wood mass than any tree for miles. A total of 6 trail miles lace the 230-acre park. However, hiking here has a downside: The trail system is shared with equestrians. In places, especially along the Middle Creek bottoms, the paths can be muddy but you can usually work around these squishy spots. To offset the negative possibilities, avoid hiking here after rainy periods. Another good way to avoid the mud is to hike here from late summer through fall, when the trails will be at their driest. Mud aside, the big trees are worth a visit any time of year, except during deer hunting season,

An old chimney is all that stands from a trailside cabin.

when the park is closed. Please consult Kentucky Department of Fish and Wildlife Resources at www.fw.ky.gov for the exact dates, which are generally in late fall.

The trail system is well signed and marked, but some user-created equestrian paths may briefly confuse. This hike follows Trail #1 most of the way since it makes the widest loop through the forest. The trailhead offers numerous shaded picnic tables and a restroom for your convenience.

The hike shortly reaches Middle Creek, bridging the clear, gravelly stream bordered by mud banks. You then cruise through bottomland floodplain forest highlighted by massive sycamores, making graceful skyward arcs. Watch your footing,

THE DINSMORE HOMESTEAD—HISTORY, NATURE, AND MORE

Just before reaching the trailhead on this hike, you will pass by the Dinsmore Homestead and the adjacent Dinsmore Woods State Nature Preserve. The preserve is part of a connected greater wild tract that includes 230-acre Middle Creek Park, where this hike takes place, and the 30 acres surrounding historic and intact Dinsmore Homestead. Known for its old-growth woodland, most notably big white oak and red oak, sugar maple, and ash trees, Dinsmore Woods State Nature Preserve, a wild parcel of the former farm, not part of Middle Creek Park, was donated to the Nature Conservancy and became part of the Kentucky state nature preserve system in 1990. But judging by the size and age of the trees the preserve was much longer in the making. The whole shooting match was set in motion in 1839 when James Dinsmore bought 700 acres of land, then built and completed the Boone County house by 1842. He'd come from a sugar plantation in Louisiana but didn't like the heat and malarial conditions. Back then malaria was a real threat in the Southern bottomlands. Before that he's been raised in New Hampshire, so his disdain for heat is well understood.

His uncle had told him about the Boone County tract here in the Belleview Bottoms near the Ohio River. Dinsmore raised a family with his wife, Martha, including one daughter, Julia, who ran the farmstead after her father had died. Much of the historic record of the farm comes from Julia's diaries and farm records. During James Dinsmore's time as an operating farmer, he raised sheep for wool, grew grapes for wine and cultivated willows. The willows were used for basket making, an unusual endeavor, out of practice in today's agricultural landscape. They also raised more pedestrian crops such as hay, corn, and oats. His daughter Julia had more troubles keeping the farm going, with the abolition of slavery. Interestingly, James Dinsmore sided with the Yankees, even though he knew the end of slavery would change the way he ran his farm. She used tenant farmers with whom she often had troubles. There were good times, too. Later in life Julia picked up writing poetry and found recognition in that field. Julia died at age 93. The homestead was purchased by a foundation and is now operated as an historic home where you can tour the house and grounds. For tour fees, information, and operating hours, visit www.dinsmorefarm.org. They also offer educational programs for children, Scouts, and adults and rent the facility for luncheons, weddings, and more.

avoiding mud spots. It isn't long before the first junction with other interior paths. Gain glimpses of Middle Creek along the way. You won't miss the double-trunked sycamore before climbing from the creek, gaining 200 feet in elevation.

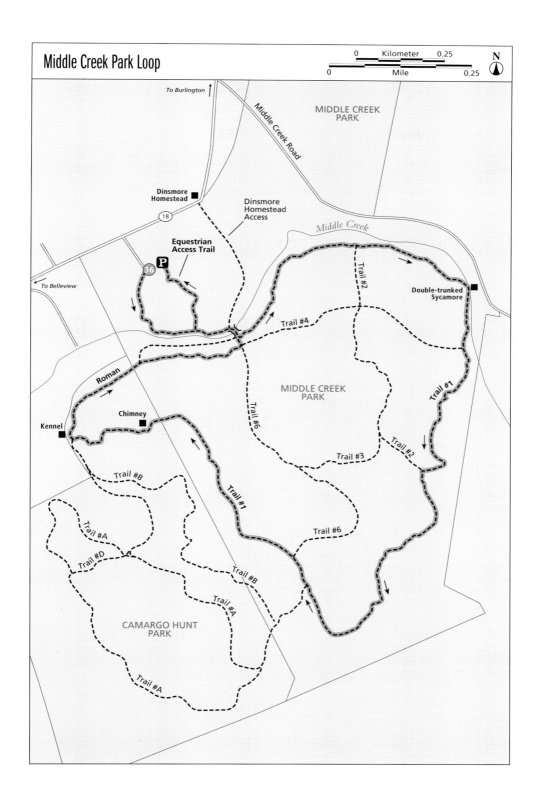

Middle Creek Park Loop

0   Kilometer   0.25
0   Mile   0.25

N

To Burlington

MIDDLE CREEK PARK

Middle Creek Road

Dinsmore Homestead

18

Dinsmore Homestead Access

Equestrian Access Trail

P

36

To Belleview

Middle Creek

Trail #2

Double-trunked Sycamore

Trail #4

Trail #1

Roman

MIDDLE CREEK PARK

Chimney

Kennel

Trail #6

Trail #2

Trail #3

Trail #1

Trail #B

Trail #A

Trail #6

Trail #D

Trail #B

Trail #A

CAMARGO HUNT PARK

Trail #A

Loop your way along ridges, under regal oaks and arrow–straight tulip trees. Reach an odd stone chimney perched on a narrow ridge. It was likely part of a hunt cabin from days gone by. The hike then descends toward Middle Creek, tracing an old roadbed back to the bridge that carries you back to the trailhead.

Miles and Directions

0.0 With your back to KY 18 take the wide path, Trail #1, heading southeast past shaded picnic tables. The other trail leaving the parking area is for equestrians. Drop off a hill to make the Middle Creek bottoms. Turn left, cruising upstream along Middle Creek.

0.1 The Equestrian Access Trail comes in from your left. Keep straight.

0.2 Make the substantial bridge over Middle Creek just after an access leaves left for Dinsmore Homestead. At the Middle Creek bridge, look for a nearby massive sycamore with a trunk so large it would take several people together to stretch their arms around it. Stay left at a four-way trail junction along the creek on Trail #1, keeping in bottoms. Maple ash, buckeye, sycamore, and tulip trees shade the trail.

0.6 Intersect Trail #2. It leaves right and uphill, away from the bottoms.

0.8 Reach the huge double-trunked sycamore to the left of the trail. Its sheer mass is amazing. Trail #1 curves right, tracing Middle Creek.

0.9 Trail #4 leaves right. Stay with Trail #1. It keeps straight, then begins ascending away from Middle Creek.

1.2 Top out on a ridge and reach a trail junction. Trails #2 and #3 leave right. Stay straight with Trail #1, undulating in hollow and hill.

1.7 A spur trail leads left into the Camargo Hunt Park trail network. Stay straight with Trail #1.

1.8 Trail #6 leaves right. Keep straight on Trail #1, making a brief descent.

2.1 Pass a giant oak to the left of trail.

2.2 Reach a stone chimney of an old hunt cabin. Sharply descend among rock outcrops and through a cedar grove.

2.4 Emerge onto a field near a kennel. Turn right here, reentering woods. Trace a shaded roadbed back toward the bridge over Middle Creek. Watch for user-created spur trails.

2.6 Reach a trail junction. Here, Trail #1 drops left for Middle Creek. Keep forward, now on Trail #4, staying with the old roadbed.

2.8 Reach a trail junction near the Middle Creek Bridge. Turn left, bridging the stream and backtrack.

2.9 Reach the Equestrian Access Trail. Take this path for added new mileage.

3.0 Arrive back at the trailhead, completing the hike.

37 Boone County Cliffs State Nature Preserve

Owned by the Nature Conservancy, this 74-acre tract preserves glacially carved hills in Kentucky's Boone County. The hike travels along a tributary of Middle Creek and through hilly woodland containing old-growth trees. The cliffs harbor some of the most biologically diverse flora and fauna in Northern Kentucky and are an important bird habitat. The preserve trail has been rehabbed. Please respect the resource.

Start: Middle Creek Road
Distance: 1.7-mile loop
Hiking time: About 1 to 1.5 hours
Difficulty: Moderate, has elevation changes
Trail surface: Natural surface path in forested woods
Best season: Late Sept through mid-May
Other trail users: None
Canine compatibility: Dogs not permitted

Land status: State nature preserve
Fees and permits: No fees or permits required
Schedule: Open daily year-round sunrise to sunset
Maps: Trailhead kiosk map; USGS Rising Sun
Trail contacts: Kentucky State Nature Preserves Commission, 801 Teton Trail, Frankfort, KY 40601; (502) 573-2886; http://nature preserves.ky.gov

Finding the trailhead: From exit 181 on I-75 south of downtown Cincinnati, take KY 18 west for 10.6 miles to Middle Creek Road. Turn left onto Middle Creek Road and follow it 1.7 miles to the trailhead on your left. Do not park on Middle Creek Road if the lot is full. No overnight parking, either. Trailhead GPS: N38 59.601' / W84 47.070'

The Hike

This gem of a wooded hilly tract not only preserves unique plants and animals of the area while harboring old-growth forest but is also simply a great hiking destination. However, the preserve was closed during 2017 and reopened in 2018, during which time some portions of trail were rerouted to make them more sustainable. Also, visitors were camping out overnight on the bluffs and illegally parking on the road outside the preserve. Please treat this place as specially as it deserves. A loop trail circles a centerpiece stream, highlighted by the 20- to 40-foot cliffs found between the tops of ridges and the stream below. Anywhere you have cliffs you are going to have elevation changes, and the singletrack path takes you on a ride that includes nearly 300 feet in elevation undulations, so be prepared for some vertical variation. The Nature Conservancy originally made their first preservation purchase of 42 acres in 1974, then expanded it in 1990. It is not only the sloping terrain that creates the special plant habitat but also the soils and cliffs, which are composed of glacial gravel outwash, rare in these parts. Birds and birders flock to this destination—over ninety species of avian life have been recorded, including resident and migratory species.

Nature abounds on Northern Kentucky's trails.

The deep hollow offers copious wildflowers in spring, and the wide diversity of trees makes for a colorful autumn display.

The trail is mostly easy to follow. Brush can crowd the track in summer, but the primitive condition of the path adds a wilderness aspect to the trek. Contemplation benches make for desirable stopping spots.

A natural surface trail leads you up a tributary of Middle Creek. The down cutting of the tributary created the cliffs of the preserve. Maple, white oak, basswood, and beech tower over the trail. Sycamores crowd the clear stream below, which gurgles over rocks and sand. The hollow tightens and soon you are in uplands, taking a short spur to an overlook that allows views into the creek below. The modest cliffs lie at your feet. Ahead you will pass through an impressive beech grove. Unfortunately, the smooth gray bark has proven too tempting for passersby who carve into the giants. Other tall trees rise from the ridgetop.

The loop continues circling around the unnamed tributary, availing views into fern-filled hollows below and views of other big trees, especially cherry. Also, look for previous signs of human habitation, such as old fence lines and faint roadbeds, especially visible in leafless winter. The circuit finally meets the creek, which is home to

PRESERVING KENTUCKY'S SPECIAL PLACES

The state of Kentucky has a special program for its special places. Run by the State Nature Preserve Commission, the program establishes areas "solely to protect and preserve rare species and the natural environment." Thankfully, passive recreation such as hiking is allowed on most preserves, but human use is watched carefully to protect the resource. Over 25,000 acres of special lands are protected, from the wetlands of the Mississippi River to the Appalachian Mountains in the east, and places in between such as here in Boone County.

The commission seeks out ecological communities that closely resemble a pre-settlement state. They are always on the lookout for new places. Once a place is identified, the commission works with landowners to purchase the plot. It isn't over then. Even the most pristine communities may have exotic vegetation within them, or have had their composition altered due to fire suppression. Land managers then set about removing exotic plants and using prescribed fire to restore the original plant communities. They will also remove exotic pests preying on native plants. For example, the hemlock wooly adelgid is devastating hemlocks in the mountainous east. But trees are being saved by killing the adelgid with a soapy insecticide within the state preserves. Plants aren't the only living things that benefit from the commission. The nature preserves also protect mammal, bird, and fish habitats, from Indiana cave bats to fish such as the least brook lamprey, located in Terrapin Creek.

Research is ongoing in these special lands, as biologists collect data to help manage the lands, examining the interplay between flora and fauna, and perhaps even find new species. But visitors are mostly people like you and me touring the area, to hike, watch birds, see wildflowers, and maybe take a few pictures. And then we can spread the word about these nature preserves in the Bluegrass State, raising awareness of the life within.

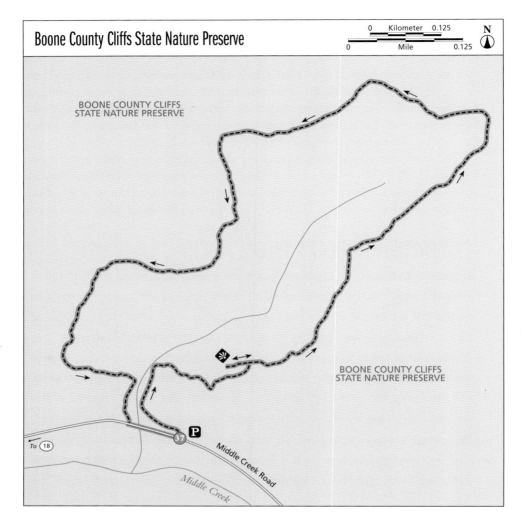

Boone County Cliffs State Nature Preserve

| 0 | Kilometer | 0.125 |
| 0 | Mile | 0.125 |

N

BOONE COUNTY CLIFFS
STATE NATURE PRESERVE

BOONE COUNTY CLIFFS
STATE NATURE PRESERVE

P
37

To 18

Middle Creek Road

Middle Creek

the dusky salamander. The amphibian needs exceptionally clean water, another reason for the preserve, the first Nature Conservancy property purchased in Kentucky. Enjoy listening to the singing stream shoals as they tumble toward Middle Creek. A very short road walk delivers you back to the trailhead.

Miles and Directions

0.0 Pass the trailside kiosk, which contains a map on its back side. Travel uphill, coming near a rocky tributary of Middle Creek.

0.1 Turn away from the stream and ascend sharply up a hill. Switchbacks ease the grade. Briefly level off at a contemplation bench then resume the climb, breaking through a cliff line.

0.3 Reach a trail intersection. Head left and walk a short distance along a ridge to a view of the watershed below. Your overlook is encircled by cliff line. Backtrack to main loop.

0.5 Enter the head of a cove, passing beneath some huge beech trees. A contemplation bench allows you to look around for the entirety of them and to absorb the natural splendor of old growth forest.

0.7 The trail turns sharply west. The major climb of nearly 300 feet is over as you tramp along the ridgetops.

1.1 The loop turns southwesterly at a ridgetop contemplation bench. The hollow to your left drops off sharply.

1.4 The downgrade steepens as it makes for the unnamed tributary. Watch your footing among the rocks and tree roots.

1.6 Come alongside the stream, continuing downhill past minor cascades. Emerge on Middle Creek Road within sight of the trailhead. Turn left onto Middle Creek Road.

1.7 Arrive back at the trailhead, completing the hike.

GREEN TIP

Love the outdoors? Show your love through action by volunteering with an outdoors-related conservation group, trail organization, or donating time to your favorite national, state, or local park.

38 Kincaid Lake State Park Hike

This hilly walk explores the rolling terrain of a hard-to-reach but easy-to-stay-awhile Northern Kentucky state park. Though a lake is the park's central feature, this loop only briefly comes near the lake after leaving developed facilities for a steep stream valley. From there, you hike into hills of cedar before returning to upper reaches of the valley. Follow a stream past small cascades before returning to the trailhead. Since the hike is short, consider camping, fishing, or boating while you are already here.

Start: Park recreation area
Distance: 2.2-mile lollipop
Hiking time: About 1 to 1.5 hours
Difficulty: Easy due to short distance, despite the hills
Trail surface: Natural surface path in forested woods
Best season: Sept through May
Other trail users: None

Canine compatibility: Leashed dogs permitted
Land status: State park
Fees and permits: No fees or permits required
Schedule: Open daily year-round
Maps: Kincaid Lake State Park; USGS Falmouth
Trail contacts: Kincaid Lake State Park, 565 Kincaid Park Rd., Falmouth, KY 41040; (859) 654-3531; http://parks.ky.gov/parks

Finding the trailhead: From Falmouth, Kentucky, southeast of downtown Cincinnati, take KY 22 east 0.4 mile to KY 159. Turn left and take KY 159 north to Kincaid State Park Drive. Turn right into the state park and follow the signs toward the camping area and recreation area. Turn right into the recreation area, just before coming to the camper registration building. The trail starts behind the basketball courts. Trailhead GPS: N38 43.464' / W84 16.950'

The Hike

The park recreation area, where the trail starts, has restroom and picnic facilities, in addition to basketball and volleyball courts. You will notice a paved trail leading right from behind the basketball courts. However, this hike picks up the natural surface trail leading left from the basketball courts. A sign indicates the Spice Bush Trail and the Ironwood Trail. Mixed woods of hickory, oak, and cedar shade the connector trail that leads to a trail shelter. From there you will descend to a tributary of Kincaid Lake. Sycamores and ash border a stone-filled watercourse. It isn't long before the connector trail reaches a bridge and a trail junction. This is where the loop portion of the hike begins. Walk across the bridge and go right with the Spice Bush Trail. The Ironwood Trail, your return route, leaves left from the bridge. A third trail, a connector, splits the loop in half. You are now following the tributary back downstream, toward Kincaid Lake.

The Spice Bush Trail leaves left from the streambed and begins climbing onto a steep hillside. Though the official name of this trail is the Spice Bush Trail, the plant for which it is named goes by the two words put together—spicebush. Spicebushes are found throughout the eastern United States and up to Ontario, Canada. The plant can be found all over Kentucky, in moist woods and marshes. It is an understory plant and blooms yellow in the spring before the trees above it leaf out. The plant is known to attract butterflies. There is even a spicebush swallowtail butterfly. Deer like to browse on spicebush twigs and leaves. In the fall the spicebush grows bright red berries that attract wildlife, especially birds.

Beech trees grow thickly on this north-facing slope. This is the hardest part of the hike. Pass through a fragrant planted white pine grove before joining the native ever-greens—cedars—on the hilltop. Watch for an old dried-up pond, evidence that this park was once farmed but has now returned to nature. Just ahead, reach a trail junction in an open field. The shortcut connector turns left toward the trailhead. Your loop stays right and uphill, still cruising quiet hilltop woods amid dogwoods and redbuds.

The Ironwood Trail takes you from these hilltops down through a moist valley back toward the trailhead. Ironwood is actually a nickname for the hornbeam tree. It is a short, usually crooked tree found in the eastern United States, including all of the greater Tri-State area. The wood is tough and dense but not commercially used.

BEYOND HIKING AT KINCAID STATE PARK

No matter your chosen route, it's a winding road to Kincaid State Park from Cincinnati. There-fore, why not explore other activities here, making the most of your time and experience? The park's number one draw is the lake. That is obvious from the park's name. You can explore the 183-acre impoundment using your own craft or a park rental boat. Choose from a rowboat, pedal boat, johnboat, or even a pontoon boat for a relaxing cruise. Fish for crappie, catfish, bass, and bluegill. If you want more civilized aquatic options, head to the park swimming pool. It is open during the summer season.

Golfers take note: There is a 9-hole course at Kincaid and you can try your hand on the links. The rest of us could settle for the putt-putt course. Looking for some friendly competi-tion between you and your fellow hikers? Head for the developed volleyball, shuffleboard, basketball, and tennis courts. No need to bring your own equipment; just check it out from the park.

When considering the above activities, it's easy to see you will need more than a day to indulge in them. Therefore, bring your tent or camper and head on down to the eighty-four-site campground. Each campsite has electricity and water. The campground is generally open from mid-March through mid-November. Call ahead for exact opening and closing times if you intend to camp during the shoulder seasons.

Author bridges streambed at hike's beginning.

Ironwood prefers rich, wetter, but well-drained sites such as this hollow. Interestingly, one of the most common plants found with the hornbeam is the spicebush, so it is no wonder these two trails got their names together. Deer also browse on ironwood, and its fruit is consumed by both birds and small mammals, such as squirrels.

The trail parallels the creek below. The limestone-bedded watercourse will flow in winter and spring but may dry up during the warmer season. In addition to flowing water in spring, you will also enjoy wildflowers. Occasional rocky drainages bisect the path as you continue downhill on a rooty single-track trail.

Kincaid Lake State Park is not far from Cincinnati—it's just there is no fast and efficient way to get there, so you might as well take your time on your route and take your time when you're here.

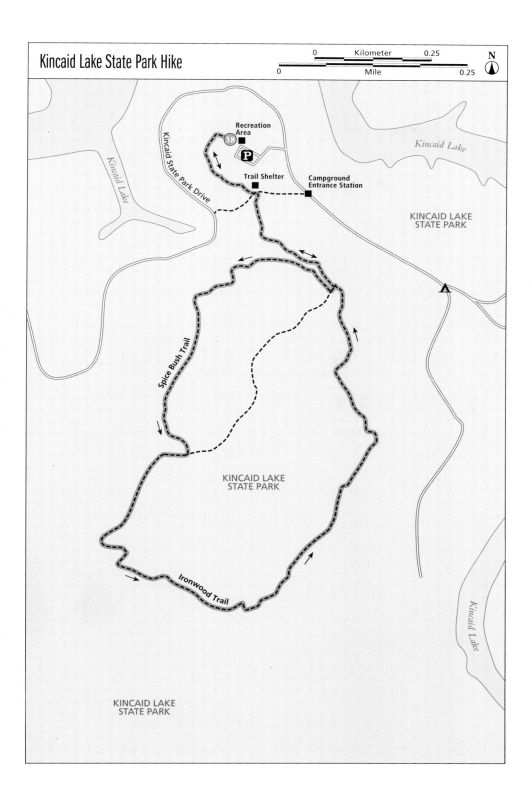

Kincaid Lake State Park Hike

0	Kilometer	0.25
0	Mile	0.25

N

Kincaid Lake

Kincaid State Park Drive

Kincaid Lake

Recreation
Area

38

P

Trail Shelter

Campground
Entrance Station

KINCAID LAKE
STATE PARK

Spice Bush Trail

KINCAID LAKE
STATE PARK

Ironwood Trail

Kincaid Lake

KINCAID LAKE
STATE PARK

Miles and Directions

0.0 Start from the recreation area near the park campground. A rocky path leads a short distance to a trail shelter, where interpretive information about the flora and fauna of the park is displayed. Watch out as a spur trail leads forward to the campground, and another trail leads right to the park road. You go downhill on wood and earth stairs on steeply sloped terrain.

0.2 The trail levels off in bottomland, next to a wet-weather tributary feeding Kincaid Lake. Cross a wooden pedestrian bridge, then turn right and join the Spice Bush Trail.

0.5 The Spice Bush Trail leaves the bottomland then climbs a surprisingly sloped hill.

0.8 Reach a trail junction near an open field. Here, a shortcut trail leads left and downhill back to the bridge. Stay right, still going uphill.

1.0 Come to a gated service road. Turn left, joining the Ironwood Trail.

1.3 Come alongside the upper portion of a rock streambed. Shortly cross the stream without benefit of a footbridge, then turn downstream.

1.9 Complete the Ironwood Trail, returning to the pedestrian bridge. Backtrack uphill after crossing the bridge.

2.2 Emerge at the park recreation area after passing by the trail shelter.

GREEN TIP

Never let your dog chase wildlife. Wild animals have it tough enough with a limited habitat. They stand the best chance to survive and reproduce if people and their pets leave wildlife alone. Keeping your pet on a leash is the best way to help wild animals.

39 Big Bone Lick State Park Hike

This hike visits historic Big Bone Lick, a place once populated by prehistoric animals, such as mastodons, giant sloths, and wooly mammoths. Their bones, left in the bogs surrounding salt licks and mineral springs, are an important archaeological site. The state of Kentucky realized the importance of the location, developing a state park with trails for you to explore the terrain, and also see a herd of buffalo, which live in the park. The museum has been improved, with all new exhibits. Stop here and give this place a shot.

Start: Park museum and nature center
Distance: 4.1-mile loop
Hiking time: About 2 to 2.5 hours
Difficulty: Moderate, does have hills
Trail surface: Natural surface path in forested woods
Best season: Year-round; museum open Apr through Oct
Other trail users: None

Canine compatibility: Leashed dogs permitted
Land status: State park
Fees and permits: No fees or permits required
Schedule: Open daily year-round
Maps: Big Bone Lick State Park; USGS Rising Sun, Union
Trail contacts: Big Bone Lick State Park, 3380 Beaver Rd., Union, KY 41091; (859) 384-3522; http://parks.ky.gov/parks

Finding the trailhead: From exit 175 on I-75/I-71, south of downtown Cincinnati, take KY 338 north. Stay with KY 338 for 7.6 miles, then turn left into the state park. Drive for 0.2 mile. The road splits—turn right toward the park museum and nature center. The trails start from the south side of the nature center parking area, near a pair of large oaks. Trailhead GPS: N38 53.033' / W84 45.173'

• Busy, heavily trafficed —
hills

The Hike

Big Bone Lick has been noted as a significant geological location for a long time. In the early 1800s, when Meriwether Lewis was en route to St. Louis to begin his memorable journey to the Pacific Ocean with William Clark, he stopped at Big Bone Lick and sent bone samples to President Thomas Jefferson. Later, on orders from Jefferson, who wanted more samples and scientific information gathered at this place, William Clark and his brother George Rogers Clark came back for a detailed exploration of Big Bone Lick. They were looking for bones of great wooly mammoths and other animals attracted to the salt licks here. This project by the Clark brothers led to Big Bone Lick being dubbed "the birthplace of American paleontology."

Since then the area has been worked over by other collectors and scientists. The mineral springs and swampy area around the salt lick held bones of the large beasts, giving the name to the area. The extraordinary concentration of animals is owed not only to the salt licks but also to the very swamps around them, for the miry muck

Viewing the buffalo is a big highlight of this hike.

sometimes trapped the animals, whereupon they died. Human artifacts have been found here as well. This makes sense, as hunters would follow the animals to their stomping grounds. In the 1800s, the mineral springs brought in visitors and a resort hotel was located here. The locale became a Kentucky state park in 1960. It was accorded national natural landmark status in 2009, a prestigious moniker, since just a few over 500 sites have been given that accolade.

Today, you can walk among the springs and wetland that was such a productive bone yard. Check out the museum for a more comprehensive understanding of Big Bone Lick. This hike first visits a bison herd that is kept on park premises. These are North America's largest herding animals. Don't crowd too close to the fence and give them ample room, even though they are on the far side of the wire. The buffalo add a living reminder of all the beasts that passed this way.

The hike then loops its way through hilly terrain above Big Bone Creek. In winter, you can look down on the valley below. Then the circuit makes an extended trip along the park boundary. Pastureland lies across a fence. Look for frequent deer paths crossing the fence, between the park and the pasture.

Next, you will circle the park lake on the Coralberry Trail. Cross the lake dam then work your way south. This area has user-created paths connecting the lake to the campground and can be troublesome to navigate, but as long as you have the

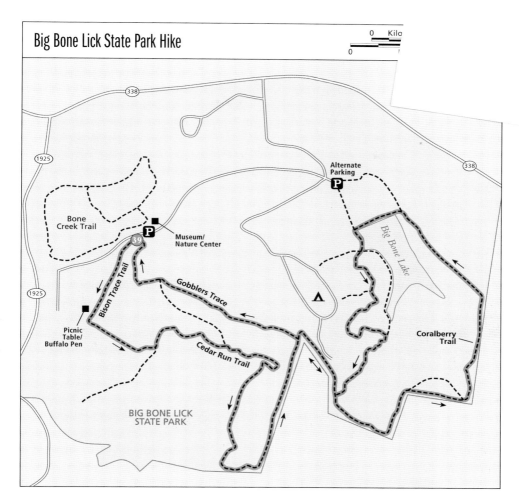

Big Bone Lick State Park Hike

0 Kilo

0

Bone
Creek Trail

Museum/
Nature Center

Alternate
Parking

Big Bone Lake

Bison Trace Trail

Gobblers Trace

Picnic
Table/
Buffalo Pen

Cedar Run Trail

Coralberry
Trail

BIG BONE LICK
STATE PARK

campground to your right uphill and the lake to your left downhill it is hard to get truly lost. Once the Coralberry Loop is completed, backtrack past the campground and pick up the east end of the Gobblers Trace.

You got it made from there. Enjoy a glorious walk on a grassy track that drifts downhill all the way to the visitor center. The ease of this ending may re-energize you to add the Big Bone Creek Trail, a short interpretive loop through the bone yard that will complete your hiking experience at this fine state park.

Miles and Directions

0.0 Start at the museum and nature center. Take time to visit if here during the warm season. This hike leaves the two large oaks on the south side of the parking area, to immediately leave right toward the buffalo herd on the Bison Trace. The Gobblers Trace Trail leaves left and is your return route. The interpretive all-access trail through the springs and wetlands of the park starts on the north side of the museum. Travel under hardwoods mixed with cedar.

0.2 Emerge at the bison viewing area. To your right stands a pen and a shaded picnic table. The main path goes left, southerly, along a fence line, as a wide track used to maintain the herd. Buffalo should be grazing in this meadow adjacent to Big Bone Creek.

0.4 Meet the Cedar Run Trail by a picnic table. The Bison Trace Trail leaves right, still along a fence line. Turn left, ascending on the single-track Cedar Run Trail, up a dry west-facing slope with cedars, red buds, and oaks.

0.6 A connector trail leaves left for the Gobblers Trace Trail. Stay right. Head up a draw.

1.1 The Cedar Run Trail turns sharply left and ascends steeply along the park boundary.

1.2 Turn left again, staying with the boundary line. The path undulates north. A field separated by wire is across the boundary.

1.5 Meet the Gobblers Trace. You will return this way, but for now, keep straight then shortly veer right.

1.6 Pass by the upper end of the park campground to your left. Pick up the Coralberry Trail, which makes a big loop you will follow.

1.7 The return loop of the Coralberry Trail comes in on your left. Keep straight, still tracing the park boundary. The path turns north and east.

1.9 Pass a mini-loop trail that rejoins the main Coralberry Trail. Stay with the park boundary. Descend north into pines and cedars. Winter views of the park lake open.

2.6 Come to a trail junction. Turn left here, crossing the park lake dam. Good views open of the lake as you walk atop the dam.

2.7 Reach another intersection after crossing the outflow of the park dam. Turn left here and head south, coming to a gravel track. Follow the gravel track uphill but soon leave left with the red blazes. Do not stay with the gravel trail, which continues climbing. This area can be further confusing, as user-created fishing trails travel along the lake's edge.

2.9 A spur trail leads right to the campground recreation shelter.

3.2 Another spur trail dips to the top of the lake. Climb away from the water.

3.4 Complete the Coralberry Loop. Backtrack right, passing the campground.

3.6 Leave right on the Gobblers Trace. The walking is easy as you ride the nose of a ridge on a grassy path.

3.9 Pass the connector trail linking the Gobblers Trace Trail and the Cedar Run Trail. Curve off the ridgeline.

4.1 Complete the loop, returning to the visitor center.

40 Quiet Trails State Nature Preserve

This hillside ramble explores a preserved parcel of Kentucky's Licking River valley. Set in serene rolling country, this loop hike wanders through a former farm, now reverting to nature's dominion. You will explore everything from cedar copses to prairie vistas before passing old farm buildings and stone walls. At your lowest point, you will visit the oft-flooded plain along the Licking, where massive sycamores hold court. Your return trip ascends hills and hollows back to the trailhead.

Start: Pughs Ferry Road
Distance: 1.7-mile loop
Hiking time: About 1 hour
Difficulty: Moderate, but does have 300-foot ascent
Trail surface: Natural surface path in mostly forested woods
Best season: Sept through May
Other trail users: None
Canine compatibility: Dogs not permitted

Land status: Kentucky state nature preserve
Fees and permits: No fees or permits required
Schedule: Open daily year-round
Maps: Quiet Trails Brochure available online; USGS Claysville
Trail contacts: Kentucky State Nature Preserves Commission, 801 Teton Trail, Frankfort, KY 40601; (502) 573-2886; http://nature preserves.ky.gov

Finding the trailhead: From the bridge over the Licking River in Falmouth, Kentucky, take US 27 south for 10.9 miles to KY 1284. Turn left onto KY 1284 toward Sunrise, and follow it for 3 miles to a four-way stop sign in tiny Sunrise. Here, keep straight, joining Pughs Ferry Road. Follow Pughs Ferry Road for 1.8 miles to the gravel state nature preserve parking lot on the right. The trailhead is bordered by a wooden fence. Trailhead GPS: N38 33.420' / W84 13.635'

The Hike

This area really is deserving of the moniker "Quiet Trails State Nature Preserve." Once a hilltop farm in the back of beyond, the primary tract was purchased by the state of Kentucky back in 1992. When state managers examined the property, the quiet must've struck them as much as the overall beauty of the silent swath—save for the birds—of the Licking River Valley.

Its origins as a preserve predate the state, however. Bill and Martha Wiglesworth owned the tract for two decades, working on the idea of operating their own private preserve. The couple knew the property was scenic, special, and historic. Their restoration work improved the property, planting native flora and improving wildlife habitat. The former homestead was reverting back to its natural state yet still harbored evidence of its past uses, such as stone fences, a well, barns, and small clearings. A picnic shelter now stands at the site of a riverside trading post, operated in the 1700s. Still other sections, in the steep hollows, remained as they were, forested havens for wildflowers.

The Licking River at this point was the site of a historic trading post.

In 1992 the Wiglesworths sold the tract to the state of Kentucky, which banked it as part of the state nature preserve. In 1997 an adjoining 55 acres was purchased. The combined parcel presents a variety of environments, from dusky cedar forests, to brushy meadows in which songbirds croon, to steep slopes carpeted with wildflowers, to maintained meadows luring in deer and turkey, to the repeatedly inundated flood-plain, where gigantic sycamores lean downstream before rising high and spreading their white branches over verdant flats.

Just above this plain is the site of the old trading post from the 1700s. River men floating lumber from the great riverside forests to market in Covington, Kentucky, stopped here to buy and sell goods, swap news and stories, too. The shelter you see uses logs from that old building. Note this site is well above the lowermost tier of the floodplain on the Licking, known to rise in brown rages and descend back to a gentle ribbon of placid green. Going farther back in time, hikers can peer into the Ordovi-cian limestone that crops up along the streambeds and hillsides of the preserve. Look for imprints of ancient sea creatures in the gray rock. The stone fence you will see, and the other rock piles, were constructed by hand, and harken back to a time when travel was slow and tough, outside distractions were few, and thus building a fence by hand was often done. Note how the fence uses an unusual upturned design, rather than the conventional stacking.

Quiet Trails State Nature Preserve

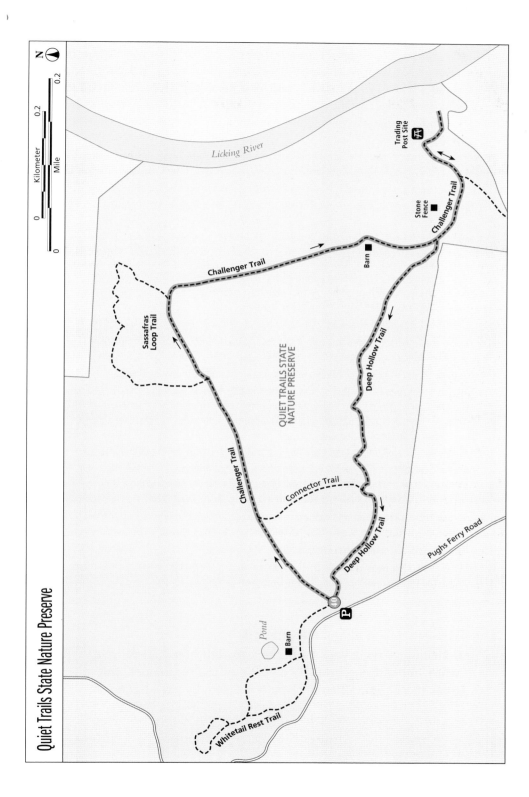

Quiet Trails State Nature Preserve

Licking River

Trading Post Site

Stone Fence

Challenger Trail

Challenger Trail

Barn

Sassafras Loop Trail

QUIET TRAILS STATE NATURE PRESERVE

Deep Hollow Trail

Connector Trail

Deep Hollow Trail

Pughs Ferry Road

Pond

Barn

Whitetail Rest Trail

Kilometer

Mile

N

Wildlife can be viewed by the patient hiker. Look for Eastern cottontail rabbits scampering away from small clearings and along grassy edges. Scan for muskrats along the shores of the Licking River. Small farm ponds add another component to the wildland mix. Listen for frogs and other amphibians. The 300-plus-foot variation in elevation fosters other ecotones. This vegetational variety increases the variety of fauna.

There was once a more complex network of pathways here at Quiet Trails, but the spider web of trails became overgrown and hard to follow, confusing hikers. In 2013, the trail network was simplified to the following loop with a spur down to the river. Enjoy all that this preserve offers, a changing menagerie of nature during all four seasons.

Miles and Directions

0.0 Start at the corner of the parking area, joining the Challenger Trail. Note the old trees bordering the former farm road you are following. Cruise along a ridgeline, easterly, toward the Licking River.

0.2 Pass the Connector Trail leaving right. Stay straight on the Challenger Trail.

0.5 Curve south along the bluff in a mix of cedars and hardwoods. Watch for a crumbling stone fence line to your right.

0.7 Pass by an old wooden barn. Begin working downhill toward the Licking River.

0.8 Intersect the Deep Hollow Trail. It leaves acutely right and is your return route. For now, stay with the Challenger Trail and look left in the woods for the impressive stone fence with the unusual vertically placed rocks. It is a time-consuming work of art. Unfortunately, falling trees have knocked over portions of it.

1.0 Reach an open clearing and the site of the 1700s trading post. An old well and picnic shelter mark the spot. To come very close to the river, you must leave the trail. Note the piled debris on the upstream side of vegetation, indicating the power of the river. The steep, muddy banks make direct access of the river difficult. Backtrack.

1.2 Return to the intersection with the Deep Hollow Trail. Stay left here, picking up the Deep Hollow Trail, and enter a steeply sloped valley centered with a limestone-bottomed stream.

1.5 Stay straight, still climbing, as the Connector Trail leaves right. This is a good spring wildflower area.

1.7 Reach the trailhead after completing the Deep Hollow Trail.

GREEN TIP
Consider carrying your trash back to your home, to recycle what you can and properly dispose of the remainder. This eases the burden of costly waste removal by park agencies.